LOVE REMAINS

LOVE REMAINS

Prophetic Writings / 2014-2015

Jeff Hood

WIPF & STOCK · Eugene, Oregon

LOVE REMAINS
Prophetic Writings, 2014–2015

Copyright © 2016 Jeff Hood. All rights reserved. Except for brief quotations in critical publications or reviews, no part of this book may be reproduced in any manner without prior written permission from the publisher. Write: Permissions, Wipf and Stock Publishers, 199 W. 8th Ave., Suite 3, Eugene, OR 97401.

Wipf & Stock
An Imprint of Wipf and Stock Publishers
199 W. 8th Ave., Suite 3
Eugene, OR 97401

www.wipfandstock.com

PAPERBACK ISBN: 978-1-5326-1241-1
HARDCOVER ISBN: 978-1-5326-1243-5

Manufactured in the U.S.A.   NOVEMBER 29, 2016

*Cover Art by Emily Jean Hood

For Joseph Hutcheson, Martyr of Dallas County

#Short Words from 2014

Married two dear friends in one of the first legal same-sex ceremonies in Ardmore, OK. -Oct. 8

Spent the morning with Sister Helen Prejean. - Nov. 3

We serve a God beyond borders. What makes us think for a second that God has anything to do with trying to keep people out of this country or any other? -Nov. 21

Spent time with one of the great heroes of the Christian faith today at the School of the Americas protest. Father Roy Bourgeois has fought against the evils of US foreign policy for decades and was defrocked for ordaining women to be Roman Catholic priests. -Nov. 22

Would Jesus remain calm in Ferguson tonight? I have a very hard time believing so. -Nov. 24

The Son of God has nowhere to lay his head on such a night. #BlackLivesMatter #Ferguson #FergusonDecision -Nov. 24

Proud to stand with two of my children aged 2 at Atlanta Protest of #FergusonDecision #BlackLivesMatter -Nov. 25

If Jesus was alive today...I have no question that we would bludgeon him to death with a cash register. #BlackThursday #BlackFriday -Nov. 28

You can kill the dreamer but you can't kill the dream. #BlackLivesMatter -Nov. 29

"People are praying all over the world for Texas to spare the life of Scott Panetti. Will you join us?" #SaveScott -Nov. 30

GOD HAS AIDS -Dec. 1

Tonight I was proud to colead with my good friend The Rev. Dr. Ray Jordan an incredibly fruitful discussion entitled "Lessons from Ferguson: Where do we go from here?" -Dec. 1

There is nothing just about killing Scott Panetti. I will stand on this corner outside the execution chamber in prayer until this thing is over. -Dec. 2

Meditation at 4 hours: "We cannot love God and kill Scott Panetti. Draw us back from our addiction to death. Save us God." #SaveScott -Dec. 3

8th hour meditation: God is here and not silent. I hear God begging us to stop. Tonight, God asks us to #SaveScott -Dec. 3

10th hour meditation: "Jesus didn't execute his enemies. Are we better than Jesus? Let us love God & #SaveScott " -Dec. 10

12th hour meditation: "You find us in our darkest hour. Be light tonight. #SaveScott from the darkness of our sin" -Dec. 3

16th hour meditation: "May the rain cleanse our souls of the death penalty in time to #SaveScott /Wash us clean God." -Dec. 3

19th hour meditation: "The light overcomes the darkness. God be our light in this dark hour. #SaveScott " -Dec. 3

21 hours into vigil: I just received word that the 5th Circuit Court of Appeals has issued a stay of execution for Scott Panetti. #SaveScott -Dec. 3

Right now, Jesus is saying, "I Can't Breathe." -Dec. 8

I refuse to believe that the best Christians can do is conversation. We must stand for justice. End of conversation. #BlackLivesMatter -Dec. 10

I'm more afraid of Christians than Muslims. #IllRideWithYou -Dec. 12

There's nothing orthodox about destroying your enemies. Matt. 5:44 -Dec. 14

Imagine if Jesus was born in Bethlehem today. The US would be a chief funder of the Israeli occupation oppressing him. #Palestinian -Dec. 14

I'm more afraid of Christians than Muslims. #IllRideWithYou -Dec. 15

Praying for peace. But how long Lord must we wait for justice? #PeshawarAttack #Pakistan -Dec. 16

If you kill people you work for evil not for God. #PeshawarAttack -Dec. 16

Boko Haram kidnaps and kills women and children as the world yawns. #BlackLivesMatter -Dec. 18

The Rev. DR. Jeff Hood / Project "The Epiphany of the Queer" -Dec. 19

Prayers for 2 dead NYPDs. Our addiction to violence and vengeance will only claim more lives. Repent. The beloved community is at hand. -Dec. 20

Gun violence, racism and police brutality are rooted in fear. We must push past the fear and learn to love each other. #AntonioMartin -Dec. 24

In a stable surrounded by shit, God got in the thick of it with us. #Emmanuel #Incarnation #Christmas #Jesus -Dec. 24

I stand with Pope Francis against the globalization of indifference. -Dec. 25

Praying for the people on board #QZ8501 / God is here and is not silent in moments like this. -Dec. 28

Change the world...love somebody. -Dec. 30

Jesus was known as a friend to sinners. Why are Christians not? #love -Dec. 30

You were made in the image of the queerest being to ever exist or that ever will exist. Don't try to be like anyone else but you in 2015. #HappyNewYear -Dec. 31

October 10, 2014

Beyond Borders: An Unexpected Trip to Mexico with a Dying Man

I didn't expect to be on a flight to Mexico. I thought I would spend most of today completing multiple unfinished writing projects that I have long neglected. Things changed when I met Ramon. Carrollton, Texas is not the type of place one would expect miracles to happen. When I pulled up to the apartment complex two days ago, I had no idea what I was getting into. I only had vague knowledge that a young man was dying of bone cancer inside and needed help. Upon seeing Ramon, I knew the situation was dire. Ramon's father seemed to be giving all the help that he could conjure up. The remainder of Ramon's family was back in Guadalajara. Then came the request..."Can you help us get him back to Mexico?"

Through much conversation and consultation, persons from the Cathedral of Hope, our Spanish-speaking congregation and Hope for Peace and Justice worked together to devise a plan to get Ramon home. I was overwhelmed and heartbroken by the whole situation. Truthfully, I was afraid and ready to get out of the apartment. When a traveling companion fell through for Ramon, one of my colleagues looked up and declared, "Can anyone travel with him?" Though words came out of my mouth, I know that I didn't speak them. It was as if I was listening to someone else. "I will go!" I heard. When I realized that it was my mouth the words came out of, I knew the Spirit had spoken. In the countenance of the universe, I realized a miraculous human union beyond the power of death and across boundaries of language and nationality was taking place.

For the last few days, I have grown angry thinking about the factors that complicate Ramon's situation. Though he has spent ten years working hard and paying taxes in this country, he does not have the proper papers to be documented. Without papers, Ramon has had an incredibly difficult time securing healthcare that could save his life. Due to his Mexican nationality, many in our country have treated him as something other than human. Ramon has relied on the charity of strangers to get through this difficult hour. Some have been charitable and some have not. From his nationality to his access to money, Ramon has lived his life on the other side of a boundary from most of us. Though he was here with us, we were not with him. We forgot that we belong to each other. We forgot that Ramon is in us and we are in Ramon. Today, I am experiencing human connection with Ramon in all fullness.

The cries of pain and sorrow that filled the air as Ramon's dad kissed his son for the last time at the airport shook my bones. In the deep love that I saw exchanged, I saw how much God loves us. I prayed for the day when death will be no more. When Ramon kissed his dad goodbye for the last time in this life, I knew that I was witnessing something eternal. Passing through security, Ramon was unable to lift his legs. I picked up each leg and helped him stand. I realized in this moment that Ramon was teaching me how to lift my legs and stand. Getting on the flight, I lifted Ramon out of his wheelchair and placed him into another wheelchair. In this moment of my frustration that he even had to switch chairs, Ramon taught me to be flexible. While I administered morphine to Ramon, I realized that he was medicating me with his presence. Throughout his groans and struggles of pain, I too groaned and struggled with the pain of knowing that a 28-year-old man was dying in front of me. What type of God would allow such a thing? When Ramon crossed himself and kissed his rosary, I embraced his faith as my faith. Throughout our deeply spiritual journey, I realize again and again that the images of God we all carry connected Ramon and I. In my moments of doubt and anger, I realized that God was with us because Ramon was with us.

Upon arrival to Guadalajara, we walked tall together. Together, we made it. There was a woman who walked up to Ramon and said she saw him on television. After giving him some money, she asked that Ramon interceded to the Virgin of Guadalupe on her behalf. From my vantage point there was no need for intercession, the heavenly saint was being made reality right before our eyes. When

Ramon encountered his brothers and friends, I struggled to maintain my composure. In the midst of a monumental sadness at an approaching death, the joy that flowed out transcended death. Though Ramon's trip had just ended, I knew it had only just begun.

Though I have only known him for three days and will probably never speak to him again, Ramon will remain with me for eternity. I don't speak such a thing to be dramatic. I speak it because it is true. Love is eternal. Though we couldn't easily speak to each other, Ramon and I shared love in our brief moments of union. In allowing borders to subside and love to come in, we quickly realized that we belong to each other. In the midst of such numerous borders to human flourishing, I pray that the world will realize the same.

Amen.

October 10, 2014

the trip // apoem

there has got to be more than this
the wheels roll toward the end
we can't stop it
we sit here helpless
watching as life leaks out
can we runaway to something more
we are loosing our grip
wasn't god supposed to help us hold on
we live on islands of fear and trepidation where no one visits
what happened to the love and grace that could bring us together

turn the car on
can we floor the gas and get out of this shit
we must rip open our bodies and pull out our souls
surely there is something left
surely there is something worth saving
are we there yet?

October 10, 2014

the pull of the seat

is your ass glued to the seat
why don't you get up
people need your help
do you not care
someone dies from some sort of injustice every second you sit here
let's go
move
is there anything I can do to motivate you to fight for justice
yes
stop talking

October 12, 2014

The Blessing of Communion at Domestic Violence Prevention Wednesday // Cathedral of Hope UCC 10/8/14

Well...I'm a little tired. I've had a hell of a day to be honest with you. I don't know if any of you share such sentiments. I had two particularly painful experiences today. One was this afternoon...I shared time with a 28-year-old man who is dying of bone cancer. There was a tremendous amount of pain involved in the situation for me. I was just trying to figure out...Where is God in all of this? Right before I came in tonight...one of the first wedding ceremonies that I ever did was one of my dearest friends...and my buddy called me tonight to tell me that he and his wife are getting divorced. We experience much pain and heartache in this life. Many situations make us feel like the world is just abusive. How is this happening? Why am I here? You know we all have similar stories of pain that we can bring to the table tonight. We could probably site similar things to what I mentioned. Yet still we come... Still we come to this church and this table expecting something....believing that something happens. I believe in a God that declares God's self to be love. I believe in a God that speaks these words, "I am the way, I am the truth, I am the life." I believe in a God that declares, "Love is the way, the truth and the life." Tonight we are talking about domestic violence. We are talking about dark spaces. But Jesus says, "I was in prison." Jesus says, "I was sick." Jesus says, "I was hurting." So tonight when we come to this table, let us remember that this broken body and this spilled blood signifies that Jesus was there...and Jesus is here. There is something magical about to take place. Open your hearts and believe in the magic. Believe in love.

This is the body of Jesus Christ. Broken...again...and again...and again...and again...for you and for all of us.

This right here is the blood of Jesus Christ. Poured out for you...again...and again...and again...and again.

I invite you tonight to come to this table and experience the magic.

Amen.

October 16, 2014

Memories of a Trip with Ramon: Words Spoken at a Cathedral of Hope

Good morning Cathedral! I think it is appropriate for me to tell you a little about my week on the same day that we are remembering and celebrating the life of Matthew Shepard. When Matthew Shepard died, there were so many of us who promised "never again." We declared, "When we meet situations of injustice we are going to stand up and do something. Never again will we let such moments pass by without action." This week I had the tremendous privilege of standing with you as we refused to let a moment of injustice pass us by without action. You see last week...Cathedral of Hope, Congregacion Latina and Hope for Peace and Justice stood together to make a difference in a young man's life. It all began when Father Alberto called us up and asked us to come to an apartment in Carrollton, Texas. When we went into the apartment, we found a 28-year-old young man named Ramon dying of bone cancer. Ramon had lived and worked in this country since he was 18-years-old without papers. In so doing, Ramon paid taxes, stayed out of trouble and committed himself to performing all of the duties of a citizen...unfortunately due to his immigration status, Ramon was not able to receive the benefits of having done that. Ramon was also not able to access the quality of healthcare that many of us are able to access. There were other pieces of the story that only exacerbated the injustice that Ramon faced. Ramon's father was desperate to help him get back to see his mother and brothers in Guadalajara, Mexico before he died. As we sat in that apartment, a number of us tried to figure out how we could help this young man get to Mexico. We asked our selves over and over, "How can we make this happen?" We decided that this was definitely something that we needed to do. We needed to find the money to get this young man to his family. We knew that a cousin was going to fly with him...then that fell through due to her passport being out of date. Father Alberto looked around and declared, "Who's going to go to Mexico? This young man needs us." I kept on thinking the same thing to myself..."Who is going to go?" Then out of nowhere, I heard someone say, "I'll go!" I thought, "Who in the hell said that?" Then I realized it was me. The next thing I know, I met Ramon and his father at the airport. Then, Ramon and I flew to Guadalajara together. Ramon was barely able to move and required constant care. When we arrived, I got to see him encounter his brothers for the first time in ten years. It was really beautiful. Throughout it all, I kept think about the beauty of the confluence of events that brought Cathedral of Hope, Congregacion Latina and Hope for Peace and Justice together to work hard and allow Ramon to die with his mother and family. This confluence of events produced a moment of unbelievable brilliance and beauty. Together we declared, "Never again!" and praise God we meant it. Now, together we must pray for Ramon and his family and be ready for the next time someone needs our help. Until then, may God continue to bless this beautiful congregation. Amen.

October 17, 2014

the confusion of the outside agitator

the you
outside agitator
the run
the stun
outside agitator

the fear

the hide

the side

outside agitator

the street

the meet

the anger

the scowl

outside agitator

the shove

the stumble

the hate

the state

the fist

outside agitator

the cuff

the stuff

the chat

the ride

the thoughts

the station

outside agitator

the door

the walk

the jail

the cell

the slam

the rights

the stare

outside agitator

which side of the bars are you on?

October 20, 2014

Sharing the Good News of Jesus with Southern Baptists: A Mission to Nashville

"It is hard for me to not believe that homosexuality is a sin when God tells us in Leviticus to kill those who perpetuate homosexual acts." In May of 2002, a fiery Southern Baptist preacher proclaimed these hateful words to be the words of God. Those in attendance cheered him on. Each time I think I'm so advanced in my understanding of the world that I can cease dialogue with persons more conservative than I, I remind myself of the words that I delivered as an 18-year-old preacher. Though many progressives and liberals would have othered me to an oblivion of irrelevance and nonexistence, God was not done with me.

When I started my educational career at the Southern Baptist Theological Seminary, I believed everything that was said. We were a people united in certainty and fundamentalist theology. My pursuit of all things conservative was interrupted by an encounter with God. On his deathbed, my Southern Baptist mentor revealed to me that he had lived his life as a closeted gay man. Though knowledge of books and ideas are often important, I believe that our stances on issues most often change when our relational knowledge changes. For the first time in my life, I was aware that I knew someone who was gay. On multiple levels, my mentor had been an incarnation of Jesus for me. After the revelation, I had to deal with the fact that the closest representation of Jesus to me was gay. How could such knowledge not change a person? I believe that God saved me from my homophobia and hate. Now, I count myself an evangelist of the inclusive love of Jesus.

From the 27th through 29th of October, I will travel to Nashville, Tennessee to attend a conference entitled "The Gospel, Homosexuality and The Future of Marriage" hosted by the Ethics & Religious Liberty Commission of the Southern Baptist Convention. Judging from the titles of the sessions, I will probably agree with very little that is said. From time to time, I will probably grow angry and struggle through difficult conversations with Southern Baptist leaders. Regardless of it all, I know there will be few inclusive voices preaching about the inclusive love of God. When I have the power to be the change that I want to see in the world, I cannot sit out a chance to respond to hate with love. Do we not believe that God can crack even the hardest of hearts? I once was really lost, but somehow God really found me. I ask that you prayerfully join me as I endeavor to share the good news of Jesus with some lost souls.

Amen.

October 20, 2014

Why I am an Evangelical that Supports Marriage Equality...

If Jesus does not support marriage equality, then the Jesus that evangelicals taught me about is not the real Jesus. In my preschool years, we sang of a God that loved the world. In my young adult years, we talked about loving our neighbors as our self. In my education at the Southern Baptist Theological Seminary, we were taught how to take the good news of Jesus to the world. All of the hate, homophobia and bad news I consistently hear being spewed by people opposed to marriage equality has nothing to do with God's love for us, our love for our neighbors or our responsibility to take the good news of Jesus to the world. What are we thinking? We have the opportunity to love God and we are choosing to worship bigotry. We have the opportunity to love people and we are choosing hate. We have the opportunity to share good news and we are addicted to bad news. We all need to get saved. I'm working so that no one gets left behind in the bad news of bigotry and hate. I can't imagine a world were my dearest friends continue to be treated like shit. I can't imagine a world where my three young children can't love who they love. I can't imagine a world where people are left to drown in their own ignorance. Today is the day of salvation. Let's pray that our fellow evangelicals get saved for the sake of our friends, children and everyone else. Amen.

October 21, 2014

The Cycle of Violence: Voting and Texas Politics

Over and over again, I listened to the voices that argued for the need to support progressive candidates that line up with progressive politics on "nearly every issue." Unfortunately, the "nearly every issue" part always seems to exclude the death penalty here in Texas. Even the most progressive candidates are for the death penalty. There is nothing progressive about killing people and I can't be a part of the charade of it all any more. Above all else, I am a follower of Jesus. I know that you can't love your neighbor as your self and vote for people who clearly state that they are going to continue supporting the State of Texas killing people. Killing and Jesus just don't go together.

We must show the world that there is a better way than killing. I believe the death penalty is one of the defining issues of our time. If the state can kill, then it has license to use every other tool of oppression. Next week, in the midst of fierce campaigning for public office, the State of Texas will execute Miguel Angel Paredes. On the night of October 28, will you be grieving the execution of another human being and demanding the cycle of violence stops or campaigning for a candidate that will stand by when the State of Texas kills another? I am ready for us to start making the right choice.

Amen.

October 24, 2014

the elements

there sits the bread
it occupies our head
there sits the wine
to fill us swine
come on down
you foolish clown
the elements are magic here
they alleviate all of our tragic fear
go now and learn
what it means to discern

October 27, 2014

When Southern Baptists Get Saved

Salvation was always such an important part of my upbringing. We were constantly begged, pushed, prodded and manipulated to go down the aisle. If I got saved once, I got saved a hundred times. When the preacher started talking about hell and the rhetorical fires started tickling my toes, I especially felt the tug to make sure I was sure about all this salvation stuff. The older I got, the more skeptical I became of the saved rhetoric. With all the oppressive language and actions that surrounded us, I didn't see anyone getting saved from anything. I actually began to wonder if getting saved actually made things worse. Then it started happening.

There was a man at our church I loved dearly. With seemingly magical powers, Brother Bobby captured my childhood attention and taught me about the love of God. Before then, I never thought that God could love me as an individual. Brother Bobby believed in me and taught me that God did too. I didn't think Southern Baptists could teach like this. I asked him one Sunday morning what made him so different and he replied, "Just like you, I am growing into who God created me to be." Months later, Brother Bobby was kicked out of our church for coming out as gay. Many years after, I saw pictures of Brother Bobby joyously smiling and holding hands with his partner. I knew Brother Bobby got saved.

I wrestled with my own sexuality for years. Whenever I found a man attractive, I just knew I was going to hell...probably penis first. Though I remained mostly attracted to women, I didn't know what to do with this other piece of me. I kept it quiet. Then I grew close to Pastor Greg. For decades, Pastor Greg led Southern Baptist churches. I decided to open up with him about my sexuality and he assured me that God lovingly created me just the way that I am. A few years later, Pastor Greg called me while I was a student at the Southern Baptist Theological Seminary and told me that he was dying of cancer. When I made it to his bedside, Pastor Greg told me that he had lived his life as a closeted gay man. With tears in my eyes, I knew that Pastor Greg was finally getting saved.

Not long after, one of my classmates asked if we could talk. When we sat down late one night, Marcus told me that he was gay. If we were at any other school this revelation would have been less of a deal, but we were students at the Southern Baptist Theological Seminary. Having contemplated suicide in the struggle to keep it quiet, I could see the visible relief in Marcus' body when he told me. Later, Marcus came out and declared that he was a gay Southern Baptist pastor. I knew he got saved.

October 27, 2014

Love is Not a Means to an End: A Surprising Revelation at a Southern Baptist Conference on Homosexuality

The Gaylord Opryland Hotel is an imposing structure. On this day, I knew that it was full of imposing figures from my past. I struggled tremendously at the Southern Baptist Theologically. For years, I couldn't decide who or what I was. The harsh teachings of my professors made things worse and led to a sustained deep depression. There are many days where I don't know how I made it. With this type of baggage, I stepped out of the car and readied for a fight.

The room was cavernous. Thousands of Southern Baptists sang praise music at the top of their lungs. To put it mildly, my stomach began to churn. Throughout the abuse and violence, I heard all of this music over and over again. I thought about turning around. Feeling that Jesus was walking with me, I went to sit down. From multiple prominent Southern Baptists, I heard many things that I starkly disagree with. Through it all, I felt like Jesus was telling me to keep listening for an opening. I struggled to remain seated. I strained to keep my heart open. Then it hit.

Glenn Stanton from Focus on the Family approached the microphone. Before I continue, I believe that Focus on the Family is responsible for much evil. After many remarks that I disagreed with, Stanton encouraged conference attendees to befriend LGBT people and loudly declared, "Love is not a means to an end." I knew immediately what he was saying. Don't just friend LGBT people to get them saved or preach to them. I also immediately knew what Jesus was saying to me, "You need to be here and love these people, for no other reason other than to love them." I couldn't believe these remarks proceeded out of the mouth of someone from such a different perspective as I. Regardless, I believe he is right.

Amen.

October 28, 2014

Jesus & the Great Cloud of LGBT Witnesses

Ever since I arrived at the Ethics and Religious Liberty Commission of the Southern Baptist Convention's conference "The Gospel, Homosexuality & the Future of Marriage," I have sensed the invisible footsteps that walk with me. The comforting whispers are constant. For days I have wondered who or what I have heard and sensed. When I started to give out tonight after a nasty and hurtful conversation with a much older participant in the conference, I sensed and heard it again. In a moment, I knew who the voice was and realized that he wasn't alone.

"Don't stop. Love is with you," came the sweet words of Jesus and the great cloud of LGBT witnesses. Instantly, I remembered why I came to the conference in the first place. I came to stand with Jesus. I came to stand with LGBT people from across the ages that have been subjugated to marginalization, oppression and terror at the hands and mouths of the Southern Baptist Convention. In that moment of glorious whispering, I was affirmed that Jesus and the LGBT saints stand with me.

Amen.

November 4, 2014

The Danger of Voting

"Give therefore to the emperor the things that are the emperor's, and to God the things that are God's" -Matthew 22:21 (NRSV)

Many years ago, religious leaders confronted Jesus about paying taxes. The group wanted to push Jesus into a corner and make him respond to their political provocations. Should they pay taxes? Jesus responded with a shrug. Picking up a coin and showing them the picture of the emperor, Jesus suggests that if it belongs to the emperor then give it back to the emperor.

Throughout this election season, religious leaders paraded candidates for various positions of emperor before their congregations. I suggest that people of faith respond to these manifestations of the political process and others in the same way that Jesus did...with a shrug. Give to the government that which is the government's, and to God the things that are God's.

Contrary to the statements of the political prognosticators, this is not the most important election in your lifetime nor will any election held by our government ever be. Whether you vote or not in a government election is a secondary issue, to whether you cast the vote that is your life with the marginalized and oppressed. The danger of voting is forgetting that your life and efforts are required of you all the time. This election cannot change the lives of people for the better. Only you can do that. In the election that is life, I pray that you will cast your ballot with those who need you the most.

Amen.

November 8, 2014

When Texas Descends into Hell: The Vulnerability of Scott Panetti

On October 30, I woke up and walked into the bedroom of our three young children. Our oldest children are twin boys. Their little bodies were contorted around stuffed animals and producing loud snores. I watched them sleep for a little while. The room was still dark. I walked further in. Our youngest was curled up in a ball. I watched him sleep for a moment. Shuffling over to a rocker, I sat for a while and let my mind wonder in the twilight.

The previous day, the State of Texas surprisingly announced that it would execute Scott Panetti on December 3. I wondered what Scott looked like when he was the age of my children. I imagined a mother watching her child sleep and dreaming about all that he child might become. I can imagine that Scott's mother never thought her child would be a paranoid schizophrenic capable of killing his in-laws in front of his estranged wife and child. The more I sat and thought, the more I couldn't help but look to my own children and wonder if they would ever commit such a crime. Who can say? I can only know what I would do if they did. I would love them.

We descend into hell when we leave love behind. The State of Texas is quickly descending into the hell of a loveless decision. Scott Panetti has suffered from documented mental illness for over 30 years. During a trial where he represented his self, Scott wore a cowboy costume and subpoenaed the Pope, John F. Kennedy, and Jesus Christ to testify. In 1986, six years before Scott killed his in-laws, the Social Security Administration of our country deemed him to be so mentally disabled that he was granted monthly benefits. In order to be competent enough to be executed, Scott must understand why he is being executed. Presently, Scott thinks that he is being executed for being a preacher of the Gospel of Jesus Christ. Over the snores of my children, I couldn't imagine letting anyone take the life out of their vulnerable young bodies no matter what they did. If we don't think it is ok to execute children incapable of understanding their decisions, why would we think it ok to execute someone who is severely mentally ill and incapable of understanding their decisions? To execute either would be a cruel injustice that serves no constructive purpose in a modern world.

In his mental condition, Scott is as vulnerable as my sleeping children. How will we respond? Will we protect vulnerable life? I invite you to think about the vulnerable people that you love. Would you want the state to kill them? Texas plans to descend into a loveless hell on December 3. Somebody please save us. Oh and by the way, the October 30 morning I spent with my children was also my birthday.

Amen.

November 12, 2014

Love Your Enemies: An Invitation from a Southern Baptist to Progressive Baptists

I am a Southern Baptist. Though I am also affiliated with the Alliance of Baptists and much more inclusive and progressive in my theology than most Southern Baptists, I don't run from the label. To discard the label of Southern Baptist would be to discard who I am. I was brought up, educated and ordained by Southern Baptists. Like many of you, this will always be a reality for me.

A few short weeks ago, I joined fellow progressive evangelicals to advocate for full celebration of all people at the Ethics and Religious Liberty Commission of the Southern Baptist Convention's multi-day conference entitled, "The Gospel, Homosexuality and the Future of Marriage." The event consisted of breakout sessions, plenary addresses and panels to provide the gathered with instructions on how to interact with a rapidly changing culture that is often unsympathetic to the views of most Southern Baptists. I presently work at the Cathedral of Hope United Church of Christ in Dallas, Texas (the largest LGBT church in the world). Before I traveled to the conference, I asked members of our congregation to stand up if they felt historically abused or mistreated by Southern Baptists. Hundreds and hundreds and hundreds of people stood up to give witness to the many theological and spiritual atrocities committed by the Southern Baptist Convention. I promised to take their stories with me to the conference in Nashville. While I was standing next to the door as people exited our church, person after person came up to me to tell me their individual story. "I graduated from Southwestern Baptists Theological Seminary and came out many years later. I lived my life terrified that someone would find out...don't forget my story." "I finished my education at Truett-McConnell College and came out this year. I felt so uncomfortable there." "I am a graduate of Midwestern Baptist Theological Seminary and was a man at the time of my graduation. No one knew what I was dealing with." The stories were endless. With a heavy heart, I jumped in the car and started the long drive.

Expecting the worse, I braced my being for a tremendous confrontation. From the time I started at the Southern Baptist Theological Seminary (SBTS) in 2007 to the time I finished in 2009, all I could remember hearing were vile and toxic remarks about gay people. As someone who felt attraction to both men and women, I remember feeling the sting of such comments regularly. Expecting to hear more of the same, I was surprised that there were people who were actually ready to talk in a loving way. I realized that the times truly have changed. On Monday morning of the conference, I participated in a press conference hosted by the Association of Welcoming and Affirming Baptists. From the stage, I declared a truth that I have long known, "I know more closeted Southern Baptist pastors than I do straight ones." The number of closeted Southern Baptist pastors out there is one of the biggest family secrets. Many people came out to me while I was at SBTS and continue to serve Southern Baptist churches. Later in the day, I participated in a civil conversation with evangelical and Southern Baptist leadership about trying to find a way forward. From pastors and leaders of some of the largest ministries in the Southern Baptist Convention, I heard a real desire to listen, learn and try to love. Many will find these words unbelievable. I did too until I experienced them.

Late on Tuesday, I experienced an angry public confrontation with a former colleague from SBTS. In a tone very close to a shout, I was told that I was going to hell and experienced all other sorts of condemnations and belittlements. In this moment, I realized that I had a choice. The events of earlier in the day also weighed heavily on my mind. Dr. Russell Moore, President of the Ethics and Religious Liberty Commission, condemned reparative therapy. Glenn Stanton of Focus on the Family declared that we must love people for the sake of loving people and for no other purpose. While these statements might not sound all that radical to you, coming from my former context, they were revolutionary. Would I listen to the vile statements made by my former colleague and others that were uttered more publicly or would I cling to the moments and statements where my attempt to engage my enemies in love seemed to make my enemies something closer to friends? I chose love. However, the choice is not just mine to make. The choice is ours. In order to live out the love of God, will we decide to follow Jesus back into the temples that almost killed us? I did and experienced Jesus more deeply there.

Amen.

November 23, 2014

The Wet God

Running late.
I am always running late.
The rain poured.
I had to get out of the car.
Stepping out
The puddle overflowed into my shoe
I kept walking
I had to get to church
Pushing into the rain
I saw someone
I didn't have time to stop
Something pulled me back

Turning around
She stood there soaking wet
I stared
She managed a smile
Smiling back
God was wet too

November 24, 2014

The Indictment of Jesus in the Flames of Ferguson

I have not looked at all the evidence. I only know that an armed police officer named Darren Wilson shot an unarmed man named Michael Brown over and over and over again. I don't need more evidence. I don't need more explanation. I don't need more analysis. I am angry. For a while after the decision of the grand jury, I prayed for peace in Ferguson. When I heard from Jesus, I stopped praying that prayer. I thought that Jesus would want all of this to go away. I don't think so anymore.

In the second chapter of the Gospel of John, Jesus walked into a space of tremendous injustice. In a space of great power, there were wealthy people taking advantage of the oppressed. Moved to both anger and action, Jesus fashioned a whip of chords and cleared out the evildoers. With great force, Jesus destroyed property. I am sure there were plenty of people who thought what Jesus was doing was too much. Unfortunately, those who passed judgment on Jesus had never stood for justice before and Jesus had to be the one to do something. We live in an age desperate for people who will do something.

I am a pacifist. I don't believe in committing physical violence against anyone. I believe that Jesus was a pacifist. I believe that there is a difference between violence against property and people. In the second chapter of the Gospel of John, Jesus forcefully destroys the property of the oppressors. In the midst of such injustice in Ferguson, how would Jesus respond?

There will be Christians who condemn the protestors in Ferguson and surrounding areas. Whether you agree or disagree with their actions, the reality is that the folks in the streets are doing something when the rest of our society has done little to nothing. There will be those who don't see Jesus in the midst of such destruction. I would encourage them to open their Bibles. In the second chapter of John, Jesus destroys the tools of the oppressor. I believe he is doing the same in Ferguson.

Amen.

November 25, 2014

Ferguson Statement for Hope for Peace and Justice

"We are a people dedicated to the pursuit of peace and justice. We realize that there can be no peace without justice. We refuse to call for peace in a situation so devoid of justice. In Ferguson, there is no justice and there will be no peace. The truth is that an armed police officer named Darren Wilson shot an unarmed teenager named Michael Brown over and over and over again. The truth remains that the death of Michael Brown is a crime against humanity that should be punished. We believe embracing this truth and demanding justice will be the path that sets us all free."

November 27, 2014

Eating Thanksgiving Dinner with Darren Wilson

Many of us will eat Thanksgiving Dinner today with Darren Wilson. Often, Wilson is someone we love tremendously. Wilson will assure us that there is not a race problem in our country. Speaking of Ferguson and other violence, they will say that those were a bunch of thugs and vigilantes. Citing their plethora of black friends, Wilson will talk about the need for people to just get along like they do with their friends. Wilson will use language that will embarrass us and make us angry. Confidently, Wilson will give example after example of how there is no power difference between whites and blacks. Ultimately, Wilson will think that you agree with him because you won't say anything. Those who sit quietly with Darren Wilson at the table this Thanksgiving Dinner should imagine that the meal they are eating on is the next Michael Brown.

Amen.

November 30, 2014

Killer Christians in Texas: The Next Victim is Scott Panetti

Has your church ever executed someone? Don't be appalled by such a question. Think deeper. Perhaps you never hung someone on the cross at the front of your sanctuary, but have you considered the consequences of your inaction? Think about all the times your church could have done something to save a life and didn't. Can't think of any? Christians in Texas should have no problem.

Texas has one of the largest populations of Christians in the nation. With a statistic like that, one might be surprised to note that Texas also executes more people than any other state. If Texas were a nation, it would be amongst the top executing nations on earth. With Christians comprising a stunning majority of people who live here, there is no ability to blame what is happening in my state on any other faith except my own. Christians are killing people.

From the Governor to the Attorney General to State Legislators to Judges to the District Attorneys to the Jurors to the Prison Guards to a whole host of others, the majority of those directly involved in the process of executing someone in this state are actually Christians. In light of this fact, I have worked over the last few years to get churches organized and talking about abolishing the death penalty. I ask the same question every time, "Would you be interested in hosting a conversation about the death penalty?" More often than not, I hear the same response, "That is too political for our congregation." When a mass movement of Christians could quickly stop the death penalty in Texas, silence remains the primary tool of execution.

The State of Texas is scheduled to execute Scott Panetti on December 3 and Christians will be his primary killers. The barbarism of our crime is exacerbated by the fact that Panetti has suffered from documented mental illness for over 30 years. From being institutionalized over and over again to being classified as disabled by the Social Security Administration to shooting his in-laws to death to dressing up as a cowboy to represent his self at trial to now thinking that he is being executed for preaching and proselytizing, Panetti is very sick. In Matthew 25, there was a man named Jesus from Nazareth who was also very sick and said that we would be judged by how we treat the sick. With just a short time to go before such an injustice is carried out, one would expect the noise coming from Texas churches to be deafening. The truth be known, most churches don't even know an execution is about to be carried out. When did we stop caring about the least of these? When did we stop talking about loving our neighbors as our self? When did we become killer Christians?

Just the other day, I drove by an old country church with a sign out front that read, "The Judgment is Upon Us." I know this to be true. We cannot continue to execute God's children and expect the results to be positive for the future of our people. On December 2, I will start a vigil outside the execution chamber in Huntsville, Texas. During the vigil, I will pray that we will be a people who will turn from our wicked ways, spare the life of Scott Panetti and call upon God to heal our land. In this most holy time of year, I ask that you join me.

Amen.

December 1, 2014

God has AIDS

Our God was born in Bethlehem. Our God became flesh and dwelt amongst us. Our God is bound to the suffering of the world. Our God is bound to us. Jesus declared that he was sick and that he would inhabit the sick. People around the world are sick and suffering with AIDS. Jesus has AIDS. The church is called the Body of Christ. People within the Body of Christ are sick and suffering with AIDS. The Body of Christ has AIDS. The very person and body of our God is sick. Can we please work together to stop this despicable disease? Our God has AIDS.

December 3, 2014

Jesus is Dead and So Are We: Eric Garner is Our Only Hope for Resurrection

On July 17, 2014, Jesus was standing on a corner. Officers confronted Jesus. After a brief conversation, Jesus was placed into a chokehold and slammed to the ground. The last words of Jesus were, "I can't breathe." I don't believe that Eric Garner lived his life as Jesus. I don't believe any of us do. Based on the exhortation of Jesus to "the least of these" in Matthew 25, I do believe that Jesus inhabits the marginalized and oppressed more fully than anyone else. In this society, black bodies are under the constant assault of all manners of marginalizations and oppressions. In the passion of Eric Garner, I believe Jesus died.

In the graveyard, Jesus lays dead along with all of us. Our society died when it chose to believe that racism is a historical artifact. The church died when it stopped talking about the oppression of racism and pretended it was dead. We die everyday when we don't do anything to stop the constant brutality that is perpetuated against black bodies. Everywhere I look in this nation, there are dead bones.

What good is a dead God laying with a bunch of dead people? I don't believe in death without resurrection. Faintly, I hear the questioning words of Jesus in the words of Ezekiel 37:3, "...can these bones live?" I don't know what to say. Racism is killing people at all levels of our society. I know I can't trust government to do better. I know that capitalism remains as prejudiced as ever. I look around and see only death. In desperation, I reply to Jesus, "I don't think so. I think we are too far gone. I don't think there is any hope. People are so racist and racism is so ingrained in all that we do." Then Jesus replied to me in the words of Ezekiel 37:9, "Prophesy to the breath...breathe into these slain, that they may live." I remembered the last words of Eric Garner, "I can't breathe." Eric Garner died because our racist dead society choked him to death. I believe in resurrection. The resurrection of Eric Garner is our only hope. We must continue to breathe life into his story and case. We must use the details of the horrific tragedy of Eric Garner's death to shock life into the people of this nation. We must keep demanding justice. Do not ever stop telling the story of Eric Garner. Get out into the streets and breathe the breath of life into this dead racist nation. Dead bones can live and in their living is our only hope of salvation.

Amen.

December 6, 2014

The Letter from the Dallas County Jail

Dear people of God,

I can't breathe.

People are so confused. Everyone thinks that protesters are the agitators across the country. Believe me, I experienced who the real agitators are last night.

You will find them next to the people who are gasping for air.

Throughout the night, over 500 people marched through the streets of Dallas to remind the populace that the real agitators in our city and nation are the uncontrolled militarized police forces that daily do violence to people of color and the wider population. The Dallas Police Department reinforced these notions over and over with arbitrary arrest and requests after arbitrary arrest and requests. Who do the police work for? There was a screaming woman of color pulled out of the middle of the crowd and arrested for no apparent reason. There was a woman arrested for standing on the sidewalk. Even though over 500 people marched up and down street after street all night, there were only a handful of people arrested for marching in the street in what was described as a "show of force" by one officer. I was one of those.

The copes were on top of us and we couldn't breathe.

When I was arrested, I didn't resist. I calmly got into the back of a van. Though I felt like the situation I found myself in was an injustice, I wasn't angry with those who arrested me. I actually have tremendous compassion for them. I feel like they are so very often unwitting pawns in a much larger game. I wasn't surprised that the police got most forceful and angry when marchers began to disrupt private enterprise. Our economic system has brutalized bodies of persons of color since the arrival of European settlers and our police have now become the chief protectors of economic inequality.

Money is choking out our conscience.

One of the officers I encountered at the Dallas County Jail informed me that pastors shouldn't get arrested. I couldn't believe the ignorance of such a statement. After I confirmed that he was a Christian, I questioned, "Did you know that the founder of our faith was arrested and executed?" The officer was befuddled. Our churches make people feel safe in the knowledge that Jesus doesn't require anything of you. Our theology often looks something like this, Jesus is Santa Clause and has a bag full of toys that he is ready to hand out. I wish that there were so many pastors willing to get arrested in Dallas that the jails would overflow. I don't think it was an accident that I had just walked past some of the most storied Baptist, Methodist and Presbyterian spaces in Dallas before I got arrested. What if all the members of those churches were out in the street? We wouldn't have a problem with police brutality. How long must we wait for churches to follow Jesus into the dangerous space of seeking justice and righteous transformation in our world?

People are choking and we call them other.

The number of people of color in the waiting room at the Dallas County Jail was astounding. If anyone needs any evidence of that our system that is unbelievably oppressive to people of color...look no further than our jail. One of the more interesting comments of the night came from an officer of color. Looking around the room, he declared the entire room to be "criminals." I think he forget the we are innocent until proven guilty piece. Regardless, I was amazed at how quickly he othered the people in the room. I think this is the primary problem of both the police and the church in our nation. These institutions survive on profiling the other and deciding that they have no value and need to be controlled at all costs. The police and our churches are a reflection of the evil in our own hearts and often live fully into this evil.

We are choking.

This is the hour to get out into the streets and create some air.

Amen.

Rev. Jeff Hood

December 7, 2014

The Real Church is in The Streets: A Speech Delivered to the Dallas Rally Against Police Brutality on December 5, 2014

Whose streets???
Our streets!!!
Whose streets???
Our streets!!!

Good evening, my name is Rev. Jeff Hood. I work out of the Cathedral of Hope United Church of Christ...the largest LGBT church in the entire world. I serve as the Minister of Social Justice of their social justice ministry Hope for Peace and Justice. Ours is a church that knows a thing or two about police brutality. Our community knows a thing or two about police brutality. Unfortunately, our church is not all that different from many churches...in that it still has much to learn about race in America. Over the last few weeks, I have looked at churches and places of faith and been so disappointed. Because I know...that churches can make a difference. I believe that churches can make a difference. So often when I have thought about the crucifixion of Jesus in the last few weeks, I feel like churches are the ones on the sidelines screaming, "Crucify him! Crucify him! Crucify him!" There is an indictment against our churches.

There is an indictment against our religious communities. That indictment is here tonight. Asking the question... How long? How long must we work? How long must we wait for justice? How long will you sit in your religious buildings and castles and do nothing? I have thought about what the church is over the past few weeks. I have decided that the buildings and the spaces don't matter. I have decided that the crosses and other religious paraphernalia are but mirages. I believe that the Spirit of God is not contained in such things. I believe that the spirit of God is right here tonight. I believe that the true church will be in the streets tonight.

I believe that what we are doing here tonight is an incredibly spiritual thing. We have a community that is broken and hurt by police brutality. You are the vessels of our redemption, sanctification and cleansing. As you walk these streets tonight, know that you are making our city a place that we will all want to live in...a place where we all matter...

I want to know one final thing from you...

Whose streets???
Our streets!!!
Whose streets???
Our streets!!!
Whose streets???
Our streets!!!

As you go out there...know that you are the future...because injustice can only last a little while... I don't believe in death without resurrection. I don't believe that the death of Eric Garner will be in vein. I don't believe the death of Mike Brown will be in vein. I believe that you are the vessels of life. Please...don't stop. Don't stop. Keep going! Awaken the conscious of this city. Awaken our souls.

Amen.

December 7, 2014

My Dear Grandmother Frances Hood Died Today and Our Love Remains

The parking lot of a restaurant is an odd place to find out that your grandmother has died. Then again, I guess it is as good a place as any to receive devastating news. The words of my dad are still echoing in my brain, "she died this morning in her favorite chair." There are few people I have loved more in this life than my grandmother. Without a doubt, Frances Hood was my patron saint. From the earliest of ages, my grandmother loved me dearly and constantly pushed me toward the truest entity she had ever known, Jesus. I credit my grandmother with much of my spiritual development. Though we disagreed monumentally at times, we always had Jesus and that was all we ever really needed.

I don't cry often. I guess I express emotions in a variety of ways other than crying. When I start to cry, water drains from my eyes profusely and my face explodes with redness. When I found out that I lost my grandmother, I had just strapped my twin sons into their car seats. I tried to keep it together for them. I didn't want to scare them. I couldn't. The tears started to flow like a river, my body started to tremble and my face turned red. The twins didn't know what to do. When Phillip asked what was wrong, I replied, "Someone I love has died." The boys didn't get it. As I was waiting for my wife Emily to get out of the restaurant, I prayed to my grandmother. I told her that I love her with all my heart. The reply was clear, "I'm home." I don't care whether anyone believes that I actually heard my grandmother or not. I did. Once I got over the supernatural and metaphysical mystery of the moment, I found it interesting that I spoke to my grandmother in a declaration and she responded with a destination. I think we are all longing for a place where love is made complete. Perhaps instead of making declarations, we need to follow the lead of my grandmother and live more into the destination. Throughout her life, my grandmother longed for a place where love exists in all fullness and I have no doubt that she is there.

Though I have had many beautiful conversations with my grandmother, I will always cherish the last one. My grandmother has never been able to understand my activism and progressive ministry. While I was at home for Thanksgiving, my grandmother brought up "the gays" (in her words). I asked her, "Have you ever been attracted to a woman before?" My question was simply too much for her. Though my grandmother was known her whole life for her ability to talk loudly and consistently, the question left her speechless and astonished. After a little back and forth, I backed off the question. The next day, we were about to leave to drive back to Texas. I had just loaded our kids into the car and was ready to go. Before I hit the gas, I thought to run inside her house next door and see my grandmother. When I knocked on the door, she opened it and said, "I was hoping you would stop and see me one last time before you left." I walked in and told her just how much I loved her. I prodded her to let me take a picture before I left. Leaning in, I gave her a soft kiss on the forehead and snapped a selfie. The moment was very special. The interaction grew divine based on the last words she ever spoke to me, "I thought about our conversation, I want you to know that I am very proud of you and love is going to be what sees us all through." Though I will miss her with all my heart, I believe her last words to me. Even in the face of death, I know that our love remains and will sustain us both until we meet again.

Amen.

December 11, 2014

A Message at the Funeral of My Grandmother Frances Hood

We gather this morning at a difficult hour. I have grown accustomed to gathering in times both good and bad in this very room. The Rock Baptist Church is an ancestral and spiritual home for the Hood family. Many of you have gathered with us over the years. I have done much questioning in these pews. Today is no different.

The last few days of my life have been filled with questions. Why would God allow my grandmother to die? Why do we have funerals at all? Why would a loving God keep allowing people to die? These are serious and difficult questions. I loved my grandmother with all of my heart. Serious love requires serious and difficult questions. We must dare ask...Why?

When my cousins Jeremiah and Jeffrey died very young...I dared ask...Why? When my Uncles Donnie Hood and Donnie Stevens died...I dared ask...Why? When my Great Grandmother Ruth Hood died...I dared to ask...Why? Last year, when my Grandfather died...I dared ask...Why? Why? Why? Why?

There are many of us sitting here with many questions. I am the chief questioner on this day. In that casket, my beloved grandmother sits in that casket cold and dead. Why?

There will be some who offer the easy answers of church speak.

Some will say: "You will see her again in heaven." I don't care about your again. I don't care about your heaven. I miss my grandmother right now. What type of God would take her from me? What type of God would take her from us? Why?

Some will say: "She is more alive now than she ever has been." She is dead. Look at this casket. There is no movement. If God is so good...what are we doing here today? Why would God do this? Why?

I could go on all morning. If I did, I would be left with a million questions and very few answers.

My grandmother had a millions reasons not to believe...but chose to believe anyways. In spite of devastating tragedies and hardships, my grandmother chose to believe.

I have felt my whole life that I can trace my faith in God to my grandmother. There was something about her reckless abandonment to Jesus that moved, shook and shaped me. Many will say that they don't believe that faith is a hereditary phenomenon. I am not so sure about that.

I found out that my grandmother died just after I finished lunch after church last Sunday in Dallas, Texas. I had just buckled my twin sons into their car seats. My dad called and said that my Aunt Jackie had just found my grandmother dead. My eyes filled up with tears, my face turned red and my body shook. I was devastated. My kids couldn't figure out what was wrong. My faith was shaken. In desperation, I cried out in prayer to my grandmother. I wanted her to know one last time that I loved her with all that I am. As clear as I am speaking to you now, I heard the voice of my grandmother declare, "I'm home." Whether you believe in such things or not is of no consequence to me, I do. I can only tell you what I experienced. I find it interesting that I made a declaration to my grandmother and she responded with a destination.

I believe that every question we ask draws us closer to a destination where there will be no more questions. I believe in home.

Jesus tells us in John 14, "Do not let your heart be troubled, believe in God believe in me. God's house has plenty of space. I would not have invited you if that wasn't the case. I will go and prepare a place for you. I want you to be where I am."

1 John 4:8 reminds us that "God is love."

I believe that it is love that prepares a place for us.
Love calls us to that final destination of home.
There is a spark of the divine in the love that we share with each other that calls us and pulls us to that ultimate destination.
Love is the victor because God is the victor. For God is love.

I am able to leave this pulpit with many questions but my faith intact because the love that my grandmother and I shared was so strong. I know that such love will continue to draw me to the source of all love until I meet my grandmother again in that place called home. In spite of the many difficulties and struggles in my soul, I choose to believe that love does save. Despite the body that lays in front of me, I dare declare at the top of my lungs that LOVE WILL NEVER DIE.

Amen.

December 12, 2014

Danny Cortez is a Dangerous Man

Darkness filled the sky and night was upon me. Throughout my drive to the airport, I thought about the death of my grandmother. I was hurting. The last thing I wanted to do was entertain a former Southern Baptist pastor from California. Though I invited Danny Cortez to speak to multiple groups in North Texas, I just wasn't in it when I pulled up to the curb at the airport. Danny is an unassuming man small in stature and quick to smile. When he got in the car, I tried to strike up some small talk. Desperate to engage the greatest theological questions of our time, Danny wasn't interested in small talk.

Our group was bigger than the venue had room to accomadate and we had to find space with more room. Upon finding a suitable location, Danny Cortez started to tell his story. From the people that he sent to reparative therapy to the lesbian that has become one of his dearest friends to his gay son, we encountered the intensity with which Danny has wrestled with questions of orientation and gender. The conversion of Danny to a place of supporting full inclusion was a process. Though he knew it would cost him his job, Danny decided to tell his Southern Baptist congregation that he had changed his mind and now supported the celebration and participation of all people in the life of the church. Ultimately, Danny persuaded his church to keep him as their pastor and agree to disagree about issues of human sexuality and gender. The Southern Baptist Convention wasn't having it and kicked them out not long after the decision. In our group, most of the people listening didn't even think that such a church was possible. Danny repeated the same conclusion over and over again throughout the visit to every group and in every venue, "As Christians, we must believe that the process is just as important as the destination."

From a home to a large progressive Baptist church to the largest LGBT church on the planet, Danny Cortez did not stop talking about love and embracing the other. Though I am much more radical and abrasive than Danny, his message caused a tremendous stirring in my soul. How do I treat those I disagree with? How do I love those who know nothing but hate? What would Jesus do in this age of polarities? The questions are not the most profound pieces of theology that I can muster, but I am more interested in following Jesus than profundity. I know that the follower of Christ must love well along the way. By choosing to believe that all people have value regardless of their beliefs and daring to seek to love them, Danny is a dangerous man for all sides. Jesus was too.

Amen.

December 16, 2014

poetic words from the struggle

frances

the deepness of the moment
the pain rolled down my cheek
you can't live forever
right now we can't speak
from the darkness I cry out
your voice is like light
something seems closer than ever
in the gap I hear something
death and life are close

the hand

why?
death takes
make the best of it
you are liar
stuck in this place

inertia of being
blindness of vision
being of nothing
I feel the hand
don't touch me
you frighten me
you are rude and careless
do you not care?
does the hand lead the way or grab to take?
I don't know
I just hold on
somehow the world becomes a meaningful place

pulpit

do you care to listen
why be here
the world is hurting
we just talk
is this a game or church

sunsets

we are never ready to say goodbye to the day
there is something that we lost just after dawn
did the hours take from us
do we donate part of our self to the sunset
are the colors us
are we looking at beauty or our own demise

only the colors know

defiance

I refused to be categorized
I refused to be victimized
I refused to be identified
I refused to be who you want me to be
Defiance

December 12, 2014

The Taliban in the Self

Shots rang out. Blood was everywhere. Bodies hit the floor. Children screamed. The images and descriptions of the scene at a school in Pakistan are more than horrific. Over 130 children are dead over an extremist religious ideology. From terrorist attack to terrorist attack, the Taliban have proven that there is no end to the barbarism of their actions. How do we make sense of such a tragedy? Our first inclination is to label those who would commit such atrocities, monsters. The problem with such dehumanizing characterization is that it fails to understand that the monster in the other is the monster in us.

How many children has our greed killed? How many children grow up without proper education? How many children are subjected to the slow deaths of racism, homophobia and sexism? How many children are dead because of our thirst for guns and violence? The questions can go on and on.

The teachings of Jesus are incredibly important to help us formulate our responses to humans that commit horrific tragedies. In the life and mind of Jesus, there was an understanding that loving your enemies is the only way to save them. Without a love for our enemies, we are relegated to an existence of hate that ultimately destroys our lives too. Do we want to be like the Taliban? The unchecked hate of the Taliban drove them to commit this great atrocity. What do you think that unchecked hate for the Taliban will do in your life? We are all capable of tremendous evil. When we allow hate to go unchecked in our own hearts, we allow the evil deeds that we perpetuate to be masked. That which we hate the most is often what we are. Our world is in desperate need of change. We cannot expect any difference if we continue to exchange hate for hate. Love is the only way to something better.

Through our desire to learn to not function as they function, the Taliban can teach us how to be more human. We can learn to love and not hate. We can learn to look for the evil in our own souls. We can learn that part of being human is holding back the monster within. We can learn to push past barriers that we think are insurmountable. We can learn.

For many years, the term Cuban functioned as the word Taliban functions now in the United States. Both words described great enemies. Today, the word Cuban describes a people that people in the United States desperately want to embrace. The love that Cubans in exile and many others have for the people on the island turned enemies into friends. I think we would be wise to follow such a path with even the worst of our geopolitical enemies. Let us never forget that our worst enemies are always going to be a reflection of what is within.

Amen.

December 18, 2014

Words of Blessing for the Dallas Youth March

I apologize for my absence this evening. During these very hours, I am graduating with my doctorate in theology tonight from Texas Christian University. I welcome your prayers as I discern how I can continue to make a difference in our world. When my friend Aleah Dillard told me about this event and asked me to send a few words, I thought about a few questions...

Is resurrection possible? Can dead bones come back to life? Is death the final word? These are important questions for anyone that is gathered in the pursuit of justice. In death, the powerful believe that Michael Brown, Eric Garner, John Crawford, Tamir Rice and many others slain by overzealous police are silenced. Tonight, I write to tell you that death has no power when people unite in the cause of justice and breathe life into the slain. Is resurrection possible? Yes, you are the resurrection. Can dead bones come back to life? Yes, you are the breathe of life. Is death the final word? No, you are the final word. Tonight and every night, you must continue to speak out against police brutality. In you words and actions, you resurrect the slain and call us forward to a brighter tomorrow.

In our present time, I believe the church has lost much moral courage. I hear a tremendous amount of silence coming from the creaky old spaces of worship around town. Where are the pastors and clergy at the marches and actions? I don't believe that such people and spaces are necessary to facilitate change anymore. I am follower of a God who stands with those who stand for justice. You are standing for justice. You are the people of God. You are the church. Tonight, you are performing a highly spiritual and sacramental practice...you are raising the dead with your voices. Be the church tonight...lead us all to a place of justice.

There will be many who say that you are too young to do the work that you are doing. Tell them that they are too old for their opinion to matter anymore. These are your streets. This is your church. Protect it from anyone who would do violence to it. Never stop demanding justice. Never stop lifting your voices. Never stop raising the dead. You are our hope of resurrection.

Amen.

December 18, 2014

Maria: A Queer Guide for Us All

If it was not for your willingness to follow God, I doubt I would be writing. I just received my doctorate from Brite Divinity School at Texas Christian University for a project entitled, "The Epiphany of the Queer: An Exploration in Theology." For so many years, you have inspired me to keep going. There are many who would say that a man married to a woman should not be doing queer theology. Often, I try to reason with those who are critical. I talk about the spectrum of sexuality and orientation and then add that I have been attracted to men and women since I was young. These words will never be enough for some. In the face of an unplanned pregnancy, I know words were never enough for your critics either. I cling to a God that is queer beyond our wildest imaginations. I know the God that speaks to me is the same God that called you. When we follow the call of God, we slowly grow queerer into the person that we were created to be. You are the queerest of them all. You rejected the normative constructions of society and lived queerly for the sake of carrying God. When anyone questions the existence of a God that is queer, I point to you.

Do you believe in the virgin birth? In living it, I guess you do. I bet it was terrifying to realize that God made you different than anyone else. Queerness is often scary when we are so accustomed to normative ways of living. You chose to step out of the closet and accept a dangerous task. In carrying the incarnation of God, you stepped closer to being the incarnation of God you were created to be in the first place. What did it feel like when they called you names? Did it feel like you were drawing nearer to God in the misunderstandings of others? When you were attacked and mocked, the queerness of God made and sustained you. People ask me all the time, "Do you believe in the virgin birth?" I don't believe in the virgin birth my dearest Maria, I believe in you. I believe that miracles come when we embrace the queer within us and live into who God calls us to be. You did. Slowly, you became ever queerer like the God who sent you. I follow your lead to God. The fruit of your womb has drawn me closer to you and all others who live and reign with the queer beyond queer, one God now and forever.
Ave Maria.

Amen.

December 22, 2014

The Shepherd from Bethlehem Speaks

Have you ever wondered what it is like to be a shepherd? Most of the time you are bored out of your mind. I sit there and watch sheep day after day. I never wanted to be a shepherd. I didn't have a choice. We have always been poor. We don't know any other way. I followed what generations before me had done. I did what I had to do to support my family. Do you know what it feels like to sit on a hill night after night to make sure that your kids have something to eat? Every morning at dawn, I go into town with shit all over the bottom of my robe. How would you like it? I guess we are all willing to walk through some shit to care for those we love.

My cousin brought some wine out to the hillside. We all got drunk watching over our flock by night. When the angel appeared and the glory of God came over us, we sobered up real quick. I just knew that we were about to be punished for being drunk. What would you do if an angel and the glory of God came upon you? Terrified and drunk, I peed in my robe. Instead of judgment, the angel spoke beautiful words. I still have no idea why God chose a drunken shepherd piece of shit like me to be among the first to see the Messiah. I didn't know if I was worthy. I guess the first step to realizing that you are somebody is to pull your self out of the shit and believe that God don't create shit.

Millions of angels filled the heavens. I couldn't believe the sight. I chanted with them, "Glory to God in the highest and peace on earth!!!" When they got to that peace part, I remembered my other addiction to violence. If I was going to go meet God, I realized that I would have to give up the vengeance I carried toward my enemies. I knew I was going to have to be about love. Would you be willing to give some things up to meet God? I decided I wanted to be different and I turned toward that bright light in the sky over Bethlehem.

When I arrived to the beautiful baby in the manger, the stable smelled like urine and shit. Since it was masking the urine and shit on my robe, I didn't care. I just kept looking at that baby. In the face of the child, I saw hope for the entire world. In those moments, I was made whole. It might sound crazy, but I got the impression that the baby could pull us all out of the shit we are in. I guess we just have to choose to love. You up for it?

Amen.

December 25, 2014

Post-Christmas Day: Get Stinky

Why did we do all of this celebrating? The spiritual reason is simple. Christmas is a time to celebrate the incarnation of God into the world. Truthfully, I don't think that most people understand what such a statement means. In our highly religious descriptions of Christmas, we often fail to tell people...Christmas is a time to remember that love was made flesh. The intersection of the divine and the human is always centered on love. The writer of 1 John 4:8 tells us, "God is Love." With love and God being synonymous terms, the description of Christmas gets simpler.

Love was born in all fullness in a stable full of shit in Bethlehem. Love got dirty in order to be with us. Love died so that others might live. Love never dies. Those who are following God or love will exist in shitty situations and places. When you choose to be like God and love people, you have to get in the shit with them.

The message of Post-Christmas Day is simple...

Go now and follow the love that is God and get stinky.

Amen.

#Short Words from 2015

Talked about abolishing the death penalty on the radio today in Houston. -Jan. 8

"All to Jesus I surrender..." The words that drew me as a child continue to draw me and my family now. - Jan. 11

Quinley Mandela started walking today. -Feb. 11

Proud to stand with Hope for Peace & Justice tonight and talk about an issue that I care about in addition to same-sex marriage as a member of the Queer Community...the Abolishment of the Death Penalty. -Feb. 20

Standing on the side of love. -Feb. 20

It's a Winter Wonderland Here in Texas Y'all! -Feb. 27

We are all excited about the release of my friend Sandhya Jha's epic new book, Pre-Post-Racial America on March 17. -March 4

Babywatch 2015. #twins #stillstanding -March 6

"NOT ONE MORE EXECUTION!" words from Texas Coalition to Abolish the Death Penalty Faith Leader Advocacy Day -March 9

Madeleine and I / The Dance -March 9

Interview I did with Al Jazeera America's "America Tonight" in June 2014 / Though the video quality is poor, this is a really good introduction to the issue of the death penalty in Texas. -March 20

"What is Theology?" - clip from "The Courage to Be Queer: An Exploration in Theology" / Keynote Address at Sam Houston State University's LGBTQ Religious Experience Summit on 3/21/15 -March 21

I am excited to announce the release of my seventh book, "LAST WORDS FROM TEXAS: MEDITATIONS FROM THE EXECUTION CHAMBER." Based on my Lenten Reflections from the Executed blog series, this longer volume contains 84 meditations based on the last words of 84 persons executed in Texas and their respective pictures. The book is dedicated to Helen Prejean, Kathy Cox and Kim Jackson, three women who are working tirelessly to abolish the death penalty. I would also like to thank my wife Emily for designing the stunning cover. -March 29

3pm (Hour1of24): The Vigil has Begun / Prayers for the Abolition of the Death Penalty in Huntsville, Texas -April 2

4pm (Hour2of24): Contemplating those who were preparing to arrest Jesus and those who prepare the materials for executions in Texas. // with Rev. Tony Lorenzen of Thoreau Woods Unitarian Universalist Church in Huntsville, Texas -April 2

7pm (Hour5of 24): Contemplating Jesus eating his final meal and the prisoners who have eaten their final meal before their execution // with Aric El in Huntsville, Texas -April 2

9pm (Hour7of24): Contemplating Jesus' washing of the disciples and our executions that make sure the feet of the executed never move again. -April 2

11pm (Hour9of24): Contemplating the betrayal of Jesus and thinking about how executions force us to betray our values // in Huntsville, Texas. -April 2

12am (Hour10of24): Contemplating Jesus' admonition that those who live by the sword will die by the sword in conjunction with our practice of the death penalty // in Huntsville, Texas #GoodFriday -April 3

8am (Hour18of24): Contemplating the chants of crucify him and our chants of execute him // with Rev. LyAnna Johnson from Servants of Christ UMC in Houston, Texas -April 3

9am (Hour19of24): "Father, forgive them, for they don't know what they're doing."
(Luke 23:34) // Who will forgive us our executions? -April 3

12pm (Hour22of24): "My God, my God, why have you abandoned me?" (Mark 15:34) // Why do we abandon those on death row? -April 3

"This is the body and blood of Jesus...shed so that we might learn how to love each other. This is also the body and blood of Tommy Sells, Lisa Coleman, Carlos De Luna and a whole host of others we have executed in this state...shed so that me might see that love and killing don't mix." // Communion thoughts at the conclusion of a 24-hour Vigil to Abolish the Death Penalty #ReclaimHolyWeek -April 3

"My children remain my greatest teachers." -April 11

"The time is NOW for BAPTISTS to get up off their ASSES and ABOLISH THE DEATH PENALTY" - Speaking to the Alliance of Baptists Annual Gathering - April 17

This morning, I will testify before the Texas House of Representatives on a bill to abolish the death penalty and I covet your prayers. I asked my son Phillip (age 3), "Why do we oppose the death penalty?" His reply: "We're not supposed to kill people." -April 29

"Unite! Rebel! Send those Killer Cops to Jail the Whole Damn System is Guilty as Hell!" / The Hoods were Present Along with Hundreds of Others in Dallas. #BlackLivesMatter #BlackSpring -May 1

"Tell Somebody!" - During the Closing Remarks at the Dallas Pilgrimage/March to the Sites of Police Murders - May 8

"It is the DUTY of ALL who LOVE JESUS to STOP the POLICE from KILLING more PEOPLE!" - During the Dallas Pilgrimage/March to the Sites of Police Murders - May 8

This is a photograph of Derrick Charles being transferred to Huntsville, Texas for his scheduled execution. Join me in prayer that we will stop killing people. -May 12

"Shouldn't liberation be the goal of any social justice movement? Are you interested in enough liberation for everyone or is that too much?" - The Courage to Be Queer -May 14

I hung out with my favorite Former Burglar, Prison Reformer, Abolitionist and LGBT Activist today...the infamous Queen of Houston Ray Hill -May 15

"Our safe spaces are keeping us from doing the work of a God who demands that we love dangerously." -May 15

"I am here representing a rainbow people. When Grapevine Police Officer Robert Clark murdered Ruben Garcia, we were reminded that police brutality can strike anyone at anytime. We must unite the rainbow of humanity to push back and get these killer cops off our streets." #LatinoLivesMatter -May 18

"I am here representing a rainbow people. When Grapevine Police Officer Robert Clark murdered Ruben Garcia, we were reminded that police brutality can strike anyone at anytime. We must unite the rainbow of humanity to push back and get these killer cops off our streets." #LatinoLivesMatter -May 21

"I just tried to be a Christian." -Legend of the Civil Rights Movement Rev. Ed King -May 30

Lunch with Rev. Mike Piazza, catalyst for growth and activism at Cathedral of Hope United Church of Christ -June 1

"For identity theories & politics in this nation...the thrill is gone. We will either learn to live together or suffocate in our categories." -June 1

Lester Bower is dead and Christians are to blame. Our atonement theologies have made us desperate for scapegoats. The blood of Lester Bower will not atone for our sin. -June 3

"We will either find freedom in our queerness or enslavement in identity." - The Courage to Be Queer in New York -June 12

Singing Lessons in Tennessee. -June 16

"There is knowledge available far beyond our words." / Pleasant Hill UCC - June 17

We made it to California! -June 24

"Jesus invited Judas to the table even when he knew the betrayal was coming...our call is to go and do likewise" -with Rev. Danny Cortez & the good people of New Heart Community Church -June 25

We spent the day handing out food on Skid Row. When I was overheard remarking that I was sad about not being in Texas to perform weddings, a prophetic woman snapped back, "Gay marriage? Baby, I'm hungry." I immediately knew we were exactly where we needed to be. -June 27

"Colonialists tried to starve us out, so we decided to embody our Native American forgiveness by doing everything we can to make sure no one goes hungry again." - Allan Espinoza, Native American Food Bank, S. El Monte, CA - June 27

Proud of the intersectional work of my friend Seek ThePoet. We must stand at the borders of identity and prophesy justice for all of God's children. Contact Seek to get your pic and join the revolution. #DualJustice -July 3

Love over Terrorism. -July 7

Quinley and I worshipping at the BeLoved Community. -July 12

"I Woke Up This Morning..." with the BeLoved Community -July 12

This is one of 3 Confederate Battle Flags in the National Cathedral (Episcopal). Dean Gary Hall has asked that they be removed. I stand with him. -July 14

"When Jesus stands at the door and knocks...he is knocking on the door of your closet." -July 14

Proud that Fox News contributor Erick Erickson has labeled me a heretic. -July 17

"Black is gay and gay is black. We will either march together or die separately." - Olinka Green -July 30

One week after the 10am August 1 incident, I prayed for justice at the exact time and in the exact spot of the jail where #JosephHutcheson was murdered by the Dallas County Sheriff's Department. -August 13

"The only path to freedom is to be the queer that God created you to be in the first place." -August 17

"Liberation should lead to further liberation not further oppression." -during interview for YES! Magazine -August 20

Emily. -August 29

Home. -August 31

"Difference is the only tool we have to make a difference." -Sept. 6

We have to do better. #LaborDay -Sept. 7

"These victims of brutality could have said, 'To hell with all y'all...' but instead they dug in deeper to work harder and that is why we call them Ambassadors of Justice." - Hope for Peace and Justice Sunday -Sept. 13

Proud to have lead a rally against Islamophobia with Mohamed ElHassan Mohamed : Ahmed Mohamed's Dad #IStandWithAhmed -Sept. 17

"In a world of normative paradigms, God will never fit in and nor should we." I invite you to explore the queerness of my first major theological work. -Sept. 23

"Killing is evil. There is no way to sanitize or medicalize it. Killing is evil." #StopExecutionsOH -Oct. 3

Walking this morning with Derrick Jamison...who was exonerated from Ohio's Death Row after spending 20 years in prison for a crime he didn't commit. #StopExecutionsOH #deathrow -Oct. 5

"Let us remember that we never walk alone." Mile79of83 #StopExecutionsOH -Oct. 9

Joined by many friends to finish up the walk this morning. Mile82of83 #StopExecutionsOH -Oct. 10

As of today, I am a Southern Baptist minister with standing in the United Church of Christ. -Oct. 17

Frank Schaefer is now the proud owner of The Courage to Be Queer. -Oct. 21

The Queer was a truly beautiful experience. This panel y'all... -Oct. 24

The Hoods were in the studio with David Person talking "The Courage to Be Queer" on 103.1 WEUP "Tennessee Valley's #1 for The Most Hip Hop and R&B" -Oct. 27

My rendition of Fred Phelps in The Laramie Project. -Oct. 29

Phillip and I walking the last steps of Joseph Hutcheson with his family on the three month anniversary of his murder at the hands of the Dallas County Sheriff's Department. -Oct. 31

"May God damn any business, church or organization that steps over the bodies of marginalized and oppressed people here in Oak Lawn to conduct their affairs as if nothing is going on." -at the March to Light Up Oak Lawn after numerous gay bashings and the murder of Shade Schuler (a Trans Woman of Color) -Nov. 1

"God we pray that you will send fire down into our hearts to bolster us in a powerful way...then can you please send a little bit of fire down beneath our asses to keep us marching for justice" #lightupOakLawn -Nov. 2

Join me in praying for the passage of Houston's Equal Rights Ordinance today! #HERO -Nov. 3

There is nothing more evil than killing the mentally disabled and call it justice. Stand down Missouri! #deathpenalty #ErnestJohnson -Nov. 3

May God show you the Way, the Truth and the Light. Amen. -Nov. 4

"Imagine for a second that God treated you like you treat everyone else..." - from a talk on relationships -Nov. 5

"Diversity is a failed construct...We don't need wider diversity...we need wider authenticity." #diversity -Nov. 5

"Claiming an identity or category doesn't make you queer...Queerness and oppression don't go together...Over the last few months, I have watched the campaign for the Houston Equal Rights Ordinance..." -Nov. 5

"Never let your wander lose that wonder" / Madeleine -Nov. 6

"I will not stop marching until these hate crimes stop!" #LightsCameraAction #LightUpOakLawn -Nov. 6

Spent the evening with Ghandi's grandson Arun and my dear friend FOR ED Rev. Kristin Stoneking at FOR's Centennial...but Madeleine still commanded most of my attention. -Nov. 7

One of the great moments of my life was to deliver the opening prayer (while holding Madeleine) at the Fellowship of Reconciliation's Centennial Gala -Nov. 7

"I stumbled on my copy of Culture Shift. I found little I agreed with until I came across this line, 'There is simply no right to not be offended, and we should be offended by the very notion that such a right could exist.'" #SBTS -Nov. 8

"So...God we ask that you take the fire that is in all of our hearts tonight and manuever it underneath our backsides so that we will race into the next 100 years." -Nov. 8

Tonight, Dallas County District Attorney Susan Hawk agreed to a meeting with the family of Joseph Hutcheson and I. The time for indictments in this case was yesterday. -Nov. 9

My latest for Baptist News Global: "I invite you to stop going to church and learn to follow. Jesus will always be out there on the margins living dangerously beyond our budgets, bulletins, buildings, baptisteries, branding and ...." -Nov. 10

"Will you commit to an impartial study that looks at the functioning of the death penalty in Dallas County?" - during a public Q&A I had with Dallas County District Attorney Susan Hawk -Nov. 10

"I don't believe in celebrating veterans. I believe we shouldn't be warring in the first place. I believe in celebrating the love of God found in people." #VeteransDay -Nov. 10

"Since those days, Love just keeps coming back. The reincarnation of Jesus Christ cannot be stopped for Love is all encompassing and eternal. Love will always win." - Nov. 12

"Would Jesus Eat Meat?" -Nov. 12

"If we want to follow Jesus, we are commanded to become what we want to save...In the coming days, our cry of love for our enemies must be, 'I am a terrorist.'" #Paris #Beirut #Baghdad -Nov. 14

"God...spare the life of Raphael Holiday. Let this be the moment that death row becomes obsolete. Let us be the people of abolition." Pilgrimage Mile 0/43 - Nov. 17

"Let Raphael Holiday know our grace." Pilgrimage Mile 2/43 -Nov. 17

"Do not let this road carry that van of death ever again. Stop the execution of Raphael Holiday!" Pilgrimage Mile 3/43 -Nov. 17

"Let the rain wash away our sins of attempting to kill Raphael Holiday and save us from the evil of the death penalty." Pilgrimage Mile 4/43
-Nov. 17

"Let Raphael Holiday know the shelter of your mercy." Pilgrimage Mile 5/43 - Nov. 17

"Excise the death penalty addiction out of Texas Christians/Southern Baptists. Jesus stands with those trying to love/save their neighbor...Raphael Holiday." Pilgrimage Mile 6/43 -Nov. 17

"Stop the execution of Raphael Holiday!" Pilgrimage Mile 7/43
-Nov. 17

"When the death van reaches this corner, may it turn back. Stop the execution of Raphael Holiday!" Pilgrimage Mile 8/43 -Nov. 17

"May we plant our feet on the pavement to stop the execution of Raphael Holiday." Pilgrimage Mile 9/43 -Nov. 17

"How can a God who died so that others might live be used to justify killing Raphael Holiday?" Pilgrimage Mile 10/43 -Nov. 17

"Raphael Holiday is a child of God and that's how I know God walks with me." Pilgrimage Mile 11/43 -Nov. 17

"Give us the strength to not stop praying for Raphael Holiday." Pilgrimage Mile 12/43 -Nov. 17

"Let Raphael Holiday know the engulfing fire of love." Pilgrimage Mile 13/43 - Nov. 17

"Raphael Holiday is not perfect and nor are we. Help us to put down our stones." Pilgrimage Mile 14/43 -Nov. 17

"Jesus died so that Raphael Holiday might live." Pilgrimage Mile 15/43 -Nov. 17

"Killing and love don't mix. Stop the execution of Raphael Holiday." Pilgrimage Mile 16/43 -Nov. 17

"Though we pass through difficult hours...let us not give up hope. Stop the execution of Raphael Holiday." Pilgrimage Mile 17/43 -Nov. 17

"Killing kills our souls. Let's save Raphael Holiday and learn to love again." Pilgrimage Mile 18/43 -Nov. 17

"Nothing is impossible with you God. Save Raphael Holiday!" Pilgrimage Mile 19/43 -Nov. 17

"We never walk alone. We know that you are with Raphael Holiday." Pilgrimage Mile 20/43 -Nov. 17

"You are the ever present help in times of trouble. Be there tonight with Raphael Holiday." Pilgrimage Mile 21/43 -Nov. 17

"Open our eyes to the injustice of the death penalty. Empower us to stop the execution of Raphael Holiday!" Pilgrimage Mile 22/43 -Nov. 17

"We pray life for Raphael Holiday!" Pilgrimage Mile 23/43 -Nov. 17

"How long must we wait God? Save Raphael Holiday!" Pilgrimage Mile 24/43 -Nov. 17

"Though I must stop for the night, I pray that the strength of our utterances for abolition will spare Raphael Holiday." Pilgrimage Mile 25/43 -Nov. 17

"Do not let Raphael Holiday be executed today." Pilgrimage Mile 26/43 - Nov.18

"May we yearn for mercy at this hour. Stop the execution of Raphael Holiday!" Pilgrimage Mile 27/43 -Nov.18

"Do not let this road carry that van of death. Stop the execution of Raphael Holiday!" Pilgrimage Mile 28/43 -Nov.18

"May Walker County rise up to lead the way to abolition. Stop the execution of Raphael Holiday!" Pilgrimage Mile 29/43 -Nov.18

"Hold us up! Give us the strength to stop the execution of Raphael Holiday." Pilgrimage Mile 30/43 -Nov.18

"Stop the killing! Save Raphael Holiday!" Pilgrimage Mile 31/43 -Nov.18

"Let someone in the execution chamber be a real follower of Jesus and save Raphael Holiday." Pilgrimage Mile 32/43 -Nov.18

"Let Raphael Holiday know our prayers and our love as he travels this road." Pilgrimage Mile 33/43 -Nov.18

"Help our Governor to follow Jesus and stop the execution of Raphael Holiday." Pilgrimage Mile 34/43 -Nov.18

"Honored to break from my pilgrimage to teach about the death penalty and queer theology at Sam Houston State University in Huntsville. Stop the execution of Raphael Holiday!" Pilgrimage Mile 34.5/43 -Nov.18

"Let our shadows not be still. Stop the execution of Raphael Holiday!" Pilgrimage Mile 35/43 -Nov.18

"Help us to keep going. Let us not grow weary. Stop the execution of Raphael Holiday." Pilgrimage Mile 36/43 -Nov.18

"I pray for Raphael Holiday to know your peace. Let us not stop pushing to save his life." Pilgrimage Mile 37/43 -Nov.18

"Help United Methodists to get out of their pews and into the streets to stop executions. Save Raphael Holiday!" Pilgrimage Mile 38/43 -Nov.18

"Raphael Holiday is still alive. I'm still walking. Will you keep praying?" Pilgrimage Mile 39/43 -Nov.18

Just received word that THE EXECUTION OF RAPHAEL HOLIDAY HAS BEEN CALLED OFF!!! Prayer can change a multitude of things. Pilgrimage Mile 40/43 -Nov.18

"Praise God!" Pilgrimage Mile 41/43 -Nov.18

"Still walking. Thankful Raphael Holiday is alive. Let's pray this holds permanently." Pilgrimage Mile 42/43 -Nov.18

"It is finished! Still praying for Raphael Holiday." Pilgrimage Mile 43/43 -Nov.18

Keeping vigil as the State of Texas is still trying to execute Raphael Holiday. -Nov.18

My last prayer of the day was with the family and friends of Raphael Holiday right before he was executed. -Nov.18

Despite my best effort, the State of Texas executed Raphael Holiday tonight at 830pm. I will continue to pray. I will continue to walk. -Nov.18

If you don't welcome the stranger/refugee then you don't welcome Jesus. Matt. 25:35 -Nov. 20

Remembering Shade Schuler on this Transgender Day of Remembrance. -Nov. 20

"In our Islamophobic society, I have no question that Jesus is so intimately incarnated with and connected to our Muslim friends that he has become one. If we want to walk with Jesus in this moment of extreme oppression and marginalization, we will too." -Nov. 20

"Since most of our local pastors and churches are chickenshit and refuse to stand up for your lives in the Battle for Oak Lawn, I say to hell with all of them...you yourselves are the church and pastors this community so desperately needs." - at the Oak Lawn to DPD, Rally for Change -Nov. 22

I spent the afternoon in Nashville advising Tennessee Death Row inmate Andrew Thomas. -Nov. 23

Praying hard this morning for my fellow freedom fighters. #4thPrecinctShutDown -Nov. 24

"I brought this Bible out here to help Dr. Robert Jeffress and the people of First Baptist understand that you cannot love your neighbor and turn your back on them in their greatest time of need. Jesus was a refugee." -Nov. 24

This is an execution. The uniformed man firing the 16 deadly shots is Jason Van Dyke and he is a terrorist. The body lying on the ground is Laquan McDonald and he should not be dead. These are simple facts and I don't see how anyone can follow Jesus and deny them. -Nov. 24

Proud to put the Bible to good use yesterday and stand against the xenophobic/racist rhetoric of Dr. Robert Jeffress at First Baptist Dallas. -Nov. 25

"Walking through the house, I blurted out, 'It feels like God is pissing on us.' 'Maybe we deserve it,' replied my wife. When I walked outside, looked to the heavens and let the rain hit my face, I wondered." -Nov. 27

Terrorism is not restricted to a specific identity...and thankfully neither is love. #PlannedParenthood -Nov. 28

"That's not very good!" -Little Jeff's response to the armed protests of Islamic Center of Irving -Nov. 29

I can think of few more exclusive/violent acts that a church can inflict on persons of color than to put a white Jesus at the front of the sanctuary. -Nov. 30

"We are here tonight to bang on these doors for justice!!!" -Nov. 30

Will Speer and I spent the morning talking and singing Christmas carols on Texas' Death Row. After deep discussion, I was shaken to my core when Will strained in prayerfully singing, "O come, O come, Emmanuel." I too groan in prayer for the God who is with us to come and save Will. Amen. -Dec. 2

"Never stop giving them hell my friend." Tonight, I was so blessed by the loving words of my friend, prophetic agitator and queer Houston icon Ray Hill. -Dec. 2

Welcome to the United States! We are a nation filled with dumbasses who believe that the only answer to our pandemic of mass shootings is to give more people more guns. #SanBernadino -Dec. 3

I spent time tonight with recent refugees from Syria. I was humbled when they thanked me for acting like a Christian. I pray that we will all learn to treat refugees with love. -Dec. 3

Merry Christmas from the Hoods. -Dec. 4

This is a video of the execution of #MarioWoods by the San Francisco Police Department. I pray for all of these murderous enemies of God to be fired and prosecuted. -Dec. 4

1 Year Ago in Dallas: "Jesus wouldn't be at home tonight. He'd rather got to jail than live quietly in this police brutality hell." I still believe this. #BlackLivesMatter -Dec. 6

"Our suggestion is to turn back to where the conversation started and try again...With all of our baggage, how can we expect to learn to be different without a turn?"-Dec. 7

"Oh God, we pray you'll move the administration and board to do right by South Oak Cliff High School and if they don't listen...then please get them the hell out of the way." -speaking at a student walkout to protest the horrible conditions at their school -Dec. 7

Earlier today, I was asked the following in a media interview, "What advice would you give denominational leaders concerning Donald Trump?" I replied, "All of these statements they've put out remind me of that old country song, 'How about a little less talk and a lot more action?'" -Dec. 8

"The gospel compels radical opposition to Trump's radically anti-gospel movement." -from an interview I gave to Baptist News Global -Dec. 9

"From the guns that are slaughtering our children...O Lord, deliver us." - The 2015 National Vigil to #EndGunViolence -Dec. 9

"The animals in Bethlehem were amongst the first to see the incarnation of God. Think about that the next time you assume they don't matter." -Dec. 9

You will never avoid what you have to push through. -Dec. 10

Tonight, I was named the Next Generation Action Network's "Person of the Year" for "relentless prophetic activism and sacrifice in the struggle against police brutality" -Dec. 11

"In the name of Jesus, put down those damn guns!" -Dec. 12

"Love your enemy and pray for those who persecute you." -Dec. 13

"I have no doubt in this contextual moment that Donald Trump is the chief opposite of Jesus...Donald Trump is the Antichrist." -Dec. 16

"Why do we keep on killing people who kill people to show that killing people is wrong? Logic like this is more twisted than a runaway tornado." -Dec. 17

"The innkeepers don't get to meet Jesus." -Dec. 20

"May this Christmas be the shittiest Christmas you have ever had!" -Dec. 20

"Do you believe that black lives matter? To answer this question, one has to look no further than this stained glass window towering over us at this very moment." #BlackLivesMatter -Dec. 28

"We are an evil people. Our hands are covered in blood. I don't see how anyone can follow Jesus and see this situation differently." #TamirRice -Dec. 29

"We don't need all white groups...Hate is diverse and so too must we be if we're going to see Justice." #HappyNewYear #whitepeople #whitefolk #blacklivesmatter -Jan. 1

January 4, 2015

"time" and "belief" / 2 poems

"time"

depression nibbles

the dogs ran away

i am haunted by the attack

blood was all they wanted

the problem was it was mine

what do you do

the only way to be in relationship is to bleed

how do you survive

how do you know

when will things go back up

i guess you learn not to die

"belief"

God is Chaos

Endless Incarnations

Endless Manifestations

God is Not Chaos

Ordered Incarnations

Ordered Manifestations

God is Chaos

Endless Truth

Endless Pain

God is Not Chaos

Ordered Truth

Ordered Pain
Chaos is the Foundation
Theology is the Experience
Thine is the Order and the Chaos Now and Forever
Amen

January 4, 2015

The Queerness of Disability: The Julian Way

The room held little light. Everyone sat in a circle waiting on something to be revealed. There were expectant thoughts buzzing inside the crania of the gathered. Squeaking along in his motorized wheelchair, Rev. Justin Hancock rolled into the center of our circle and commanded our attention. In a room full of people with diverse sexual orientations and gender identities, Rev. Hancock talked about having cerebral palsy and what it looks like to celebrate the self no matter what. In those beautiful moments of intersectionality, we learned more deeply what it looks like to live into exactly who and what God created us to be. In our world of crippling normativity, Rev. Hancock helped us to understand that the queerest way of being is to celebrate the self no matter what. Through Rev. Hancock's refusal to see his body as a problem, we heard a word from God illustrated in the flesh that night. We all walked out of the room a little bit queerer than we came in.

Regardless of the normative circumstances of death and destruction going on all around her in the 14th Century, Julian of Norwich believed in the power of God to partner with us in liberating the self through love. In discovering the love that God showed us in creating us exactly as we are, we can believe that we are perfectly made in God's image and can begin to live into such perfection. For many years, Rev. Hancock and his wife Lisa have partnered together to dream about what it would look like to make space for disabled families to see their families as made in God's image and together learn to live into that perfection. Tired of the pressure to pass their family off as normal and desiring to offer hospitality within the fragmented and isolated experience of the disabled community, Rev. Hancock and Lisa started to plan for the creation of a community with an identity based on the celebration of disability. In their estimation, disability should be treated as a natural part of God's creation and never as a stigmatizing label. Believing that the time is right for a radical expression of love and community, the Hancocks recently announced their intention to found an intentional Christian community and missional worship epicenter for disabled families called the Julian Way. Much like the love of God, the authenticity and beauty of the experiment is overwhelming.

Rev. Justin Hancock made a lasting impression on many of the people he spoke to on that special night. One person asked her partner to marry her. One person came out as transgender. One person made a career change. One person made peace with their mental illness. One person kissed his boyfriend for the first time. Inspired by the message of being who you are no matter what, person after person made the decision to be the queer that God created them to be in the first place. Rev. Justin and Lisa Hancock are queer pioneers of self-exploration, compassion, mercy and grace. I pray that you will join them at http://thejulianway.org

Amen.

January 5, 2015

Dangerous Theology in Houston: Excerptible Words from Speaking Tour on the Death Penalty

- Excerpt from address to Texas Coalition to Abolish the Death Penalty Houston Chapter on Speaking Tour of Houston:

Christians have blood on their hands. Here in Texas, our historical theology has made a way for the death penalty. We taught over and over that the wrath of God was not to be satisfied without the blood of Jesus. Unfortunately, a theology based on blood teaches humans that blood is required when blood is spilt. Vengeance becomes the basis of faith. We created this theology and we can fix it. How?

We begin to deconstruct a theology of death by repenting of our sins and engaging the lunacy of the death penalty head on. People are not going to pay attention to a theological argument. How many of you feel like you are most effective in this work when you are arguing with someone? I didn't think so. We cannot expect people to take big steps unless we are willing to take big steps. Many of you have asked me about the 200 miles I walked back in June against the death penalty. Why did I do it? I guess I felt like I needed to take a few big steps to show others the way.

The reason we still have the death penalty here in Texas is because we are afraid to take the big steps. Most people don't know how to take the big steps. Most people need people like you to show them. You must be the guides for them. We must be willing to travel to dark places if we are going to share the light. Do not be afraid. You are the light of the world. You are the reason that we will win.

Amen.

January 7, 2015

Dangerous Theology in Houston: Who or what gives you the right to kill?

People often begin their arguments for the death penalty with one simple phrase, "That person committed a crime so heinous they deserve to die." We must begin our reply with one simple question, "Who or what gives you the right to kill?" In order to kill someone, one must other or dehumanize the person to the extent that the person is comfortable pulling the switch or the trigger. Gov. Perry has consistently called people on death row, "Monsters." The person who committed the heinous crime is something other than human. Those who are something other than human deserve to die. This line of reasoning creates a world where the proponent of execution becomes judge, jury and executioner or God. The self-deification leads to a place where no one is more deserving of both life and vengeance than the proponent of execution is. When God says that we should have no other Gods but God, I believe that God was also warning us against creating a God out of our self too. The time is past due to quit thinking that we know enough to know who to kill or who not to kill. God commands us to, "Love our neighbor as our self." Can't nobody love their neighbor as their self and kill them.

Amen.

January 10, 2015

Prayer at the Dallas 5th Circuit Hearing on Marriage Equality Rally

Good evening. I want to introduce you to someone. I brought my son Phillip with me tonight. Phillip is two years old. I want Phillip to grow up and be able to grow up and marry whomever the hell he wants to marry. I want Phillip to grow up and be able to love whoever the hell he wants to love without fear of any legal limitations or repercussions. Most of all though...I brought Phillip here tonight to see what love looks like in the flesh. I believe that God is love and I believe that we incarnate the presence of God when we share love with each other. I believe that God is present at this rally tonight.

In the spirit of a God who is present and speaking, I ask that you pray with me. God of love...God of hope...God of light...join us here at this most holy hour of demonstration and yearning. Give us the strength to stand firm in the face of injustice. Help us to love those who hate us. Help us to love those refuse to do nothing for this cause. Help us to love. In this moment of prayer, I ask that you give to each other words that you would want for the people in this space to take with them tonight...

Love. Hope. Shalom. Heartbreak. Joy. Peace. Courage. Perseverance. Tenacity. Fortitude.

The words are countless and varied. God, I ask that you gather all of the words that we have heard and those that were left unsaid...may they come to fruition in our lives and make us whole. We need some help down here to love each other. Make all the actions, emotions and future desires that these words represent come to fruition. We believe that you are love. Give us the strength to go and make some love tonight.

Amen.

January 11, 2015

Freedom of Speech is Divine: Westboro Baptist, the Gay Christian Network and Paris

In the beginning, God created freedom of speech. If you follow the Genesis account, God placed humans in the Garden of Eden and gave them the right to agree or disagree. One of the primary ways that we express agreement or disagreement is through speech. I believe the most divine thing that we do on any given day is express who we are and what we believe. When societies suppress free speech, we suppress the divine. We take away the opportunity for people to express and live into all that God created them to be. The uncensored word is what makes us human and is also one of our closest connections to emulating God. God could have controlled speech from the very beginning. God did not. God made us in God's image to speak how we felt led to speak...even if it is too our detriment.

The Gay Christian Network is currently meeting in Portland, Oregon. The folks from Westboro Baptist Church showed up with their typical hateful signs and posters. The posts on social media championed those who stood in front of them and shouted them down. Confrontations with Westboro have consistently produced videos and images that are very powerful. While I hate what they speak about, I am so glad that they can and do say it. I am convinced that the people of Westboro Baptist Church are responsible for the dramatic advances in marriage equality and gay rights over the last decade. Over and over again in my work, I have been able to sit down with Christians and ask them, "Do you want to be like the folks at Westboro?" The answer is always a resounding, "No." With the ability to see what hate looks like in the flesh, I am convinced that Westboro has helped many Christians change their mind on human sexuality and gender orientation. On some level, I am thankful that God can use the lunatics among us to bring about God's will. If the people at Westboro were silenced in the past, I doubt the Gay Christian

Network would be holding a conference in as favorable of a national climate as they are right now.

The events in Paris over recent days remind us that freedom of speech is under attack. I spent part of this afternoon looking at the cartoons of the Prophet Muhammad that were published in Charlie Hebdo. While I found some of the drawings and captions to be disrespectful and distasteful, I don't believe that anyone should die over what was drawn or said. People should be able to express their thoughts even if it is to their own detriment. The uncensored word is the only way that we are going to have honest interaction. True progress is not possible when people are not free to express their thoughts. God knew this at the moment of creation and so should we.

In the midst of thinking about free speech, the image of French Muslim police officer Ahmed Marabet being shot point blank on a Parisian street is etched into my mind. Why was Marabet killed? The short answer is that people were enraged over speech and desired to silence it. I believe we must stand with Ahmed Marabet, the cartoonists and writers at Charlie Hebdo, Westboro Baptist Church, the Gay Christian Network and all other groups of people that desire to express their thoughts. Followers of Jesus know "...out of the heart the mouth speaks" (Luke 6:45). When you don't know the hearts of people, you don't know who needs to be saved. Furthermore, to be silent in the face of terror is to extinguish pieces of the divine in the self. People of faith must stand for free speech. God is with us in this effort.

Amen.

January 12, 2015

IF THE WAGES OF SIN IS DEATH...: The Case of Andrew Brannan

The weather was cold. Winters in Georgia are always a strange kind of cold. The stated temperature never reflects the discomfort most people feel. In 1998, Andrew Brannan murdered Laurens County Deputy Sheriff Kyle Dinkheller during a traffic stop. I was in eighth grade. Most of the people I was around believed the killer should die for the crime. Two years later, the weather was similar in Georgia when a jury found Andrew Brannan guilty of killing Dinkheller and sentenced him to death. I grew up and lost track of the case. When I heard Brannan was scheduled to be executed on January 13, I realized that the sin of vengeance in Georgia does not have an expiration date.

The wages of sin is death. Many people in Georgia believe this verse and desire to practice it. Believing that Andrew Brannan is guilty of a horrendous sin, many Georgians want to execute him. The problem with such an approach is that the wages of all sin is death. We all deserve to die. Who deserves to live? Well, no one actually. We are all responsible for tremendous evil. If the wages of sin is death, who deserves to be the last one standing to inject the last needle? An eye for an eye and a tooth for a tooth will leave us all blind and toothless.

The United State of America sent Andrew Brannan into a combat zone called Vietnam that forever scared his mind and psyche. We trained him to be a killer and he killed. What do we expect? When you teach someone to kill and cause them to lose their mind, you cannot expect them to be able to discern who to kill and who not to kill. Minds are a terrible thing to waste and we waste them all the time on violence. We created Andrew Brannan and we are responsible for his crimes.

Barring a miracle, Andrew Brannan will be pronounced dead in Georgia on the night of January 13. The collective conscious of a state and nation should be pronounced dead too. We have lost all sense of morality and justified our killing spree. By God's grace, I don't believe in death without resurrection. If the wages of sin is death, Andrew Brannan will be standing at the gates of heaven to forgive all of us for what we are about to do.

Amen.

January 15, 2015

The Other Rev. King

Make no mistake, there truly are ghosts in Mississippi. Most often, they inhabit long forgotten places and toil with hopes that their mortal lives have not been lived in vain. A few years ago, I first traveled to a forgotten place to meet a forgotten man. "For his sake I have suffered the loss of all things, and count them rubbish, in order that I might gain Christ and be found in him..." Though I had heard the words of Philippians 3:8 many times before, I had never heard them like this. We all know that the setting and the speaker often increase the magnitude of words. I knew the man speaking to me was someone that had sacrificed his life to be on the side of justice. A veteran of the Civil Rights Movement and many other struggles, Rev. Ed King is a complicated man. Long forgotten by everyone except the most meticulous of historians, Rev. King truly has suffered the loss of all things in order to authentically gain and be found in God. While I went down to Jackson to collect and tell his story, Rev. King ended up changing mine.

We have very little cultural space for alternative heroes of the Civil Rights Movement. In an age of certainty, we have constructed clear lines of what we think an authentic hero is supposed to look like. Rev. King believed that the only line that should have consequence on the way that we engage the world is the one between justice and injustice. Desiring to stand on the side of justice, Rev. King was mentored early on by Medgar Evers. Serving as chaplain of historically black Tougaloo College, Rev. King helped to strategize, organize and lead the Civil Rights Movement in Mississippi. There are few other figures as close to almost every major event in the Mississippi Movement. From talking to Evers before he was assassinated to being a part of the demonstration at Woolworth's Lunch Counter to being heavily engaged in Freedom Summer to being an early participant in and candidate for the Mississippi Freedom Democratic Party, Rev. King was consistently there and paid the price. Why do so few people know who he is?

From experiencing numerous acts of violence (including the crash that left his jaw mangled) to enduring constant threats and psychological torment, Rev. King is forever scared by the Civil Rights Movement. In the fifty years since, Rev. King has divorced, sometimes been broke and struggled to find his place in the emerging historical consciousness of the Movement. There were four people in the service when I met Rev. King. When I left, I felt sad that so many people were missing out on a chance to interact with such a historical figure. Sometimes, I still feel sad when I talk to him. I guess I shouldn't. Rev. King has chosen to suffer the loss of all things and count them as rubbish so that he might be found in God. Through Rev. King I have learned that true discipleship is costly, especially in a society that has such strict interpretations of what authenticity is supposed to look like. During this time of celebration of the life of the Rev. Dr. Martin Luther King, Jr., let us not forget that there were other Kings and that life is about engaging in our own authentic pursuits of justice no matter what the cost.

Amen.

January 15, 2015

The Rape and Death of a Baby: The Grace of a Mom

Adrianna Waller was a beautiful baby. On August 22, 1997, Charles Warner was supposed to be watching her. Instead of protecting and caring for her, Warner proceeded to rape and murder little Adrianna. During the trial, Warner's own son testified against him. A jury convicted Warner and sentenced him to death. Tonight, January 15, 2015, the people of Oklahoma put Charles Warner to death. Despite the heinous nature of the crime, there was one person who stood adamantly opposed to the execution...the mother of little Adrianna.

Not long ago, Shonda Waller asked the people of Oklahoma to spare the life of Charles Warner in video testimony before the Board of Pardon and Parole. Unsurprisingly, the Board did not listen and proceeded with the execution. Over the last few days, I have watched interviews of Christians anticipating and reacting to multiple executions throughout our nation and declaring, "An eye for an eye and tooth for a tooth..." In her recorded remarks, Shonda Waller said that her faith in Jesus would not allow her to support the execution of Charles Warner and declared, "I don't hate him. I have forgiven him." I wish that we had a few more Christians like her.

Amen.

+http://www.nbcnews.com/storyline/lethal-injection/oklahoma-execution-babys-mom-says-killer-charles-warner-should-live-n285436

January 16, 2015

Save the Date: Jesus is Getting Married

"What you have done to the least of these you have done to me..." The words of Jesus from Matthew 25 remind us that Jesus endures every oppression and marginalization. For most of the modern era, many queer people have been oppressed and marginalized for their sexuality and identity. This afternoon the Supreme Court agreed to hear the case that I believe will finally allow same-sex couples to be in legalized marriages in the United States. Throughout the oppression and marginalization, Jesus stood and continues to stand with queer people. Jesus is always on the side of love. Since Jesus stood with queer people thus far, I have no doubt that Jesus will also be standing with everyone who gets married after the Supreme Court rules. I encourage you to save the date. Jesus is getting married!

January 18, 2015

A Prophetic Convergence: The Rev. Dr. Martin Luther, Jr. & The Southern Baptist Theological Seminary

On April 19, 1961, the Rev. Dr. Martin Luther King, Jr. delivered a stirring sermon in a most unlikely place. Though not his most famous address, Dr. King's words to the Southern Baptist Theological Seminary or simply Southern Seminary pushed the audience to do more to accomplish racial justice. Delivered to the flagship theological institution of the flagship denomination of Southern Culture, Dr. King would never again give another address like this.

The Southern Baptist Convention originated from a desire amongst Southern Baptists to keep their slaves and Jesus too. For many of the early years, Southern Seminary reflected the staunch racist and segregationist attitudes of Southern Baptists. After many years of secret and segregated courses, Garland Offutt became the first African-American graduate of Southern Seminary in 1943. By 1947, Southern Seminary was fully integrated. To put this in perspective, Duke Divinity School did not integrate until 1961 and Candler School of Theology at Emory University did not integrate until 1965. Who would have thought that the flagship seminary of Southern Baptists led the way amongst major theological institutions in the South on race?

In December of 1960, Dr. Henlee Barnett secured an invitation for Dr. King to deliver the Julian Brown Gay Lecture from the Guest Lectureship Committee. Knowing that the invitation would be controversial, Southern Seminary President Duke McCall told the committee, "Boys, it is your call, but you do realize you are going to cost us hundreds of thousands dollars if you proceed." Dr. Barnette replied, "If so, it will be money well spent." Dr. King accepted the invitation and responded with a title, "The Church on the Frontier of Racial Tensions." By the time April arrived, there were security concerns and controversy brewing throughout the Southern Baptist Convention.

Arriving with a full police escort, Dr. King was greeted by professors Henlee Barnett, Nolan P. Howington, Willis Bennett, Wayne Ward and James Leo Garrett. Dr. Ward remembered Dr. King being deeply reflective. The group stopped to take a picture that still hangs on the wall of my office. When Dr. King climbed into the pulpit, an overflow crowd of 1500 people greeted him. Former student Rev. Charles Worthy remembered, "The mood was absolutely electrifying."

The Dr. King that is heard at the beginning of his address to Southern Seminary is not the same Dr. King that was later remembered as one of the greatest orators ever. Stumbling over his words, Dr. King is clearly nervous. However, once he got in the flow, Dr. King never turned back. Speaking about the role of the church, Dr. King pushed the gathered to "...develop a world perspective." Speaking about race relations, Dr. King declared that racial injustice is "...diametrically opposed to the underlying philosophy of Christianity." Speaking about economic injustice, Dr. King declared that people must, "...learn to live like Jesus." Pushing the congregation out the door, Dr. King declared, the gathered must be "...maladjusted to the evils of this age." The only African-American seminary student in attendance at the time, Dr. Emmanuel McCall remembered, "It was powerful...I felt like the direction of many lives were altered that day." Though controversy did cause Southern Seminary to lose money, I have to agree with Dr. Barnette that it was money well spent.

In 2008, close to fifty years after Dr. King's sermon, I was a student struggling at a radically different Southern Baptist Theological Seminary. Following denominational conflict, Southern Seminary became one of the most fundamentalist theological institutions in the nation. Due to some radical changes I experienced, I dramatically changed my perspective on a number of issues of social justice. When I was searching for direction and didn't have many places to go, I discovered the story of Dr. King's sermon. Realizing that there was a way to follow Jesus beyond the narrowness and bigotry I had known, I started following the advice contained in Dr. King's sermon and began working to develop a world perspective that equipped me to fight against injustice and be maladjusted to the evils of this age. Presently, I work as the Minister of Social Justice for the social justice ministry of the Cathedral of Hope United Church of Christ, the largest LGBT church in the world. Without the courage of the early professors from the Southern Baptist Theological Seminary and the witness of Dr. King, I doubt I would be here. I pray that maladjustment to injustice continues to spread.

Amen.

January 18, 2015

Why weren't they at your church?

Thanks to a group called The Official Street Preachers, "Homo Sex is Sin" was the message that congregants at the Cathedral of Hope United Church of Christ were greeted with this morning. Unfortunately, our family was not at church this morning. Our son Phillip has the flu and the rest of the kids are considered carriers until the Tamiflu runs out. I would have loved the opportunity to show my children how foolish people look when hate takes over. Regardless, I felt like I got much of the experience from the numerous videos and pictures people shared. Ever the preacher, I started to wonder what the message of the moment was? Then, I saw all the posts from people at other churches expressing their disgust. Thinking about the protestors and naysayers that followed Jesus around, I knew what the sermon of the day was. Why weren't they at your church?

Amen.

January 19, 2015

Poetics for a King

The Pledge

Please stand for the Pledge of Allegiance
What for?
What does it mean?

What will my standing say?

I only pledge allegiance to God alone

I don't have allegiance to any nation

How can a follower of Jesus pledge allegiance to a nation?

I especially find it hard to have allegiance to this nation

So full of...

Inequality

Oppression

Marginalization

BUT

This is my home

I guess freedom is what I believe in enough to pledge allegiance to

I stand for freedom

Which is why

I refuse to stand

Amen

The Playground

Daddy look at the plane

I'm scared

Why?

Planes drop bombs

How do you know that?

You are only 2

I'm scared

To the white clergy of Birmingham:

King asked you to move
What are you doing now?
Why is it still the same?
What have you been doing all these years?
Do you notice the lingering inequality?
Do you notice the segregation?
If you won't move after hearing word after word from God...
Who will you move for?

January 21, 2014

No More Murders! : Stop the Supreme Court and the People of Georgia with Prayer

There is an old story about Jesus. During one of his marathon sessions, the entire house he was teaching in filled up and everyone wanted to share a moment with Jesus. Hearing that he had the power to heal people, a group across town picked up their disabled neighbor and carried him on a mat to the house where Jesus was. After being unable to find an entrance or a way to get into the place of healing, the group carried their neighbor to the top of the house and worked to make a hole in the roof big enough to lower their friend to Jesus. I wonder what people thought when dirt started to fall on their heads? After some work, the hole was finally big enough to lower the neighbor through. What if the story took a terrible turn at this moment? What if the group decided they were tired of their heavy neighbor and just dropped him? Instead of the beautiful story of healing, the story becomes about a group of people who abused a vulnerable person and dropped him to his death.

Rather than heroes for carrying their neighbor to a place of healing, we would rightfully call the group murderers.

Warren Hill is a murderer. Warren Hill has been convicted of killing two people. The names of Myra Wright and Joseph Handspike must never be forgotten in this conversation. As a person of deep religious faith, I believe that murder is evil. I pray for the redemption of all think about committing or who commit murder. Right now I am praying for the people of my home state, Georgians are preparing the execution chamber to be the scene of an atrocity...the murder of an intellectually disabled man named Warren Hill.

With an IQ of 70, Warren Hill is every bit the same as the disabled neighbor in the aforementioned story. In order to function, Hill needs the help of people around him. Doctor after doctor after doctor has consistently testified that Hill is intellectually disabled. In the coming days, the United States Supreme Court will have another opportunity to weigh in on this case. The Court is standing above a place of healing and has the opportunity to lower Hill or drop him to his death. When the life of someone so vulnerable is at stake, there is nothing to call someone who would allow Hill's death to take place except for a murderer. I pray for the redemption of the Supreme Court, the people of Georgia and every other player that could save the life of Warren Hill. Join me. We do not need any more murderers walking around.

Amen.

January 22, 2015

Prayer at the Inauguration of Jeff Hood as Chief of the Hall County Fire Department

Good evening. I am the Rev. Dr. Jeff Hood from Denton, Texas. I have come a long way to pray with you. Will you please oblige me by bowing your heads? God we come to you from many different religions, nationalities, races, classes, orientations, genders, abilities and various other categories and identifications...some ascribed by our self and some ascribed to our self. Regardless of where we come from, we come together tonight knowing that the only way that we will see justice and righteousness played out in this world is through coming together. Tonight is an occasion of both celebration and expectation. We celebrate the accomplishment of Chief Hood...but we also stand firmly in expectation of the mighty movements of justice and righteousness that are coming to fruition through this administration. God thank you for this moment. Let us all depart from this place with the confidence of knowing that our new Chief has been your child for a long time. Let the children of God say Amen...say Amen...and glory glory hallelujah Amen.

January 23, 2015

The Lethal Nature of Moderate Theology

Week after week, pastors and staffs of churches deliberate about what message they intend to purvey to their community with their church sign. The sign is intended to share with the community the most important thoughts of the congregation for the week. While visiting my home state of Georgia this week, I drove past a church sign advertising, "Moderate Theology." The sign sparked my curiosity. Later in the day, I asked a friend in ministry in Atlanta about the sign. "They think that God calls them to be moderate," she explained.

In the coming days, the people of Georgia are scheduled to execute Warren Hill. If the intentional execution of a human is not enough to spark your moral outrage, Hill has an IQ of 70 and would be considered mentally disabled by most fair standards. For fear of upsetting people in their congregations, pastors and churches in Georgia with a moderate theology will choose to remain silent this Sunday in the face of the Warren Hill tragedy. Based on the simple number of them, moderate churches could save Warren Hill's life. I have no doubt that if the people of Georgia execute Warren Hill...moderate theology will be responsible. When will we understand that moderate theology in the face of injustice kills?

This will not be the first time that moderate theology will have failed to react in the face of injustice and remained silent in the face of death. Racism, classism, sexism, homophobia and a whole hose of ists and isms go unchecked and even encouraged due to an inability of churches to embrace the radical message of Jesus. Jesus never said, "Love your neighbor as your self moderately." Jesus said, "Love your neighbor as your self." When will we step up and stop hesitating to love people? Our neighbors are dying to find out.

Amen.

January 25, 2015

On the Power of Preaching...

I woke up this morning with my mind set on the things of God. When the majesty of God truly comes over you, there is a tingling in your physiological construction.

While I wouldn't call it nervousness, I can say that it makes you shake. Today was a preaching day and like all preaching days I was overcome with the sense of responsibility that comes with standing before the people of God and purveying the words of God. The drive is always the worst. I was thinking a million miles a minute about the structure, content and flow of what I was about to preach. I try to keep praying over and over in the midst of all this. With my mind and prayers so fixed on the sermon, it is a wonder that I don't slam into the car in front of me. Though I had a few hard brakes that scared the shit out of me on the way, I made it safely to the church. No matter the location, there is something about walking into a sanctuary and seeing where the preaching moment is going to take place. There is beauty and magic in the place where people gather to hear a word from God. The closer the moment of proclamation got, the more I felt the magic. By the time my sermon started, I knew what was coming. I could feel it. In spite of my limitations, I knew that God showed up and showed out. I left changed. Regardless of our modern sensibilities, I was reminded today that there is still tremendous power in preaching.

Amen.

January 28, 2015

The Execution of Our Conscience

When the time comes to consecrate communion, most celebrants approach the altar and read from a prepared liturgy. In the moment when Jesus is supposed to be closest to us, I have always felt like the consecration of communion is a time to explain what the incarnation means. Based on Jesus' promise to inhabit the least of these amongst us, I feel like the incarnation changes and transforms constantly with the changes and transformations that go on in the world around us.

Consequentially, I approached the altar last Sunday and declared, "I know some people are not comfortable with body and blood language when it comes to communion. Some find it ancient and repulsive. This week, the people of Georgia are prepared to execute Warren Hill. Warren has an IQ of 70 and is intellectually disabled according to every doctor who has ever examined him. I believe that Jesus is closest to those that we marginalize and oppress. On this day, Jesus is with Warren. When you take communion this week, I want you to remember Warren. If we want to stop using body and blood language in communion, then we need to stop killing those that Jesus inhabits. We execute Jesus and our own consciences every time we shed someone's body and blood. Jesus was executed in a state-sponsored execution and will be executed again if we execute Warren Hill."

In the midst of person after person coming to receive the body and blood of a Jesus that we keep on killing, I realized that these executions have become most effective at executing our consciences. The performed and scheduled executions this week give us a moment to push back and reflect.

Though I expect more from our whole society, I am saddened and outraged that most of the executions in our country are carried out by states that are predominately Christian. In Georgia, people who claim to follow Jesus are largely responsible for executing Warren Hill. At every step of the way, Christians could have stepped in and stopped the killing of an intellectually disabled man. Like the disciples before them, few people said anything. In their race to execute their own consciences and pretend that this execution was justified, the followers of Jesus forgot that Jesus said that he would be with the least of these. It wasn't just Warren Hill that was executed.

Richard Glossip was convicted of murder based on the testimony of one person. Though Justin Sneed is the one who actually committed the crime, he testified that Glossip hired him to do it and got a life sentence. Recently, Sneed's daughter sent a letter to the Oklahoma Clemency Board that said her father lied in his testimony and was afraid to formally recant for fear of getting the death penalty. Our execution system encourages the execution of the conscience in order to save your own skin. In a case of possible actual innocence, we can't know the truth because we have already decided what we want to happen and created a system that will make it happen. The execution of Jesus was similar.

The authorities are ready for another execution in Texas. Robert Ladd has a measured IQ of 67 and has qualified for special needs most of his life. Texas is still determined to kill him. People don't care about who Robert is. We simply declare that he is a murderer. In our othering of Robert, we other Jesus and execute our consciences. Robert is a child of God who deserves our help not our violent retributive hate.

Who are the killers and who are the victims in these processes of execution? If we can somehow develop a tiny sliver of conscience, we will understand that this process makes us all killers and victims. I thought our existence was about giving life and not taking it. There is an antidote to our vengeance and hate. Love can awaken the consciences that we have executed and set us free from this madness. Would you open your heart for the revival of your soul?

Amen.

January 29, 2015

A Prayer from the Execution of Robert Ladd

God. Why? Why do I have to keep coming down here? Why was Robert Ladd born with intellectual disabilities? Why were people murdered? Why are we about to murder Robert Ladd? Why? Do you care? Are you here? Is there a reason why you don't stop this? Are you addicted to death and suffering? Do you even exist? I don't know the answer to these questions. I only know that I have chosen to believe. I believe that you are there with Robert. I believe that you will walk with Robert down the hallway. I know that you will lay down with Robert on the gurney. I know you will feel the needle. I know that you will die with Robert. You have taught me to believe that death doesn't happen without resurrection. I know that you will not leave us here as murderers. I know that you will resurrect us to meet Robert and ask for his forgiveness for our sins tonight.

Amen.

January 30, 2015

Texas Muslims are the Real Christians

"All Muslims aren't terrorists, but all terrorists are Muslims." A woman shouted these words into the camera in one of the many videos of Christian protests of Texas Muslim Capitol Day in Austin. During the over hour and a half event, Christians consistently shouted down Muslim speakers and at one point came close to assaulting some of the speakers. Muslim children from Texas were screamed at and told to return to their home country. If that wasn't disgusting enough, Christian Texas Rep. Molly White posted on Facebook, "I did leave an Israeli flag on the reception desk in my office with instructions to staff to ask representatives from the Muslim community to renounce Islamic terrorist groups and publicly announce allegiance to America and our laws. We will see how long they stay in my office." While there are some who might argue with my use of the word Christian to describe these protestors and Rep. White, I think it is important for fellow Christians to realize that this is a mess of our creation. Starting with our belief in an exclusionary God and our promotion of the idea that there are people who are damned for all of eternity, we have promoted theology that constructs a God that is identical to the Christian protestors. If we want to change the perception that people have of Christians, we have to promote theology that offers no quarter for those who believe God hates some people enough to send them to burn in hell for all eternity. If you need an idea of what a loving God looks like, look no further than the Muslim speakers who sought to love those Christians protestors that treated them with hate yesterday.

One of the speakers was Mustafaa Carroll, the Executive Director of the Council on American-Islamic Relations in Houston. Having no idea who he was, I first met Mustafaa about six months ago at an Iftar hosted by the Texas Muslim Democratic Caucus. I knew very few people at the event. While I was standing alone, Mustafaa came up to me and confirmed that I didn't know many people at the event. I explained that I came at the invitation of my friend and that he was busy getting the event going. "So you really don't have anyone to hang out with?" Mustafaa replied. "I guess not," I replied. After the exchange, Mustafaa made sure I felt welcomed and engaged with everything that was going on for the rest of the night. I will never forget his kindness. I am thankful for his continued friendship. Yesterday at the Texas Muslim Capitol Day, a Christian protestor pushed Mustafaa and other speakers out of the way and spewed hate into their microphone. When I saw the events transpire, my heart really hurt for my friend.

When I think about all that has happened over the last few days and consider that love is the core of what it means to be a Christian, I think that Texas Muslims are the real Christians.

Amen.

January 31, 2015

The Courage to Be Queer

*Delivered at the Virginia-Highland Church in Atlanta, Georgia

Life is about questions. Sometimes these questions have answers and sometimes they don't. Who are we? Why are we here? Do we even matter? These are human questions. On this day, I intend to engage these questions from a queer perspective. The Gospel of John in the first chapter says, "In the beginning was the Word and the Word was with God and the Word was God." I guess you could say that the Word for me is Queer. There are some who might quarrel with my use of the word Queer. Though this word has a checkered past, I do believe that we serve a God who has a history of taking broken things and making them whole. Today, I will use a primary definition of outside of what is normative to describe Queer.

Circling back to our fundamental questions... Who are we? Why are we here? Do we even matter? I think the answer lies in our origins. I turn my attention to Genesis 1:1, "In the beginning..." Beginnings are a curious phenomenon. To think that there are moments where before there was nothing and then there is something boggles the mind. We always want to know what the cause of a beginning is. I believe that God created the heavens and the earth. In a modern age, such a statement sounds silly or even downright Queer. The problem with God language is that God language is often deficient. The true God is always the God beyond God. The true God is always indescribable, uncontainable and beyond our wildest dreams. I believe that the best way to capture both the majesty and mystery of God is to call God Queer. I believe that God creates us Queer in God's very image. According to Genesis 1:26, we have far more in common with God than we have ever been given the permission to realize. I believe that our creation in the Image of God is the most important piece of our faith. If we are created in the Image of God, then we are created totally beyond any normative constructions and beautifully and magically Queer. There are no duplicates...there are only Queers. There are many who would call me a hedonist for making such statements, I simply tell them that in all actuality I am an Edenist. Regardless of whether you believe Eden was or is an actual place, there is something to be learned by what took place there and maybe a place to return to.

Why do we spend so much time trying to define our self? Why not be who God created us to be in the first place? We have a false impression that identities, categories, borders and boundaries make us safe. I would disagree. Furthermore, I would argue that there is no safer place for us to be than in the arms of the God that created us to be every bit as Queer as God is. The power of the Queer or should I say the answer of the Queer or should I say the Queer origin of the universe is bubbling inside of us and desperate to come out. Why do we waste our time chasing anything other than what we were created in God to be? Everybody wants to talk about spending time with your Bible. I want to tell people that it is time to spend some time with your self. You are a walking testament to the beauty and majesty of the creator of the universe. You are the living incarnational masterpiece of a Queer God.

There in the beginning...right around Genesis 1:27...God creates humanity male and female. Most people want to talk about this gender construction as a binary. I think they're wrong. In the beginning, I think that each person had a gender that was unique. God created them male and female in the same person. I have often thought that if their gender was blurred then so was everything else. These first persons would not fit into our lines of race or sexuality or any other category that we have created. These were people who were who they were. They were Queer...just like the God that created them. We better not try to push our lines on them. These folks were free and full of unique non-normative Queer life.

Everything was going great. The first humans were living into all the queerness or holiness that God created them to live in. Unfortunately, the Queer party got busted up. The Queers met a temptation they could not resist. The tempter was a snake...but the temptation was the evil that we all fall victim to. In Genesis 3:5, the snake tells the human, "If you eat of the tree, then you will be made like God..." The human ate the tree and the rest is history. Most people think that the first sin was one of disobedience BUT the reality is found in the factuality that the first sin was in choosing to believe that God could be found in a tree and not in the very place where God has always been...INSIDE OF US. Inside of that Queer creation that we are. Inside of God's Queer Image that we carry. We are the revelation of the Queer.

I believe all evil in this world stems from a failure to locate and embrace the Queer within. You are perfect. God has made us perfect and we have chosen to chase the normative constructions of this world. We have chosen to believe that our value comes from fitting in. We have chosen to believe that our safety comes from staying in closets of our own construction. Let me tell you something...God never intended for anyone to live in a closet. There ain't nothing safe about closets. People die in closets. People don't live in closets. So how do we bust the door of the closet down and get back to that place where all of humanity came from? How do we connect with the Queer that God created us to be in the first place?

In our scripture from Mark this morning, Jesus calls Peter, Andrew, James and John to leave normativity behind. Jesus calls them to be Queer. Jesus calls them to embrace the very Image of God within them. Jesus calls them to fall in love with God. Does anybody know anything about falling in love? I am talking about when your entire body tingles. Does anyone fall in love normally? Do you ever look at the one you love and declare how normal they are? Jesus tells the people that the realm of God is here. The time for love in all fullness is here. The time of life in all fullness is here. The Queer is here.

In the movie *Big Fish*, Edward Bloom is accused of living in a fairy tale by his skeptical son Will. The interesting thing is that when we live into the Queer that God created us to be...people think that we are crazy and living in a fairy tale. I don't believe that the wholeness of queerness has to wait until heaven. We can be who

God created us to be right now! The realm of God is a fairy tale and you are being called to be the Queer fairies.

Jesus says repent...stop trying to be like everyone else...be who you are. Let go of all the normative identities, categories, borders and boundaries. Repent! Be Queer. Believe the good news. Believe the Queer news that you are perfectly made to be a beautiful Queer creation. Peter, Andrew, James and John dropped everything to find and cultivate this new Queer way being whole.

Later, Paul tells the Corinthians that the present forms are passing away. Stop clinging to all of this shit that doesn't matter...the present forms are passing away. Leave all the normative borders, boundaries, boundaries and other bullshit behind...be Queer...follow God.

Friends, we can't change the world until we are ready to change our self. True social change and social justice begins within. The great theologian RuPaul once said, "How the hell are you going to love somebody when you can't love your self?" The COURAGE TO BE QUEER is the COURAGE TO CHANGE THE WORLD. Embrace the power of the Queer. Follow Mary, Peter, Andrew, James, John, Paul, Ghandi, Buddha, Malala, Martin and a host of others...BE QUEER...and you will not only discover the Queer within...you will discover the Queer in whose image you are made. Let the Queer Revolution begin today. Walk through those doors with a newfound courage to be Queer. Don't look back...Don't turn back...to the way things used to be.

BE QUEER. BE QUEER. BE QUEER. Amen. Amen. Glory. Glory. Glory. Hallelujah and...

Amen.

February 1, 2015

A Magical Moment of a Hidden Sickness

I am sick. I am not talking about the kind of sick that you are able to get over. My sickness is chronic. Though I take medicine twice daily, I will never be healed. Then again, I don't know that I want to be. The construction of my mind is terribly important to who I am. Though some people would call my condition Bipolar Disorder, I would call it me.

Apart from the intermittent mania and depression, my condition manifests most strongly around major life events. For those who don't know the present circumstances of our lives, my wife Emily is pregnant with our fourth and fifth children. To give some additional context, our oldest twin son Jeff is aged 2.5 years. We are filled with life these days. My mania or depression manifests around different things on different days and often not at all. Today, I thought about death.

I woke up this morning thinking about Frances. I lost my grandmother just last month. Frances was a beautiful strong woman. When she, my grandmother gifted me her glasses. Through the glasses, I look back and into the future. I miss her.

To get the kids out of Emily's hair for a little bit this afternoon, I took the twins down to the park. For over an hour, the kids played and played. When I came to the playground revelation that my kids will not live forever, I started to get depressed. No one wants anyone they love to die. I started to cry. No one else could see me. I began to pray for some sort of sign of hope. When the kids ran to the basketball court, I got it. The sun blasted through the trees and the kids ran toward it. In the beauty of the moment, I realized that God is always calling us to go deeper into the light of love and the light of love is eternal. If we always run to the light of love, we will never taste death. Phillip even turned around and said, "Coming daddy?" In their running, the boys were the theologians today.

Amen.

February 2, 2015

A Christian Perspective of Polyamory: A Conversation Between Rev. Danny Cortez and Rev. Dr. Jeff Hood

J: Is there room in the Bible for polyamorous relationships?

D: I don't see polyamory spoken of positively at all in scripture. When polyamory is mentioned, it is not approved or valued.

J: I think we are going to disagree on this. There are multiple points in the Old Testament were intimate love is shared equally by more than two people. I see love as the thrust of scripture. Throughout the scriptures, love being confined to a couple and only shared within that couple is not the normative construct. In the Old Testament, you have all of these plural relationships. In the New Testament, we are encouraged to not get married at all. Despite what evangelicals and fundamentalists would have us to believe, marriage and family is not the chief end of the scriptures at all.

D: The polyamorous relationships in the Old Testament are not motivated by love. These relationships are motivated by money and power. The polyamorous relationships in the Old Testament seem destructive. The men function as misogynistic and patriarchal dictators of multiple women.

J: There is no question that the way that polyamory was practiced in the Old Testament is problematic. When Jesus comes and shows us a new way of being, I have to wonder if that doesn't open the world up to new and equal ways of sharing love. On some level, I think the disciples and Jesus were involved in some sort of polyamorous relationship. Love seemed to be pretty free flowing around Jesus.

D: First, I don't believe the disciples had any type of sexual relationship with Jesus. Second, Paul makes it clear that marriages are to be made up of two people. Paul places a premium on singleness and calls all that are able to remain as such

J: I find Paul's patriarchal words to be derogatory, demeaning and dismissive.

D: I get it. It's like... If you can't control your body then go ahead... I don't think that is what Paul meant to convey. When you share your self with more than one person, the intimacy factor begins to go down. Love begins to lesson when it is shared beyond the intimate partner.

J: I disagree. I think that it is quite possible for love and intimacy to grow the more that it is shared.

D: How about an analogy? I think the more limited something is the more valuable it becomes.

J: Would you not say that love is a limited commodity anyways? I think love is something to embrace with all that we are whenever we find it.

D: It is true that love should be cultivated wherever you find it, but I am talking about the sexual intimacy part. When I think about my relationships with people, there are different levels of intimacy that I embrace with different people...but there is only one person that I am most intimate with...my wife. There are things that I do with my wife that I don't do with anyone else. If I were to expand that, the intimacy would diminish.

J: I experience deep intimate relationships with persons who are not my wife. Danny, I would say that our friendship is an intimate relationship for me. I have been really blessed by knowing you. The more difficult piece of this is that many polyamorous relationships are situations where our culture has pushed closeted LGBT people to get married and instead of getting divorced from someone they have grown to love...some people decide to bring a third partner into the relationship. This situation is a result of our oppression. How can lovingly tell these folks that what they are doing is wrong? Some of these polyamorous relationships come from a desire to do no harm.

D: I will have to admit that I don't know anyone in a polyamorous relationship. I feel like I can only speak from a distant theoretical understanding. This is a subject that I have little experience with.

J: Would you welcome a polyamorous family into your church?

D: I would receive them without question.

J: Would you bring all three parents or four parents up during a baby dedication or any other special church service?

D: I have no desire to police the relationships of our people.

J: I am not interested in condemning love. If people have learned to love each other and not do violence to each other, I just want to let them be. I love my neighbor as my self by letting them be.

D: I don't think that scripture gives a robust position on this topic.

J: I don't think that scripture gives any position on this topic.

D: I don't think there is enough evidence in scripture to outright condemn polyamory. I just don't believe it is the ideal that scripture is pointing us towards.

J: What about celebrating it? How would you help them to feel a part of the community?

D: I would invite them into my home. I would treat them the same as I would a relationship made up of two people. I would respect whatever they wanted to be called. I would love them.

J: You know we don't believe in the holy couple. We believe in the Holy Polyamorous Trinity.

D: Throughout the world, we have spent so much time trying to manipulate and control people's relationships. Whatever they look like, we need to spend more time helping people strengthen their relationships. I do believe that.

J: I don't believe that the polyamorous struggle for equality is all that different from the LGBT struggle for equality. Love is love. I believe that the people of God must always stand on the side of love.

February 3, 2015

Does Ty's Life Matter? : The Betrayal of Silence Following the Murder of a Transgender Woman of Color

Ty Underwood. Most people don't know her name. Most people don't know her story. Most people would just prefer not to know and keep going on about their lives. I can't. Last week, Ty Underwood was brutally murdered somewhere near 24th Street in North Tyler, Texas. In addition to the murder, Ty faced the numerous struggles and oppressions that come with being a transgender woman of color in our society. When I first heard about the case, I immediately believed that it was a hate crime. Anyone who lives here in Texas knows the charged atmosphere that exists regarding anything perceived to be queer.

When I revealed to a woman that I was going to be a part of a vigil in North Tyler for Ty, she insinuated that transgender people often use drugs. I couldn't let a comment like that go and replied, "Are you insinuating the gender expression of a person has to do with their propensity to use drugs?" To be transgender in our society is to be oppressed in life and death.

After the murder of black lesbian couple Britney Cosby and Crystal Jackson in Port Bolivar last spring, I helped organize a vigil in Fort Worth that four people attended. Though there was strong suspicion that Britney's father murdered the couple, one of the leaders in the community questioned our insistence on holding the vigil and concluded, "You know this is not a hate crime?" I replied, "I had no idea that one of the stipulations of hate crime legislation was that the victim had to be white." To be black in our society is to be oppressed in life and death.

"Black lives matter!" We have heard the demand for equality over and over the last few months. One would think that such demands would extend to transgender women of color. During the same period as our growing national conversation on race, numerous transgender women of color have been murdered. When police brutality has brought people into the streets, the death of transgender women of color has garnered little reaction. Who is there to demand justice? Presently, I am preparing to travel down to North Tyler, Texas to participate in a vigil for Ty Underwood and I will be thinking the whole time, "Does Ty's life matter?"

Amen.

February 4, 2015

Texas Killers: Pushing Back Against a Culture of Death

In John 14:6, Jesus said, "I am the way and the truth and the life." Texas has the largest population of Christians of any state in our nation. You would think that the words of Jesus would be something that are lived out here on a daily basis. Today, I am attending two vigils to provide witness to two situations, that contrary to the vision of Jesus, are characterized by misdirection, dishonesty and death.

By many accounts, Ty Underwood was murdered last week for being a transgender woman of color. Regardless of what proof is found of this assertion, we live in a state that consistently makes life unbearable for transgender people. When Christians consistently contribute to the rhetoric of violence against marginalized and oppressed people, we should not be surprised when actual violence occurs. I will be attending a vigil tonight in North Tyler, Texas to apologize for the behavior of a church that is not apologetic about the consistent mistreatment it perpetuates against transgender people. I can just hear the replies, "We hate the sin and love the sinner." If such rhetoric was helpful in any way, transgender people wouldn't consistently face death in this state. I apologize with the hope that our future is better and closer to the love of God, but the apologies must not stop there.

The people of Texas will execute Donald Newbury tonight. No one outside of our state government knows where the lethal substances that will be pumped into Donald's body came from. Killings and secrets go to together in Texas. On the way to his execution, Donald will pass under a cross. In Texas, the cross of Christ is much more associated with death than it is life. I must apologize that a state full of Christians continues to want to kill people. Jesus is about life not death.

I apologize and pray that we will get saved from our addiction to violent oppression and death. I think God can save killers too.

Amen.

February 4, 2015

Prophetic Words at the Rally for Ty Underwood: Transgender Woman of Color Murdered in Tyler, Texas

I have lived in Texas for about three years now. My wife Emily and I have three children. We have another two on the way. We have a big family. I am always thinking about their future and what it would be like for them to grow up here. When we first moved to Texas, it took me a few days to realize that difference was not welcome in this state. The people of Texas simply cannot handle difference. What is normative and expected is valued and what is different is silenced, run off and sometimes even disposed of. The chief perpetuators of such backwards thinking...such unchristian thinking...are churches...the people who say that they are the people of God...who say that they have the message of God...the word of God.

Tonight, I think we are here due to the words of hate that the people of God have spoken and the actions of hate that they have caused.

We can talk until we are blue in the face about the circumstances of the death of Ty Underwood. We can talk about what actually happened when Ty was killed and what didn't happen...who was involved and what the motives were. We can speculate about Ty's death all we want to and not be sure...but we can know one thing for certain...Ty lived in a state that did not value her life and shunned her for her difference.

I am incredibly moved to be here tonight...because looking at Ty's life from a distance...I can tell she lived her life authentically. I believe the way she lived her life tells us much about what it looks like to follow God...to follow Jesus...to live as God calls each of us to live...to be who God has created us to be. I want to encourage you tonight...don't let any church...don't let any pastor...don't let any religion...tell you that you have to be anything other than what God has called you to be. God is right. They are not.

In conclusion, I call on the Baptist, Methodist, Lutheran, Presbyterian, Catholic, Jewish and many other pastors, priests and religious leaders of this state of Texas...of this city of Tyler...to do right by those who are different. Stop persecuting people. Stop the oppression. Stop the violence. When you talk violently and say violent things...you can expect violent outcomes. Let us be a people whose chief concern is love. Let's be like Ty. Let us live lovingly as Ty lived. I know that if we follow Ty, we can also say as God would have us say and we can also be as God would have us be and we can also do as God would have us do.

Amen.

February 6, 2015

Pope Francis' Ignorance on Spanking

A few days ago, Pope Francis endorsed spanking. Believing that one can spank children and leave them with dignity, Pope Francis even called such a means of punishment, "beautiful." Unless there are records or evidence of the Pope spanking children that are not his own, I don't think that the Pope has much direct knowledge with this subject. In an age of serial and often unreported abuse of children in the Christian world, I can think of few more ignorant statements than for the Pope to give his blessing to the abuse of children. Some might argue that the language of abuse is too strong. I would argue that abuse always begins with the violent exercising of power over someone who is powerless and this is what the Pope has just endorsed.

I grew up in a Christian context where spanking was normal and often turned into abuse. There was nothing beautiful to me about being hit. I cannot imagine being hit in a way that was not demeaning or abusive. I remember the sting. I remember the lines. I remember the blood. I remember the bruises. I remember the pain. I remember being told that God endorsed and commanded what was happening to me. I remember despising any God that would be for the abuse of children. I almost left God altogether. I could not believe in a God that promoted the hitting and abuse of the innocent. Thankfully, I lived long enough to find out that God has nothing to do with the promotion of violence toward children.

Perhaps unwittingly, Pope Francis has given some parent out there the freedom to keep hitting and abusing a helpless and defenseless child tonight. I wish Pope Francis would follow the example of Jesus and realize how ludicrous it is to tell a child to "love their neighbor as their self" as they are getting hit. What do you think that a hit, spanked or abused child will do when they have to make a decision about hitting, punching, shooting or bombing later on in life? If you begin with violence, you should not be surprised when the violence continues. The abuse of children begins with spanking. The continued violence in our world begins with spanking. "Those who live by the sword will die by the sword," declares Jesus in Matthew 26. Doesn't Pope Francis know that those who live by the hand will die by the hand? While I appreciate the many denunciations of violence and abuse proclaimed by this Pope, as a follower of Jesus I cannot endorse the hitting of children. With every fiber of my being, I believe that Christians must act to stop the cycle of violence and take a strong stance against hitting children for any reason. What type of world do we want to live in? What type of God do we believe in?

Amen.

February 8, 2015

The Queer Resurrection of Alabama

The year was 2005. I was a junior at Auburn University in Auburn, Alabama. The Glomerata or our yearbook had just come out. I remember sitting at my fraternity house and hearing people laugh about a picture in the Glomerata. While I don't remember the exact name of the organization, the picture was of the LGBT organization on campus. There were three LGBT people who were willing to take a stand at one of the most conservative public universities in the nation and have their pictures placed in the Glomerata. While I was still incredibly conservative at the time, I wondered if God was not somehow present in the courage of these three individuals? Nearly a decade later, I have no doubt.

Did God forget about Alabama? Through the years, I have wrestled with this question over and over. From slavery to segregation to continued hate, Alabama is no stranger to evil. After earning two degrees from Auburn and a degree from the University of Alabama, I have direct knowledge and experience of how hateful Alabama can be. However, God always leaves a remnant. Throughout the state, I have met courageous people who are living their lives authentically and challenging the evils of Alabama.

I can think of no more authentic of Alabamians that Chi and Jessica Peoples. Recently the subject of a Freedom to Mary commercial, I met this beautiful couple about five years ago. In their persistence to live and be who God created them to be in their home state, I believe is Alabama's hope. When same-sex couples start filing out of the courthouses, I encourage the people of Alabama to look to them for who and what God wants you to be...love.

For so long, Alabama has been dead in hate and prejudice. As a Christian, I don't believe in death without resurrection. I think LGBT people are birthing a queer resurrection in Alabama. I know it will spread even further. I can't wait to see the beauty of God in the land of the living. Who would have ever thought that Alabama would be one the Southern states leading the way?

Amen.

February 8, 2015

The Midnight Christ

Did you know who you were?
Or was who you were something different than who you are?
Did you perform those miracles?
Or did those miracles perform you?

Did you know how it was going to end?

Or did the end choose you?

Are you the Messiah or is this the biggest hoax of all time?

Or are we a hoax?

Am I real?

Do I exist?

Can I know anything?

Thine is the truth, the way and the light...

In the midst of an existential wondering, could you please stop by tonight?

Amen.

February 12, 2015

The Lynching of Sureshbhai Patel

The video is horrific. Madison, Alabama police officer Eric Parker slammed Sureshbhai Patel into the ground hard enough to paralyze him. There was a time when lynchings were carried out by mobs. Now, we have created a much more formal process of carrying out violence against oppressed and marginalized people. Badges and uniforms are handed out so that those we place in authority can intimidate and repress those that we think are less worthy of life. The temptation is to say that Eric Parker is an animal and dismiss the entire situation. The truth is that Eric Parker was simply doing what we paid him to do.

The dirty secret about the lynching of Sureshbhai Patel is that a homeowner called in and reported him as, "...a skinny black guy, he's got a toboggan on, he's really skinny." There was also an ominous report that he was getting close to a garage. The police showed up quickly for "a skinny black guy" in a white neighborhood close to a garage. These are racist thoughts perpetuated in white neighborhoods around our nation every day. The police first thought they were going after a black man.

Upon arrival, Officer Parker realized Patel did not speak English. Instead of having patience, Officer Parker grew more aggressive. How many times does this same situation play out over and over again throughout our nation? People who are unable to understand and speak English are treated like shit. What makes us think that our language is superior to every other language on earth? The truth of the matter is that the only language that our whole nation is fluent in is the language of violence and oppression. Officer Parker simply played out the way that we treat immigrants all the time...we push them around, treat them with suspicion and tell them to go home. What began as racism, turned into xenophobia and ended up in a crime of hate.

Ever since I heard about the story, I have not stopped praying for Sureshbhai Patel. When I told a religious friend of mine how concerned I was about this story, I was chastised, "If he is Hindu, then you need to first and foremost pray for his salvation." Who the hell is going to pray for our salvation? We are an evil, intolerant and oppressive people in desperate need of an antidote. The first step of recovery is admitting you have a problem. For the love of God, can we please stop and admit that we need help?

Amen.

February 14, 2014

Love: A Theology of Emily

If God is love, our theology must be Love. Love is a strange word that is more often than not thrown about to reflect the intensity of emotions between people. "I'm in love." "I love you." "I fell in love." "I don't love you anymore." "We made love." The interesting thing is that the way of God or the way of Love is more about a state of being and less about a state of feeling. Please don't get me wrong...feelings matter to the way that we journey through life...but for God...Love is. No matter the circumstance or situation, the Love of God is. What feelings or actions can separate us from the Love of God? God is Love. God is here. God is not silent. I like to put it like this: "For Love so Loved the world that Love gave Love's only begotten Love that whosoever believes in Love will not perish but live in everlasting Love." Love never dies. God never dies. Love is constantly pursuing us. Love is in us. Love moves and shapes us. Love will eventually guide Love to completion.

I didn't think like this until I met Emily.

The Love of Emily simply is.

In this magical journey of life, the Love of Emily made me believe in a God called Love.

Though I have studied at the finest theological institutes in the world, it was the Love of Emily made me a theologian.

Blame her.
Amen.

February 15, 2015

Christians: You Have 5 Months

Last November at the Church of God in Christ's 107th Holy Convocation in St. Louis, Andrew Caldwell stood at the front of the auditorium and infamously declared, "I ain't gay no more. I am delivered! I don't like mens no more. I said I like women. Women women women women!" and went on to add, "I would not date a man! I would not carry a purse! I would not put on make-up! I will, I will love a women." To add insult to injury, not long after Andrew shouted these words, the presiding pastor declared, "God said he's going to bless you because of your commitment. Just to prove it, He just told me to give you $100." The spectacle of the scene reminded me of the many hyperemotional evangelical Christian services of my youth. We spent so much time trying to convince our souls that God hated us and we needed to get saved. Upon having a salvation experience, our next job was to convince our souls that God hates everyone that church leaders did. If we hated properly, either our self or our neighbors, we would be rewarded, just like Andrew was. Unfortunately, Christians in our nation have consistently built churches and denominations to reflect this cycle of hate. When anyone stops and questions the lunacy of it all, they are dealt with severely.

When Drew Cortez came out, his father Danny lovingly accepted him. If not for the Southern Baptist Convention, this would be a beautiful story of a father's love for his child. When this story started to receive attention, the Southern Baptist Convention kicked New Heart Community Church out for retaining Danny Cortez as their pastor after he accepted his son. In addition to Pastor Danny, a local Baptist association in Huntsville, Alabama affiliated with the Southern Baptist Convention recently moved toward kicking out Weatherly Heights Baptist Church for not kicking out Rev. Dr. Ellin Jimmerson, who performed one of the first same-sex marriages in Alabama.

If you are tempted to assume that Southern Baptists have a monopoly on hate, United Methodists have regularly disciplined ministers for performing same-sex marriages, including the infamous case of Frank Schaefer that has played out over the last 14 months. Just recently, the Evangelical Covenant Church pulled funding, support and fellowship from a church plant in Portland. The Cooperative Baptist Fellowship has a firm policy of not hiring people in same-sex relationships. World Vision also discriminates against persons in same-sex marriages. From mainline to evangelical churches to Christian organizations to everything in between, the stories are endless and hate still seems to have a strong foothold in the national Christian conscience.

Unfortunately for those who love hate and fortunately for those who love love, judgment day is rapidly approaching. The signs of the times are all around us. Court after court and judge after judge has ruled in favor of marriage equality and wider interpretations of civil rights. Recently, even Clarence Thomas spoke of marriage equality as a forgone conclusion. I believe we can expect a national marriage equality from the Supreme Court in June. So what is a Christian to do in such a circumstance? The short answer is to get saved.

We are about to see the beauty of love set free. Now is the time to learn how to choose love over hate. Now is the time for the people of God to get delivered from these hateful ways of being. I call on all Christians to lay down your scriptures, dogmas, doctrines and interpretations long enough to learn how to love your neighbor as your self. With 5 months left until the Supreme Court decision, the end of societal protection of hate is near and you don't want to get left behind.

Amen.

February 16, 2015

Learning to Die

There was a moment in my journey of faith that I realized that following Jesus meant death. In that moment, I realized that, "death is the way, death is the truth and death is the light." One has to die in order to experience the fullness of Jesus. On occasion, I am vividly reminded of what the consequences of following Jesus can be. When I saw the brutal beheadings of the Coptic Christians in Libya, I was reminded of the Apostle Paul's words in Philippians 1:21, "...to live is Christ and to die is gain." As a follower of Jesus, I believe that in death is life. I thank God for the beauty of the sacrifice of these 21 Coptic Christians and know that they are now dwelling in the eternal peace of God. I simply don't believe in death without resurrection. I look forward to meeting these saints in glory one day. I also look forward to meeting their murderers. If ISIS or anyone else ever asks for my head because of my faith, I hope that I will remember that Jesus loves my murderer as much as Jesus loves me. On that day, I hope that I will have the courage of these Coptic Christians and that Jesus will be the last name on my tongue.

Amen.

February 17, 2015

The Ashes of Rodney Reed

"Remember that you are dust, and to dust you shall return." The words will be repeated over and over again across Texas tomorrow. Texan after Texan will be reminded of their own mortality. In addition to the introspection, I pray that God will add a little outerspection to Ash Wednesday here in Texas and pierce the hearts of Christians about the approaching March 5 execution of Rodney Reed.

For 18 years, Rodney Reed has maintained his innocence in the murder of Stacey Stites. In his latest appeal, three of the most respected pathologists in the country declared that they "have re-evaluated the case and determined that Mr. Reed's guilt is medically and scientifically impossible." In addition to a cadre of supporters from around the world, Stites' own cousin Heather Stobbs is very vocal about her belief that Reed is innocent. Stites was white and Reed was black. With DNA left untested and a variety of other exonerating evidences left unmitigated, Texas is rushing to execute an innocent man.

The ashes always come before the execution. May the feeling of the ash on our foreheads remind us that we are responsible for whatever happens next. I believe that if we will allow the ashes to manifest and become more than just an empty ritual in our lives, we can free Rodney Reed.

Amen.

February 18, 2015

Lenten Reflections from the Executed: #484 Marvin Wilson / August 7, 2012

*These reflections are taken from pieces of the last words of the last 40 persons executed in Texas.

Marvin Wilson-

"Ya'll do understand that I came here a sinner and leaving a saint."

In his final moments, Marvin Wilson wanted the room to know that he was a redeemed child of God. In the midst of a world that called him a criminal and a sinner, Wilson still found his way to God. Sometimes in the midst of a world that so desperately wants to nail us to the wall with our past mistakes, we have to push toward where we are going and not dwell on where we have been. The lesson that Wilson left us with is that all of us can be a saint if we want to. Do you want to?

I invite you to pray the last words of Marvin Wilson:

"Ya'll do understand that I came here a sinner and leaving a saint."

Amen.

February 19, 2015

Lenten Reflections from the Executed: #485 Robert Wayne Harris / September 20, 2012

***These reflections are taken from pieces of the last words of the last 40 persons executed in Texas.**

Robert Wayne Harris-

"I'm going home, I'm going home. I'll be alright, don't worry."

Robert Wayne Harris wanted everyone to be at ease as he finished his journey. In John 14:1, Jesus speaks to the disciples in the same way, "Let not your hearts be troubled..." Though there was still pain and suffering to face, Jesus knew that he was going home. What if we lived as if we were just on our way home?

I invite you to pray the last words of Robert Wayne Harris:

"I'm going home, I'm going home. I'll be alright, don't worry."

Amen.

February 20, 2015

May Love Win: The Queerness of Working to Abolishing the Death Penalty

*A Short Speech Delivered at Hope for Peace & Justice's "I'm Queer and I Care Rally" at the Legacy of Love Monument in Dallas, Texas

Good evening, my name is the Rev. Dr. Jeff Hood, Minister of Social Justice for Hope for Peace & Justice. I am grateful for this opportunity to be out here tonight talking about issues that have impact on the wider queer community...beyond same-sex marriage. Certainly same-sex marriage is an important issue that we spend much time on, but we want to take this opportunity tonight to talk about some other issues. An issue that is near and dear to my heart is the death penalty. Here in Texas, we are executing more people than any other state in the country. Since the death penalty was reinstated in the late 1970s, we have had 100s and 100s of people executed...some of whom were guilty of their crimes and some of whom were not. Regardless, as a person of faith, I believe that Jesus calls us to love our neighbors as our selves and our enemies. I don't believe that you can do either while killing or executing someone. I am here tonight to push Texas to stop the cycle of violence...from the top to the bottom. The State of Texas cannot expect people to stop killing each other due to gun violence and other violences if the State continues to set the example by killing more people and perpetuating more violence. I struggle against violence because I believe that God is love and love is ultimately what can bring us together. We must work together...so that at the end of the day...love not only wins with regard to same-sex marriage but love also wins as we abolish the death penalty here in Texas. Amen.

February 20, 2015

Lenten Reflections from the Executed: #486 Cleve Foster / September 25, 2012

*These reflections are taken from pieces of the last words of the last 40 persons executed in Texas.

Cleve Foster-

"Over the years I have learned to love."

When Cleve Foster was about to die, he wanted everyone to know that he had learned to love. Sometimes love takes some growing into. We live in a cruel world and love seems to be a precious and endangered commodity. Often, people just learn to live and survive by being just as heartless as everyone else. Cleve wanted to live differently and worked hard to learn to love. The God who is love wants us all to learn to love. How are your love studies coming along?

With great expectation for what God can and will do in your life, I invite you to pray the last words of Cleve Foster:

"Over the years I have learned to love."

Amen.

Lenten Reflections from the Executed: #487 Jonathan Green / October 10, 2012

***These reflections are taken from pieces of the last words of the last 40 persons executed in Texas.**

Jonathan Green-

"It hurts bad."

In his final moments, Jonathan Green wanted to give voice to the pain that he was suffering. On the cross, Jesus screamed out in pain, "My God, My God, Why have you forsaken me?" (Matt. 27:46). In the midst of our pain, why do we feel the need to go through life silent about it? We make life all the more torturous by not naming the pain. Tell people that it hurts. Remember, God is with the hurting.

I invite you to pray the last words of Jonathan Green:

"It hurts bad."

Amen.

February 22, 2015

Lenten Reflections from the Executed: #488 Bobby Lee Hines / October 24, 2012

*These reflections are taken from pieces of the last words of the last 40 persons executed in Texas.

Bobby Lee Hines-

"Please forgive me."

Forgiveness is a powerful phenomenon that can set both the offender and the offended free. Shortly before he was executed, Bobby Lee Hines asked for forgiveness. While it is impossible to know if Bobby was forgiven by those associated with his crimes or not, we can only know that God generously forgives all who ask for forgiveness and we are taught to do the same. In Luke 6:37, Jesus also says, "If you forgive others, you will be forgiven." We are called to forgive all who seek forgiveness. If we dare forgive others, perhaps we might be able to forgive the most horrible sinner of all...our self. Do you have the courage to engage in radical forgiveness?

I invite you to pray the last words of Bobby Lee Hines,

"Please forgive me."

Amen.

February 23, 2015

Lenten Reflections from the Executed: #489 Donnie Lee Roberts, Jr. / October 31, 2012

***These reflections are taken from pieces of the last words of the last 40 persons executed in Texas.**

Donnie Lee Roberts, Jr.-

"God knows I didn't want to do what I did."

If we allow it, evil can possess and overtake over our lives. Upon possession, we do not necessarily do the things that we want to do. In his final moments, Donnie Lee Roberts, Jr. wanted the world to know that he didn't want to kill anyone. I believe him. There have been times in my life that I let evil in and didn't necessarily do the things that I wanted to do. Can you think of moments in your life where you didn't want to do the evil things that you did? God knows we wanted to do better and stands ready to forgive us.

I invite you to pray the last words of Donnie Lee Roberts, Jr. as a means of release and request for forgiveness,

"God knows I didn't want to do what I did."

Amen.

February 24, 2015

Lenten Reflections from the Executed: #490 Mario Swain / November 8, 2012

*These reflections are taken from pieces of the last words of the last 40 persons executed in Texas.

Mario Swain-

Silence.

Mario Swain offered no words when he was executed. Why didn't we speak up to save him?

I invite you to spend a few moments pondering the silence of Mario Swain:

Silence.

Amen.

February 24, 2015

Giving Our Bodies to Kelly Gissendaner

In February of 1997, Kelly Gissendaner orchestrated the brutal murder of her husband Doug in Gwinnett County, Georgia. Sentenced to die in 1998, Gissendaner's appeals process is about to run out. Barring a miracle, Gissendaner will be executed by the State of Georgia on Wednesday night (2/25/2015). Those of us who grow up in the South know well how this process of execution plays out. Over and over again, we watch society dispose of what we perceive to be our most brutal killers. Unfortunately, we fail to realize that no one has a right to kill anyone.

One day at the temple, Jesus met a woman similar to Kelly Gissendaner. The woman was tossed at his feet. The religious and government officials outlined her crimes and started to raise their instruments of execution. Instead of spending a bunch of time trying to convince or persuade the gathered government and religious figures, Jesus got down in the dirt with the woman. Now, if the religious and government officials were going to kill the woman they were going to have to kill Jesus too. With great boldness, Jesus wrote the crimes of the religious and government officials in the dirt. In the midst of the confrontation, Jesus declared, "Let the one who is without sin cast the first stone." The religious and government officials realized they were not without sin and walked away. We all are just as guilty as Kelly Gissendaner and no one has the right to take her life.

Most people think that the turning point of the story comes when Jesus writes in the dirt or maybe when he speaks to the religious and government officials, I disagree with such assertions. Regardless of the outcome, the life of the woman was saved when Jesus placed his body in the dirt and was prepared to face the same punishment she was sentenced to. If we are willing to place our bodies into the conversation, Jesus shows us that we can save lives. Over the next two days, I pray that enough bodies will be placed into the conversation to save the life of Kelly Gissendaner. Bodies matter and enough of them could abolish the death penalty once and for all. May God make it so.

Amen.

February 25, 2015

Lenten Reflections from the Executed: #491 Ramon Torres Hernandez / November 14, 2012

*These reflections are taken from pieces of the last words of the last 40 persons executed in Texas.

Ramon Torres Hernandez-

"Can you hear me?"

Before Ramon Torres Hernandez was executed, he wanted to know if anyone could hear him. I cannot count the late nights of prayer where I have laid awake pondering whether I was heard. Is God real? I don't have robust proof. There are moments where I think I know and there are moments where I know I don't. Regardless of my confused thoughts, I can only tell you that for some strange compelling reason I keep talking to whatever is out there. Maybe every step of faith begins with having the courage to ask if anything is there to listen?

I invite you to pray the last words of Ramon Torres Hernandez:

"Can you hear me?"

Amen.

February 25, 2015

Who Are the Real Killers?

Eddie Ray Routh will spend the rest of his natural life in jail for murdering Chris Kyle and Chad Littlefield. When I watched the families of Kyle and Littlefield celebrate what they considered to be a triumph of justice, I couldn't help but wonder about another 160 families who will never get their day of justice. We are a confused people. Chris Kyle kills 160 people and we call him a hero. Eddie Ray Routh kills 2 people and we call him a monster. I guess in this nation you just have to make sure that you kill the right people in order to be celebrated. In a paraphrase of Matthew 26:52, Jesus has a warning for all those who believe in all this killing, "Those who live by the gun will die by the gun..." I guess the real killers are those who somehow are crazy enough to still believe that guns and killing will make us safe.

Amen.

February 26, 2015

Lenten Reflections from the Executed: #492 Preston Hughes / November 15, 2012

***These reflections are taken from pieces of the last words of the last 40 persons executed in Texas.**

"...fight for my innocence..."

Have you ever been falsely accused of something? Until the very end, Preston Hughes maintained he was innocent. Even in death, Hughes wanted his family to fight for his innocence and clear his name. Regardless of the veracity of his claims, I believe that we all begin innocent. Unfortunately, there is an accuser out there who constantly wants us to believe that we are guilty and condemned. Hughes refused to believe the accusations and fought for his innocence. I wish we would have the courage to fight back against the accusations and start living into the person God created us to be. No matter what has happened, you started innocent and pure...go back there. Do you have the courage to fight for your innocence?

Thinking of both yourself and those who love you, I invite you to pray the last words of Preston Hughes:

"...fight for my innocence..."

Amen.

February 27, 2015

The Execution of a Graduate: Struggles from Candler School of Theology

I needed a theological education that could save my life. For years, I struggled to survive under the weight of what I was taught at the Southern Baptist Theological Seminary. I just couldn't believe that God hated so many people. How could a God called Love only have love for those whose minds and hearts were closed to the world around them? I couldn't give up. I had to take one more chance on God and life. When I arrived at Emory University's Candler School of Theology, I got the jolt of existential electrification that I needed. In classroom after classroom, I met a God that knew my name and desperately sought to breathe life into me. Just when I thought it might be over, a little theological education got me moving again. Though there were difficulties, I can say in no uncertain terms that my tenure at Candler School of Theology saved my life.

Most people would not think of the largest women's prison in Georgia as a center of theological education. When I first heard about Candler's Certificate of Theological Studies, I thought that someone had really lost it to try and construct theological education in a prison. Then, I met some of the graduates of the program. God shows up and shows out in some of the strangest places. Upon encountering some of these women, I realized that theological education was saving their lives too.

In 1997, Kelly Gissendaner was sentenced to death for orchestrating the murder of her husband, Doug. If we think about it logically, Gissendaner probably deserves to die for her crimes. I guess we all deserve to die for our crimes to some degree or another. Struggling to find life in dark spaces, Gissendaner started her theological education from the same place that I did. From lesson to lesson, Candler School of Theology taught Gissendaner that the love and grace of God never fails. I never grew tired of that lesson. Knowing that she would be probably executed, I wonder if

Gissendaner thought that theological education would save her life? In a spiritual sense, I suspect it already has. Yet, Gissendaner is still scheduled to be killed on March 2. In the midst of such a crisis, what are we to do with our theological educations?

The Candler School of Theology taught me that I was learning in order to give life to others. Today, I am struggling with the value of such education when the state is preparing to kill one of the graduates. How could this happen? Where were we? Maybe we were in prison when she was there. Maybe we will be with her until the bitter end. Maybe we will be the ones who keep her memory alive. All of this theology is well and good, but I would still like to save her life. If theological education cannot both raise the dead to life and keep the guilty from being slaughtered, then what good is it? For the sake of Kelly Gissendaner, I pray that we figure this piece out before Monday.

Amen.

February 27, 2015

Lenten Reflections from the Executed: #493 Carl Blue / February 21, 2013

*These reflections are taken from pieces of the last words of the last 40 persons executed in Texas.

"We all have to die to get to heaven."

When I think about heaven, I think about the overwhelming and intoxicating embrace of love. Sometimes, I think we get glimpses of extravagant love on earth. Regardless of when we are talking, I don't think love comes without death. We have to die to our self in order to be able to love anything else. We have to die to our self in order to experience the full love of God. Carl Blue knew about love and wanted to share his knowledge of love in his final moments. Love won in his life and love will win in all of our lives if we stop holding on to the illusions of control and embrace the limitless power of love.

I invite you to pray the last words of Carl Blue:

"We all have to die to get to heaven."

Amen.

February 28, 2015

The Existential Crisis of Birth: Waiting in the Midst of Doubt

Depression stalks me before every birth. The existential questions taunt me over and over again. Why are we here? Do we matter? Where are we going? Death becomes a trusted friend. For I know, there will be a day when I don't have to deal with these questions anymore. While I still take the pills, existential crises are not easily cured. Hope is difficult to cultivate in a world of doubt. I just keep searching.

The snow piles up. I have been here before. In the cold firm wetness of the precipitation, I feel the absence of God. Do you care about me? Why am I here? The moisture falls. Are you there? I hear the crunch of snow. Could that be God finally walking up to cure me? I hear the birds chirp. Is God taunting me with such close flight? I hear a car about to drive up. Is it ridiculous to wonder if God will pull up in a car? I only know the void of absence. People are dying and where are you? Love seems like a charade when you let the innocent be slaughtered. I guess a spiritual relationship is like lying prostrate in the cold wet snow and not knowing whether you are going to freeze to death before God shows up.

The diagnosis and treatment of my Bipolar Disorder only helps soften my reaction to these questions, but it doesn't make them go away. I guess I am able to remain sure of my love of God through my experience of longing for God. I have only known for sure a few times in my life. I could use one of those moments. In the name of the shadow, the whisper and the dream.

Amen.

February 27, 2015

Lenten Reflections from the Executed: #494 Ricky Lewis / April 9, 2013

***These reflections are taken from pieces of the last words of the last 40 persons executed in Texas.**

"It's burning."

When the poison started to flow through the needle, Ricky Lewis said that his body was burning. Lewis is just one example of a great many executed persons who have reported a burning sensation before they died. Though the burning is used to argue that the execution process is a violation of the constitutional protection against cruel and unusual punishment, I am hungry for the day when we realize that killing people is always evil. Shall we light the fire and let our bodies burn boldly with love for all of God's children?

With the idea that the fire of love can save us from all this killing, I invite you to pray the last words of Ricky Lewis:

"It's burning."

Amen.

February 28, 2015

For the Association of Welcoming and Affirming Baptists:

50 Years After Selma: Jesus is Transgender

The most terrifying substance known to our world is difference. When people can't control or contain it, they want to destroy it. The fall of humanity is centered on a failure to love and respect queerness. The God that exists queer beyond our normative ways of being and thinking must be weeping. 50 years after Selma, queers are still being slain in the streets and the silence from the church is deafening.

Growing up in Atlanta, I constantly heard people talking about marching or getting arrested with Dr. King. The truth of the matter is that everyone always marched and got arrested *after* the victory has been won. In every movement of justice, there are always only a few people who choose to be different in order to make a difference.

The voices of moderation filled the air during the struggle in Selma. When Jimmie Lee Jackson was gunned down during a march for civil rights while protecting his mother and grandfather, you can bet all that you own that there were those sympathetic to the movement who responded by saying that he shouldn't have pushed so hard. People like gradualism not real change. A few weeks later, Rev. James Reeb was beaten to death for not wanting to be like every other cowardly minister who sat trembling in church offices and did absolutely nothing to advance the cause of justice. People like safety and want to steal courage from the actions of others. Driving back from Montgomery, Detroit resident and mother of 5 children Viola Liuzzo was murdered by the Ku Klux Klan. Can't you just hear the people saying that Liuzzo should have stayed home with her kids? I suspect that Luizzo did as much or more to instruct her kids on how to live their lives in her death than she could have done in life. People always want to talk about death in Selma, but my God there was a hell of a lot of life packed into those days.

Now, I look around and wonder whether the bones that are pilling up in our churches are even capable of life anymore. Can any of these damn bones live? I pray daily that we will somehow find the queerness that those in Selma found. While there is certainly no shortage of avenues of oppression, one would be hard pressed to point to a pandemic more severe than the marginalization and slaughter of our transgender neighbors.

50 years after Selma, our response to violence against transgender bodies is the same old cowardice and gradualism from so many years prior. Since the beginning of the year, at least 9 transgender persons have been slain. These courageous people, who chose to live their lives queerly in the face of tremendous normative pressure, deserve our admiration and celebration and not our fear and silence. A few weeks ago in Tyler, Texas, I spoke at a vigil for a murdered black transgender woman named Ty Underwood. I was appalled at the lack of participation by clergy and churches in the community. For them, I guess the lives of transgender people matter less than those people who are paying the bills to maintain these dens of normative safety and apathy. There will be more deaths and it will be because the church has nothing to offer but more silence and inaction. With bills criminalizing transgender use of public restrooms, hate is slowly becoming the law of the land. We have moved so slowly on equality for lesbian and gay people that we have all but

left the transgender population behind. Now, the violence and ostracization has reached a level that cannot be easily be ignored.

50 years after Selma, the church is failing again in the presence of queerness. In the face of such evil, how many more lives will have to be taken for us to realize Jesus is transgender? There is no need to quarrel about her genitals. We all just need to know that Jesus is always going to be with the persecuted. The presence of God with the marginalized and oppressed is never a gradual phenomenon...it is a lived reality. 50 years after Selma, Jesus is still calling us to grow queerer. Will we heed the call and finally give our bodies to the struggle for liberation?

Transgender Lives Matter.

Amen.

February 28, 2015

Lenten Reflections from the Executed: #495 Ronnie Threadgill / April 16, 2013

***These reflections are taken from pieces of the last words of the last 40 persons executed in Texas.**

Ronnie Threadgill-

"I am going to a better place."

I can think of no more depressing of a place to be than lying on a gurney and waiting to die. With the executioners swarming, Ronnie Threadgill wanted everyone to know that he was going to a better place. How often do we live our lives consumed with all of the morbid and depressing shit going on all around us and forget that we are going to a better place? Look to the sky my friends! God has given us the ability to imagine the fruition of all our hopes and dreams for a reason.

No matter what you are going through, I invite you to pray the last words of Ronnie Threadgill:

"I am going to a better place."

Amen.

March 1, 2015

Lenten Reflections from the Executed: #496 Richard Cobb / April 25, 2013

***These reflections are taken from pieces of the last words of the last 40 persons executed in Texas.**

"Life is death, death is life."

Matter is never created or destroyed. So what happens when we die? With the needle in his arm, Richard Cobb declared that there is life in death. The matter of Cobb or us will never created or destroyed. Life never dies.

In the juxtaposition of your daily striving, I invite you to pray the last words of Richard Cobb:

"Life is death, death is life."
Amen.

March 2, 2015

Kelly Gissendaner Lives. Everyone Else Too?

The drugs were cloudy. Though I can imagine, I have no idea what that really looks like. With a question about bad drugs being what postponed this execution, I know that this is not just about Kelly Gissendaner anymore. This is a moment that could have real repercussions for the many other people on death row. I pray that this is the moment that abolitionists in Georgia have been looking for and that these cloudy drugs will slow down the entire process or even lead to a moratorium. Brian Terrell is scheduled to be executed on March 11. We need #kellyonmymind to start thinking in the direction of #brianonmymind and #deathrowonmymind. This could be the moment we have all been working for. I pray so.

Amen.

March 2, 2015

Lenten Reflections from the Executed: #497 Carroll Parr / May 7, 2013

*These reflections are taken from pieces of the last words of the last 40 persons executed in Texas.

"I'll be back."

To believe in an afterlife is to believe that you will be back. Maybe you won't be back to the exact same spot that you left. Since death is a tragedy for most people, I doubt that most people would want to go back to the exact spot of their death. I think that the back is actually where you started. If God is love and we started in the mind of God then I guess we just collapse back into love.

I invite you to pray the last words of Carroll Parr:

"I'll be back."

Amen.

March 3, 2015

Why Kelly Gissendaner *Almost* Died.

Kelly Gissendaner *almost* died for the sins of Christians. When word came in that Kelly's execution was postponed, I knew why she was *almost* executed beyond a shadow of a doubt. Having grown up in Georgia and now living in Texas, one grows familiar with these execution processes. Though there was much publicity around Kelly's case, most people are executed with little public resistance and scant media attention. If you look back a week to the night before Kelly was originally supposed to be executed, there was little attention being paid to the case. Then something spiritual happened. Christians in Georgia started to wake up.

The orchestrated effort to save Kelly's life was incredibly impressive. Post after post tagged #kellyonmymind filled social media. Popular Christian writers and bloggers offered their words of encouragement and resistance. The traditional media was full of stories about the changes that occurred in Kelly's life over the last few years. Professors, students, former inmates and others created films that were incredibly compelling. The pictures that came out of the efforts of the last few days were unbelievable. With all of this unbelievable effort and attention, Kelly was only saved by cloudy drugs not public pressure. Now, we are left to wonder how we ever let her get so close?

When I say that Kelly *almost* died for the sins of Christians, I am being quite literal. The last death penalty case to get this type of attention was Troy Davis. I stood across the street from the prison in Jackson and watched the hundreds of people demand that the State of Georgia spare his life. I remember thinking that if we could keep up this moment then we could abolish the death penalty all over the country. There have been five executions since the execution of Troy Davis. Most people could not name one name of the executed let alone two. If Christians had been as excited and energized about these last five executions as they were about Kelly, I don't think there would have been a death penalty to even talk about in this case. The lack of engagement from Christians around the country is what causes the heinous practice of executions to continue. Kelly *almost* died for the sins of Christians or the lack of engagement in the previous cases and efforts that could have saved the lives of everyone on death row. Will we now rest until they try to go through with the execution of Kelly or will we stand with the hundreds and hundreds and hundreds of people on death rows all over the nation facing execution?

After some of these cases garner tremendous public attention, I go back to my work as an abolitionist. I always pray that everyone will stay engaged and we can together abolish the death penalty. With seven executions scheduled here in Texas before the end of May, the lives of Kelly Gissendaner and Brian Terrell still on the line and numerous executions scheduled across the country in coming days, abolitionists could sure use the help. #kellyonmymind must become #deathrowonmy mind if we are going to end this heinous practice once and for all. Though I want to have hope, I always have to be realistic and tell myself that most of these Christians will probably just go back to doing what they were doing and not care about the wider sickness that is the death penalty. I pray that I am wrong. Amen.

March 4, 2015

Lenten Reflections from the Executed: #498 Jeffrey Williams / May 15, 2013

*These reflections are taken from pieces of the last words of the last 40 persons executed in Texas.

"I ain't got no love for anyone that don't love me."

How often do you feel this way? I'm only going to love those that love me and then I will be safe. The problem is that Jesus calls us to the dangerous spaces of a reckless love for the world. With his last words, Jeffrey Williams held on to the illusion that he could control and manage love. When he met the love of God or the God whose name is love, I am sure that Williams learned that he was no longer in control.

I invite you to pray a prayer of confession using the last words of Jeffrey Williams:

"I ain't got no love for anyone that don't love me." and add forgive me.

Amen.

March 4, 2015

God in the Waiting: The Final Hours of Emily's Pregnancy

We are nearing the final hours of a long journey for our family. Emily has carried our fourth and fifth children almost forty weeks and should give birth within hours. The last few weeks were particularly tough. Due to the weather, we were consistently stuck in the house. In tremendous pain and discomfort, Emily waited. Battling a new but familiar bout of depression, I waited. Not totally realizing exactly what was about to happen, our children waited. At the end of our journey, I know we will find the beginning of our journey. We will have waited for the soft cries of new birth and in those cries we will find hope in new life.

In the midst of these late stages of waiting, I looked for comfort in an old book. I read scripture listening for the soft cries of new life. When I find those words of new life, I cling to them with all that I am.

Tonight, God spoke words of life to our family. "Those who wait upon God will gain new strength; they will rise up with wings as eagles; they shall run and not be weary; and they shall walk and not faint." As we prepare to leave for the hospital, the words of Isaiah 40:31 remind us that the presence of God is real in the waiting and grows more real as new birth takes over.

Amen.

March 4, 2015

Lenten Reflections from the Executed: #499 Elroy Chester / June 12, 2013

*These reflections are taken from pieces of the last words of the last 40 persons executed in Texas.

"A lot of people say I didn't commit those murders, I really did it."

Before he gave the Warden the go ahead, Elroy Chester wanted to make sure that everyone knew that he killed a number of people. Upon hearing Chester's confession, it is easy to label him a monster and be done with it. The harder task is to see how you are like Chester. In Matthew 5:21-22, Jesus compares and equates murder and anger. How many times have you been angry?

In confession of your anger, I invite you to pray the last words of Elroy Chester:

"A lot of people say I didn't commit those murders, I really did it."

Amen.

March 5, 2015

A Real Christian in Arizona Saved Jodi Arias' Life

Wielding a knife and gun, Jodi Arias brutally killed Travis Alexander. By the time her case went to trial, Arias garnered much media attention. Ultimately convicted of murder and facing the death penalty, Arias was saved by a hung jury and prosecutors decided tried again. After the second sentencing proceedings and a long deliberation, jurors voted 11 to 1 for the death penalty. In Arizona, that lone juror saved the life of Jodi Arias.

When I heard a juror stood against death, I realized that there is at least one real Christian in Arizona. Whether the juror knows it or not or even believes it or not, they follow the teachings of Jesus more closely than all these other folks who claim to be Christians and keep on killing. Followers of Jesus are called to love their neighbor as their self. Does anyone realize that it is impossible to love your neighbor as your self and kill them? The teachings of Jesus are about creating and maximizing life not taking it. If you are interested in discovering how to follow Jesus in our culture of death, look no further than the lone juror who prophetically stood against execution.

Amen.

March 5, 2015

The First Throuple

Three men married each other in a traditional Buddhist ceremony on Valentine's Day in Uthai Thani Province, Thailand. Joke, Bell and Art have become famous sharing their beautiful story of love and commitment. While critics have said their relationship makes a mockery of marriage, I can only say that the Thai throuple has strengthened my belief in the magical and mysterious ways of love. With the dawn of legal same-sex marriage, we can expect more and more proponents and defenders of a new normative couple-based way of viewing relationships and marriage. I would argue that these folks are just as wrong as those fighting same-sex marriage. If love is love for same-sex couples, then surely love is love for the throuples. Person after person who has shared the story of Joke, Bell and Art have called them, "The First Throuple." This is the only part of this story I couldn't disagree with more. We all know that the first throuple was God, Jesus and the Holy Spirit.

Amen.

March 5, 2015

Lenten Reflections from the Executed: #500 Kimberly McCarthy / June 26, 2013

*These reflections are taken from pieces of the last words of the last 40 persons executed in Texas.

"I am going home to be with Jesus."

Why are we so embarrassed to talk about Jesus? We work so hard to make sure that people don't think we are too spiritual or religious in our modern age. There is something absurd about hiding love. Kimberly McCarthy was home sick for the great love of her life and the next, Jesus. Maybe we need to get a little home sick. Maybe we need to learn that love is something to be expressed and not hidden.

In anticipation of that great reunion of love, I invite you to pray the last words of Kimberly McCarthy:

"I am going home to be with Jesus."

Amen.

March 6, 2015

If She Had a Penis...

For over 40 weeks, Emily has carried our son and daughter. We walked all day. With every step, I held Emily's hand and she engaged every contraction with grit and determination. Over and over, I looked into her eyes and knew that my home will be wherever she is. Despite the pain, today was about a beautiful love that only seems to grow deeper and wider. Nearing the end of a long journey, we had some beautiful moments to reflect today. One stands out.

We stopped for a second at a small chapel. During an impromptu photography session, Emily sat down next to a beautiful array of light flowing in from a stunning stained glass window. Often, God speaks to me through rainbows of light. Looking at her stomach, I realized that she has two vaginas and a penis now. In that moment of revelation, I knew that I would love her no matter what sexual organ she has. I have fallen in love with the soul of a person. In the beauty of the moment, God reminded and affirmed in me that love is love and love is what will set us free from all our silly categories that hold our minds and hearts back. I pray this beautiful revelation for the world.

May we embrace and celebrate love wherever or however we find it.

Amen.

March 6, 2015

Lenten Reflections from the Executed: #501 John Quintanilla, Jr. / July 16, 2013

***These reflections are taken from pieces of the last words of the last 40 persons executed in Texas.**

Who do you love? If you had a needle stuck in your arm about to pump poison through your veins, who would you express your love to one last time? John Quintanilla, Jr. wanted his wife to know how much he loved her. Though Quintanilla was executed, the love he had for his wife lives...for love never dies. Who do you love?

Thinking about the ones you love, I invite you to pray the last words of John Quintanilla, Jr.:

"...tell my wife that I love her..."

Amen.

March 7, 2015

Lenten Reflections from the Executed: #502 Vaughn Ross / July 18, 2013

*****These reflections are taken from pieces of the last words of the last 40 persons executed in Texas.**

"I don't fear death."

We are a people paralyzingly afraid of death. We are diseased with an inability to see life in death. For Vaughn Ross, life was far scarier than death. Ross was ready to depart this life for the experience of the beauty of the next. The courage of a convicted killer facing death in the execution chamber reminds us that there can be more life in dying than we could ever imagine.

I invite you to pray the last words of Vaughn Ross:

"I don't fear death."

Amen.

March 8, 2015

Thank You: A Prayer in Crisis

The natural birth of Lucas was amazing. Madeleine was a little slower to make her appearance. Emily was experiencing contraction after contraction and nothing was happening. After close to four hours, I noticed something dripping on the floor. I don't know why, but I assumed that it was water for a moment. When I realized that it was blood, I told Lauren (the doula) and ran out into the hall to yell for the nurse. Emily was in trouble and so was Madeleine. As medical professionals rushed into the room, my anxiety grew exponentially with each passing second. When I started to pray, there were no words coming out. I just kept sending thoughts and emotions to God. Somehow out of my hope that God would see our family through, I managed to whisper, "Thank You."

The more the doctor worked, the more it became apparent that this was not going to be a natural birth. Emily made the decision to go ahead and have an emergency caesarian section. While she was being prepped for surgery, I stayed back in the room and struggled to keep it together. From her appearance, I could tell that Emily was not in a good place. When I arrived into the operating room, there was blood everywhere. After a few moments, the doctors handed Madeleine to me and told me that she had been stuck face first in the birth canal. Emily was under anesthesia and unable to provide too many lucid thoughts, but she did manage to let me know that I was going to be getting a vasectomy as soon as possible. Though the nurses wanted me to go with Madeleine, I couldn't leave Emily. When it was finally over and we got back to the room, I softly cried. Looking up, from a deep place, I managed, "Thank You."

This morning, Emily's doctor came in and told us just how close we came to having a funeral instead of a celebration. Madeleine was stuck and could not have come out on her own. If Emily had chosen to keep pushing, she would have broken Madeleine's neck. By the grace of God and the medical professionals at Denton Presbyterian Hospital, I am looking at Lucas and Emily feeding on Emily's chest as our other three children, Phillip, Jeff and Quinley, run around the room. There are not enough words available to describe the magic of these moments. I can only say, "Thank You."

For many years, I have sought to pray more fervently and effectively. I have shouted out prayers. I have repeated ancient prayers. I have written prayers down. I have forced out difficult prayers. I have spent hours upon hours trying silent prayer. I have been mentored in prayer. I have even spoken in tongues a time of two. Through it all, I have prayed and prayed and prayed. Yet, despite all of my strivings and searchings, I think I just got all the prayer education I will ever need. In a moment of crisis, "Thank You" was enough.

Amen.

March 8, 2015

Lenten Reflections from the Executed: #503 Douglas Feldman / July 31, 2013

***These reflections are taken from pieces of the last words of the last 40 persons executed in Texas.**

"I hereby protest my pending execution and demand immediate relief."

Douglas Feldman was a remorseless killer. Before he uttered his last words, Feldman declared that his killing of innocent truck drivers were a justified death sentence that he was forced to carry out. Why would anyone care about his last words? Feldman protested his execution and demanded relief. We didn't give it to him. We chose to look away in the face of a forced death. We can do better.

I invite you to pray the last words of Douglas Feldman and think about how you can give the next person to be executed some relief:

"I hereby protest my pending execution and demand immediate relief."

Amen.

March 9, 2015

Lenten Reflections from the Executed: #504 Robert Gaza / September 19, 2013

*These reflections are taken from pieces of the last words of the last 40 persons executed in Texas.

"It's not easy, this is a release."

Sometimes the most freeing things are the most difficult to endure. In the hardest of moments, Robert Gaza pointed to the the release that was upon him. I believe Gaza felt the presence of God. One does not have to be strapped to a gurney or lying in a hospital bed to feel like they are dying. Regardless of your circumstance, know that God is with you and you can always point to your release.

I invite you to pray the last words of Robert Garza:

"It's not easy, this is a release."

Amen.

March 10, 2015

Not One More! : Words from Texas Coalition to Abolish the Death Penalty Faith Leader Lobby Day

Good afternoon. My name is Rev. Dr. Jeff Hood. I am standing right outside of the Governors office here in Texas. We just dropped off a faith leader sign on letter with over 550 signatures of Texas faith leaders...who are committed to abolishing the death penalty. I am so proud to be standing with people who are willing to put their careers, their livelihoods, their wellbeings on the line for this cause. I ask that other faith leaders not only join us in their comfort...but walk out of your churches, walk out of your offices, walk out of the safety of your surroundings to get more deeply involved. Jesus commands us to love our neighbors as our selves....friends, we cannot accomplish this and execute people. This past summer, I walked over 200 miles from Livingston to Huntsville to bring awareness to the immorality of the death penalty. I was inspired to walk by a Buddhist monk named Tashi Nyami at a prayer breakfast last spring. Tashi told us, "If we want to change the world, then we have to place our body in the conversation." With my walk in mind, I know that every step all of these faith leaders are taking here today is one step closer we all take to abolishing the death penalty. Today is about advocacy. Tomorrow must be about advocacy. The next day and all the days after that must be about advocacy until we finish this thing. Not one more. Not one more execution in this state. Wednesday Manuel Vasquez is supposed to be executed. I pray to God that that day will be a day of tremendous beauty when our legislators and governor wake up to the immorality of the death penalty and stop executing people. We can save Vasquez's life and we can save the lives of others. No more! Note one more! Not one more! Not one more!

Amen.

March 11, 2015

Manuel Vasquez Deserves to Die

If the wages of sin is death, then Manuel Vasquez deserves to die over and over. A member of the Texas Mexican Mafia, Vasquez strangled Juanita Ybarra to death with a telephone chord over illegal unpaid drug taxes. One prior conviction involved the beating of a man who died after his body was set on fire. During the sentencing phase of his trial, prosecutors provided evidence that Vasquez was involved in at least two other murders. To make it plain, Vasquez was a very violent man before he was sentenced to death and maybe still is. With this said, I don't fault anyone for thinking that this man deserves to die.

Later this evening (3/11), the State of Texas will kill Vasquez. The media will acknowledge the many victims of his crimes and insinuate that his death is a direct result of his actions. After the deed is done, various pundits will talk about what a relief it is that Vasquez is dead. I can just hear them, "Now, he won't be able to kill anyone else" or "The family of the victim can now move on." The words of justification will be many.

The problem is that all the people talking will have just killed someone.

Manuel Vasquez deserves to die.

Who wants to become a killer?

You can't stop the killing by killing...only love can do that.

Amen.

March 11, 2015

Lenten Reflections from the Executed: #505 Arturo Diaz/ September 26, 2013

*These reflections are taken from pieces of the last words of the last 40 persons executed in Texas.

"I have no hate for you."

Are there people out there that you simply can't stand? Do you think you could keep from hating someone who was actively trying to kill you? In the midst of a room full of his executioners, Arturo Diaz declared, "I have no hate for you." What would it look like to live your life with such grace? You can begin to find out today.

Thinking of those you despise the most, I invite you to pray the last words of Arturo Diaz:

"I have no hate for you."

Amen.

March 12, 2015

Lenten Reflections from the Executed: #506 Michael Yowell / October 9, 2013

***These reflections are taken from pieces of the last words of the last 40 persons executed in Texas.**

"I love you."

The world is complicated. Evil and love mix on the inside and outside of every person. Michael Yowell was no different. Though he was a confessed killer, Yowell spent his final moments telling his children that he loved them. Who are we to say that the love of a killer isn't just as salvific as the love of anyone else? We spend so much time judging the love of others that we fail to live love out.

I invite you to practice love by praying the last words of Michael Yowell:

"I love you."

Amen.

March 13, 2015

Lenten Reflections from the Executed: #507 Jamie McCoskey / November 12, 2013

*These reflections are taken from pieces of the last words of the last 40 persons executed in Texas.

"And if this takes the pain away, so be it."

While in the Garden of Gethsemane, Jesus kept asking God if there was any other way to take the pain away. Jamie McCoskey used similar words. There is something divine about giving our bodies to others. Though McCoskey didn't have a choice of whether or nor to die, he wanted the sacrifice of his body to mean something. We give our bodies to something daily. Why not give your body to alleviating the pain of others?

I invite pray the last words of Jamie McCoskey:

"And if this takes the pain away, so be it."

Amen.

March 13, 2015

Border Blindness

I graduated from the Southern Baptist Theological Seminary in 2009. Though I have kept only a small portion of the theology, I still occasionally read material from people I knew there. Earlier today, I came across an article by my old ethics professor Southern Baptist Ethics and Religious Liberty Commission President Dr. Russell D. Moore entitled, *Left Behind in America: Following Christ after the Culture Wars*. For a second, I resisted reading the article. Some old wounds take a long time to heal. After a minute or so, I stepped blindly across the border I erected and started reading. Though there are multiple problematic assertions and conclusions to be found in the article, I did agree with Dr. Moore that there is a stark difference between Christian values and the Gospel. Jesus calls us to be right and not just act right. Throughout my day, I have wondered what it would mean to leave Christian values behind and simply embody the Gospel.

This evening, I got a call from a buddy asking me to sign a petition for someone facing deportation. After revealing a few details of the case, he asked if I would still sign it. I didn't hesitate. I don't believe in borders. I feel like borders blind us to the humanity of the other. Our categories of undocumented or documented are absolutely ludicrous. In the eyes of God, we are humans. While I am able to espouse Christian values, I am still yearning to develop a broader case of border blindness. The Gospel of Jesus calls us past the false lines we have drawn in our lives to places of deeper engagement. We are not called to engage Christian values. We are called to give our lives. When we are completely given over to Jesus, no border formed against us will prosper.

Talk of traversing borders is not vogue in most Christian contexts. Everyone wants to talk about spaces that are in one way or another safe. Conservatives, evangelicals and fundamentalists have constructed borders around issues of doctrine and dogma. Liberals and progressives have built borders around being right on Christian values. What all of these groups of people don't understand is that the most dangerous place to be is in the prison of our own borders. We cannot achieve Jesus' call to the world or even the self unless we develop a border blindness that makes the prisons of our borders obsolete. I remember Billy Graham saying a time or two, "...give up everything that is holding you back and follow Jesus." I think he was right. You simply can't follow Jesus and hold on to your borders.

Amen.

March 14, 2015

Lenten Reflections from the Executed: #508 Jerry Martin / December 3, 2013

***These reflections are taken from pieces of the last words of the last 40 persons executed in Texas.**

"God is the ultimate judge"

Why do we worry so much about the opinions of others? If God is the judge, then none of the finite opinions floating around us matter. Our job is to please God not humanity. In his last words, Jerry Martin wanted everyone to know that he feared God more than the judgments of humanity. Do you?

I invite pray the last words of Jerry Martin:

"God is the ultimate judge"

Amen.

March 15, 2015

Lenten Reflections from the Executed: #509 Edgar Tamayo / January 22, 2014

*These reflections are taken from pieces of the last words of the last 40 persons executed in Texas.

Silence.

Mexican national Edgar Tamayo decided to remain silent during his execution. After looking back at other cases, I realized that a considerable amount of persons being executed in Texas that have remained silent are from Mexico. I have to believe that Mexicans exercising silence in the execution chamber is emblematic or an expression of the oppression faced by Mexicans throughout this country. Mexican immigrants are too often without voice or hope in the United States. Jesus calls us to do better. How can we lift up the voices and hopes of Mexican immigrants?

I invite you to ponder the plight of Mexican immigrants as you experience the lack of last words from Edgar Tamayo:

Silence.

Amen.

March 16, 2015

Lenten Reflections from the Executed: #510 Suzanne Basso / February 5, 2014

*These reflections are taken from pieces of the last words of the last 40 persons executed in Texas.

Silence.

Suzanne Basso refused to speak. Have you ever wondered why women are silenced?

I invite you to ponder the oppression of women around the world in the silence of Suzanne Basso.

Silence.

Amen.

March 17, 2015

Lenten Reflections from the Executed: #511 Ray Jasper / March 19, 2014

*These reflections are taken from pieces of the last words of the last 40 persons executed in Texas.

"...stay strong and faithful to God."

Sometimes we deny our own strength. Unbeknownst to us, God has placed deep reservoirs of strength within every person. Upon the culmination of many hard years on death row, Ray Jasper knew about these reservoirs. In encouraging faithfulness to God, Japer wanted everyone to know the source of his strength. For Jasper, God and strength went together. What about for you?

I invite you to pray the last words of Ray Jasper:

"...stay strong and faithful to God."

Amen.

March 18, 2015

Lenten Reflections from the Executed: #512 Anthony Doyle / March 27, 2014

***These reflections are taken from pieces of the last words of the last 40 persons executed in Texas.**

Silence.

Anthony Doyle refused to speak in his final moments. Will we remember the silence that we caused?

In the silence of Anthony Doyle, I invite you to experience the silence caused by capital punishment:

Silence.

Amen.

March 18, 2015

When Inclusion is Exclusion : Radical Ecclesiology

The church is the church is the church. Right? Ecclesiology is the study of what the church is. At our present hour, one cannot study the church without hearing the word 'inclusion.' In books, sermons and articles people consistently write and speak about a need for greater inclusion. For many Christians, being inclusive has become synonymous with being a Christian. In fear of losing what they think or claim is church, groups have formed within congregations and denominations to push for full inclusion. The salvation of institutions through greater inclusion is of the highest priority. With church after church and denomination after denomination declaring they are now fully inclusive, many believe that the church is finally being saved or as one of my friends put it, "...we are moments away from full inclusion in the church." Unfortunately, I think it all might be a trap.

Not far from our home, there is a road with nine churches in a row on it. Driving down the road, I passed building after building of every major Christian denomination. After some prayer for guidance, I realized that these spaces were not really churches. When Jesus placed his person with the least of these, Jesus located the church outside of walled institutions of safety and comfort. In staring at each building and thinking about the denominations, I realized that these spaces exist for the comfort of the members.

For within each building and broader denomination, walls are erected to keep people safe and any interaction with the real church in the streets is carefully scripted and limited. The walls of these buildings and institutions that people thought protected them are really the walls of prisons that keep them from being with marginalized and oppressed people or where Jesus actually is. The message of Jesus calls for a radical ecclesiology or a bold understanding that the church is always going to be in the streets with those we call dangerous or other.

For far too long, Christians have defined the church based on buildings and denominations. There is a desperate need for radical ecclesiology. Jesus was never about the project of institutional upkeep. Jesus was about the people. Jesus will always be about the people. With battles raging for inclusion, one has to begin to wonder if inclusion is worth the energy? Jesus warned us about a time when inclusion would actually mean exclusion or when being a part of the comfortable would mean not being with Jesus. Do our efforts at inclusion mean that we are leaving Jesus for comfortable prisons? Even if it costs us inclusion in the very churches and denominations we love, we are called to be excluded and stand with those who are standing alone.

Amen.

March 18, 2015

Lenten Reflections from the Executed: #513 Tommy Sells / April 3, 2014

*These reflections are taken from pieces of the last words of the last 40 persons executed in Texas.

Silence.

Tommy Sells was a serial killer. Do you realize this system of execution makes you one too?

In the silence of Tommy Sells, I invite you to repent:

Silence.

Amen.

March 19, 2015

The Call: A Reflection.

I was in the library at the Southern Baptist Theological Seminary when I got the call. Though I had known he was sick, death was in his voice and he needed me. Time after time, my Southern Baptist mentor called and chatted with me about all sorts of subjects. I had heard the call before, but never like this. The doctors treated my grandmother's cancer a few years ago and she made it out fine. Why couldn't my mentor just get well? The hour was late, but I knew that this couldn't wait and ran to my car. I hit the accelerator to the floor and screeched out of the parking lot. Passing exit after exit, I couldn't stop...I had got the call.

Pulling into his driveway, I rushed inside. My mentor was asleep and his wife let me rest on the couch until he woke up. Sleep? Who in their right mind sleeps when they have heard the call? In those hours of darkness, I prayed and waited to fulfill the call. When I heard the birds chirp, a jolt of nervous energy sent me into motion. I got up as quickly as I could. I had heard the call.

There was a gigantic hospital bed in the room. "Pull up a chair," my mentor whispered and motioned next to the bed. When I grabbed his hand, I was startled by the cold sweat. To say that I was frightened is an understatement. Regardless of feeling like my stomach was a basket of knots, I received the call and there was no turning back. Pulling me closer and closer, my Southern Baptist mentor offered words that would forever change my life and solidify the call, "I'm gay and I always have been." I have never felt the presence of God so strong. Before I could reply, my mentor added, "Go back to seminary and never stop fighting for those who have no voice." Though I followed the call of God many times, I think this is the call that saved me. I have never stopped following the call.

Amen.

March 19, 2015

The Genocide of the Mentally Ill

Jason Harrison is dead. Jason Harrison is not dead because he was holding a screwdriver and made a movement toward Dallas police. Jason Harrison is dead because we live in a society that refuses to value and protect the lives of the mentally ill. If Dallas police officers had engaged the situation with the needed care and restraint of dealing with someone who is sick and in desperate need of help, Jason Harrison would have been restrained in a nonlethal way and taken to the closest mental health facility. Instead of an outcome where Jason Harrison could get help, we are left with the wailing cries of his mother, "Oh, they killed my son! Oh, they killed my son!" In the midst of the horror of it all, our society shrugs and another one bites the dust.

If you think I am being dramatic, I invite you to engage a few other tragic cases. In 2011 in California, members of the Fullerton Police Department beat unarmed homeless schizophrenic Kelly Thomas to death. Thomas' last words were, "Daddy, help! They're killing me!" In early 2014, a North Carolina police officer, fed up with an inability to subdue teenage schizophrenic Keith Vidal, declared, "We don't have time for this" before shooting him to death. In March of 2014, mentally ill and homeless James Boyd was shot and killed by New Mexico police officers while camping in an illegal space and displaying camping knives. In St. Louis, mentally ill Kajamie Powell was shot to death after stealing pastries and energy drinks from a convenience store and displaying a knife. There are hundreds if not thousands of stories just like these. If law enforcement was trained to deal with the mentally ill, most of these situations could be avoided. With little training coming and a lack of empathy from the public, we are beginning to have genocide on our hands.

Living near Dallas, the murder of Jason Harrison has deeply affected me. In my prayers, I have consistently pleaded with God to open the eyes of our society to the plight of those suffering with mental illness. I suffer from bipolar disorder and have had periods of time in the past when I was out of my mind. Looking back, I am really glad no one ever called the police to get me under control. This morning, I got out of bed and went to the bathroom to take my medicine. When I picked up the little pill, I stared at it for a long time. For the first time in my life, I wondered if this was all that was separating me from being the next victim. I took the pill and tried to move on with my day. When I walked downstairs and looked at my five children, I knew statistically that at least one of them is going to deal with some of the same mental health problems that I do. What happens one day when one of them doesn't take their medicine? I can't just sit back and hope that if that day comes we meet a police officer with the proper training and empathy.

Jason Harrison's mother shouldn't be screaming alone. We should all be demanding justice and protection for the mentally ill amongst us. The genocide must stop.

Amen.

March 19, 2015

Lenten Reflections from the Executed: #514 Ramiro Hernandez / April 9, 2014

*These reflections are taken from pieces of the last words of the last 40 persons executed in Texas.

"All I have is love."

We go through life thinking we need so much. Unfortunately, the more we accumulate the more we think we need. People fail to realize that love will make you richer than anything else one could ever accumulate. When Ramiro Hernandez was strapped to the gurney and asked for final words, everything had been taken from him. In his last moments, Hernandez realized that love was all that he had and all that he needed. I pray that the world will learn the same lesson.

With deep understanding of just how rich you are, I invite you to pray the last words of Ramiro Hernandez :

"All I have is love."

Amen.

March 20, 2015

Lenten Reflections from the Executed: #515 Jose Villegas / April 16, 2014

*These reflections are taken from pieces of the last words of the last 40 persons executed in Texas.

"I am at peace."

In a world of violence and fear, we work so hard for peace. Unfortunately, I think that peace is far more about being and trusting than it is working. Jose Villegas understood that lesson. In his final moments, Villegas wanted the world to know that he was at peace.

After you stop working, I invite you to pray the last words of Jose Villegas:

"I am at peace."

Amen.

March 22, 2015

Lenten Reflections from the Executed: #517 Lisa Coleman / September 17, 2014

*These reflections are taken from pieces of the last words of the last 40 persons executed in Texas.

"Tell them I finished strong."

Life is about finishing strong. Do not let the failures and disappointments distract you. You are capable, but you must stay committed. Despite her circumstances, Lisa Coleman stayed committed and finished strong. I pray that we will follow her lead.

With thoughts about how you want to finish, I invite you to pray the last words of Lisa Coleman:

"Tell them I finished strong."

Amen.

March 23, 2015

*This address was delivered on March 21, 2015 at the LGBTQ Religious Experience Summit at Sam Houston State University in Huntsville, Texas

The Courage to Be Queer: A Theological Exploration

May this be a wild experience for us all...perhaps even a queer experience if we are lucky. Let's begin by talking about theology. What is theology? Most people think that theology is primarily about doctrines and dogmas. Folks, this couldn't be further from the truth. Theology is an exploration and adventure in being. Learning to be. Theology is about how you experience the divine within the self. Theology is rooted in story. We forget that we all have stories. We forget that we all have powerful stories. We forget that our stories have the potential to change the world. Good theologians are always storytellers.

Let me begin with a story. I grew up at a large Southern Baptist church. We were conservatives amongst conservatives. By the time I was in middle school, everyone in our youth group was talking about the possibility of getting left behind in the rapture. During this time, I remember seeing piles of laundry in our house and thinking that I had been left behind. I would flip out and get saved. This happened over and over. I just took church so seriously. I believed every word of it. One of our youth teachers told us one time that our penises would fall off if we masturbated. Thankfully, one of my buddies was able to lean over and assure me that that wasn't the case. To make a long story short, I constantly felt a tension in my childhood between the doctrines and dogmas that I learned at church and the pull of love that pushed me to treat people better than such beliefs would allow.

In high school, I remember thinking that a guy was attractive and believing that the simple attraction to a guy was enough for me to end my life over. This was the first time in my life that I had to struggle with what it would look like to have an alternative sexuality. I tried to forget about all of it. By the time I arrived at Auburn University in Auburn, Alabama, I was a fervent evangelical and determined to stay that way. Though most people don't believe me now, I was a frat guy back then. Our fraternity was made up of elite guys from elite families. For me, the thought of being wealthy and successful like everyone else was simply too great of a temptation. In that context, I definitely wasn't telling anyone that I had ever experienced any attraction to men. Our fraternity was probably one of the worst places on earth that you could have let that be known.

In the midst of it all, somehow God still found me. I felt called to the ministry and decided to go to seminary. As a good Southern Baptist, I decided to go to the apex of theological education in Southern Baptist life...The Southern Baptist Theological Seminary in Louisville, Kentucky. The president of the institution is Dr. Albert Mohler. If you google Dr. Mohler, you would find hundreds of articles criticizing everything we are gathered here to do today. When I got there, some of these attractions to men came back. I flipped out again. I worried and worried and worried. I just knew that I was destined for hell. Thankfully, God found me once more and I got saved.

Late one evening, I received a phone call from my Southern Baptist mentor. With sharpness in his voice, he told me that he was dying. I traveled through the night to get to him. Driving through town after town, I thought about my faith and how I couldn't reconcile it with all the evil coming from my denomination. When I arrived at his home, I went into his room and walked up beside his hospital bed. With death lingering, I was very uncomfortable. In probably one of the most profound moments of my life, my Southern Baptist mentor told me that he had lived his life as a closeted gay man and challenged me to be a voice for the voiceless. While it was a tremendous moment of calling, I had never had anyone share such things with me. For so long, my mentor had been a representation of Jesus for me and now I had to deal with the fact that Jesus was now gay.

Upon returning to Southern Seminary, I started asking questions. Isn't it funny how questions often lead to revelations? I bet I know more closeted Southern Baptist pastors than I do straight Southern Baptist pastors. Regardless, I graduated rather quickly from Southern Seminary and moved on to Emory University's Candler School of Theology. I thought all the liberal Christians would embrace me with open arms. I was wrong. Truth be known, I traded one fundamentalism for another...that really wasn't all that progressive. Having just arrived from the land of Southern Baptists, I didn't have many friends and people were consistently skeptical of me. I feel like God has always brought people around me when I need them the most. In that context, queer persons of color befriended me and the relationships that followed proved transformative. Though I had started to shift, I wasn't fully celebrating of all people and these friends sat with me until I was. Though it was my mentor's revelation that saved me, I can say without hesitation that queer persons of color have taught me how to be queer.

I never wanted to move to Texas. We moved here for my wife Emily to teach and do her PhD at the University of North Texas. I was depressed for a little while. I couldn't find my place. Things started to change when I began studying with a gentleman named Steve Sprinkle, who is the Professor of Practical Theology at Brite Divinity School. Though my thinking had been increasingly headed in a queer direction, I learned to really systematize and structure it with Steve. So you can blame him for what comes next...

I firmly believe that our constructed identities are problematic and divisive. I intellectually operate out of a place of queer theory and queer theology. There are a few events that have firmed up my beliefs in recent years and help illustrate where I am coming from. A few years ago, I had a young man come to me and tell me that he didn't think that he was gay enough. Unable to ascertain what he meant, I asked, "What do you mean?" He replied by explaining that he didn't feel like he was culturally gay enough. I realized that culture was the problem and not this young man. There was another situation in which a lesbian lost her partner of decades and started dating a man many months later. Instead of being happy for her, the community attacked the lesbian as a fraud and truly shunned her. Within my own life, I have been attracted to men and married a woman. Our identities leave people thinking that they must fit within construct created by others instead of allowing them the freedom to define their own person. I believe that sexuality and gender a fluid constructs and we would do well to let people be without limited definitions and identities. God did not create us to be so limited and simple. God created us to be queer because God is queer.

The God who is queer exists outside of all of our categories and binaries. When we try to define God...we fail. The reason is that God is too immense and unique. Who can describe a love beyond love? Who can describe a hope beyond hope? Who can describe grace beyond grace? Who can describe justice beyond justice? There in the beginning we were created to be in God's image. As God cultivated humanity in the Garden of Eden, God creates humanity to be queer in God's image. I believe that every human to ever exist is a queer construction of a loving God.

Now, you know that things got sideways in the Garden and humanity got pushed out of this right relationship with God. There was a moment of temptation. The serpent slithers up and tells the human that if they eat of the tree then they will be made like God. The human ate and the rest is history. Ultimately, I believe the first sin is always the act of believing that God can be found somewhere other than within. Theology is about being. Queerness is about being. Queerness is about the courage to be who God has created you to be. We are taken out of right relationship with love and each other when we fail to be queer. Failing to be queer is failing to be.

Jesus is a construct that comes to show us how to be. How to be what? How to be queer. Jesus is not easily defined. In the life of Jesus, we are shown what it looks like to live in a place of fluidity and movement beyond identity. With the knowledge that safe spaces are never free spaces, Jesus lived dangerously in a society of normativity and paid the price. Until queerness wins, there will always be those who persecute the queer. If you are not being persecuted, then you have to wonder if you are really queer. Jesus shows us that queerness is a way of being beyond identity.

I believe that the Spirit of God works to take us deeper into the spectrum and make life more mysterious by the day. The message of God as revealed in Jesus is an invitation to embrace the mystery of queerness and become immortal in your very being. The Spirit of God is drawing us to each other in the unity of difference. The world will be made right when people learn to live queerly.

Claiming an identity doesn't make you queer. Living into the core of your being is what makes you queer. Let me set forward the example of the Cathedral of Hope United Church of Christ. Most people think that our congregation must be the queerest spot around. This is not even close to the truth. In fact, if you took out the sexual orientation and gender identities of our folks...you would not be able to tell the difference between First Baptist Dallas and Cathedral of Hope. We have developed a normativity that would rival any congregation. In many ways, we have lost our first love.

Queerness is about claiming something beautiful and unique in who God has created you to be. We fail when we create communities and identities that push everyone to be the same. Why do people get so pissed off about queerness? There are identity patrols out there who think it is their job to make everyone fit within the lines. I think it is because queerness is not easily contained or controlled.

You can change the world if you will just be honest. Our identities create dishonesty. The constructs of our identities cannot contain all of who we are and we are forced to lie. Tell the truth! Stop trying to fit and learn to be! It takes courage to be honest. It takes courage to be queer.

My prayer is that the courage to be queer will transcend sexuality and gender. I am ready for these issues to be over with. I am ready to be at a spot where people can be who they are. We've got a tremendous amount of work to do. Texas is executing more people than most nations on earth. People are dying trying to get across our borders for a decent job. We are manufacturing weaponry and bombs with the capabilities of destroying our world millions of times over. We can solve or even speak to these issues until we are ready to be authentic and honest with each other...until we are ready to be queer.

Queer people save the world because queer people are the world...if we are honest with our self.

Amen.

March 23, 2015

Lenten Reflections from the Executed: #518 Miguel Angel Paredes / October 28, 2014

*These reflections are taken from pieces of the last words of the last 40 persons executed in Texas.

"I hope you let go of all of the hate because of all my actions."

How do you pray for those who hate you with good reason? When we name hate we probably make the hater hate us more. Yet, how can we not name hate for what it is. If we have been freed, how can we let anyone stay enslaved in hate? Miguel Angel Paredes knew that there were people out there who hated him and he wanted to name it before he died. We don't have to wait for death to acknowledge hate that we have caused and pray for the haters.

With the haters in mind, I invite you to pray the last words of Miguel Angel Paredes:

"I hope you let go of all of the hate because of all my actions."

Amen.

March 23, 2015

The Church in the Dirt

The Pharisees caught a man and woman fucking. Under the religious law of the time, fucking outside of marriage was a capital offense. So the Pharisees brought the woman and slung her in the dirt at the feet of Jesus.

Notice, I said the woman. Where in the fuck was the man? The Pharisees were a bunch of pampered religious leaders who led with their own prejudices. Sound familiar? How many of you have ever felt rejected by traditional churches? With nowhere else to go, you are out here meeting in the dirt. The Pharisees stand all around you in judgment. The men and women represent the United Methodist Church, Roman Catholic Church, Southern Baptist Convention, United Church of Christ and many other religious bodies. In their arrogance, the Pharisees have slung you out of their churches and into the dirt. Though they can't legally kill you, they treat you as if you are dead. This is the nature of being a church slung in the dirt. The good news is that you have landed right at the feet of Jesus.

When Jesus saw the woman, he got down in the dirt with her and started writing on the ground.

I have no question the woman was lower than whale shit. Do you know how low whale shit is? Let me put it this way, it don't get any lower. Have you been made to feel this way by religious leaders? The traditional church sits in judgment of people like you. You are made to feel like you don't belong. Does anybody believe that a room full of rich white people is what the realm of God looks like? Thankfully, the economy of God is different than the economy of the Pharisees. When the Pharisees tossed the woman in the dirt, they didn't realize that she was now closer to Jesus. When you have been thrown out of traditional churches, you have been thrown ever closer to Jesus. Exclusion equals inclusion in the economy of God. Jesus said, "What you have done to the least of these you have done to me..." So, if you are being included...that's the point that you should be worried about where Jesus is...or whether you are standing with the Pharisees or are in the dirt with Jesus.

Instead of picking the woman up, Jesus gets dirty. So often, people concentrate on what Jesus was writing in the dirt. Though I am somewhat curious as to what was being scribbled, I think the more important piece of this conversation is that Jesus was placing his body into the conversation. Jesus was willing to be stoned and die with the woman. How often do we place our bodies into the conversation? How often are we willing to die so that others might live? As far as the traditional churches go, you can't save someone you have no contact with. The real church will forever be the church in the dirt.

Jesus looked at the Pharisees and said, "Whichever one of you is without sin can cast the first stone."

In a world where institutionalizations and hypocrisies have overtaken the church and threatened to choke the very life and love out of the Gospel of Jesus, you sit and stare back in judgment. For those who dare raise their stones, you let them know that Jesus stands more fully with you than he will ever stand with the comfortably safe and included. Pilgrims in the Park...you are the light of the world...you are a city set on a hill that will not be hidden. On this day, you have reminded me anew that the salvation of Jesus is always in the dirt. Thank you.

Amen.

March 24, 2015

Lenten Reflections from the Executed: #519 Arnold Prieto / January 21, 2015

*These reflections are taken from pieces of the last words of the last 40 persons executed in Texas.

"There are no endings, only beginnings."

For Jesus, the ending was just the beginning. For Arnold Prieto, the ending was just the beginning. What about for you?

I invite you to pray the last words of Arnold Prieto:

"There are no endings, only beginnings."

Amen.

March 24, 2015

Lenten Reflections from the Executed: #520 Robert Ladd / January 29, 2015

*These reflections are taken from pieces of the last words of the last 40 persons executed in Texas.

"Let's ride."

We stop. We are afraid. We don't want to move an inch. Danger is a paralyzing force. In the face of certain death, Robert Ladd looked danger in the eye and shrugged. If we place our trust in God, we too can have such confidence.

Staring down whatever danger you face, I invite you to pray the last words of Robert Ladd:

"Let's ride."

Amen.

March 25, 2015

Teaching God to Love Lucifer: A Review of Jim Forest's "Loving Our Enemies: Reflections on the Hardest Commandment"

Forest, Jim. *Loving Our Enemies: Reflections on the Hardest Commandment.* Maryknoll, New York: Orbis Books, 2014.

Lucifer got jealous of the boss. Haven't we all made this kind of mistake before? God kicked his ass out of heaven and never let him come back. Ever since Lucifer got banished, he has been raging all over the earth. Every time God tries to get something good going, Lucifer tries to destroy it. Every time Lucifer tries to get something good going, God tries to destroy it. I have no question that the two are entrenched mortal enemies. So, where does God get off telling us to love our enemies? Jim Forest helped me engage this deep theological question.

Though all of *Loving Our Enemies: Reflections on the Hardest Commandment* is fabulous, I was most impressed with the nine disciplines of active love. When I started thinking about the toxic relationship between God and Lucifer, I realized that these nine disciplines could help.

First, Forest encourages us to pray for our enemies. Can you imagine God spending all of his celestial time praying for Lucifer? Every day, ruminating and meditating on how much he loves and misses his buddy. If God answers the most fervent prayer, maybe God isn't praying hard enough for reconciliation with Lucifer. If Lucifer is the problem, perhaps God just needs to keep praying until Lucifer comes back. Prayer can change things.

Second, Forest encourages us to do good to our enemies. Though Lucifer did some bad things, it was not very nice to throw him out of heaven. While God can't take back that failure at reconciliation, he can invite Lucifer back. What would it look like if God started acting as generously with Lucifer as we are expected to act with each other? Even if it is not reciprocated, one has to do good to their enemies in order to expect good to come about.

Third, Forest encourages us to turn the other cheek. While I guess God could destroy Lucifer if he wanted to, God should stop slapping Lucifer's cheeks by leaving him outside the gates of heaven. Lucifer should also stop trying to destroy God and his people. Turn the other cheek folks!

Fourth, Forest encourages us to practice forgiveness. I wonder if God has really forgiven Lucifer? There must be real forgiveness in order for real reconciliation to happen. I know that God and Lucifer have it in their hearts to forgive each other. There is just going to have to be effort.

Fifth, Forest encourages us to break down the wall of enmity. If God won't let Lucifer back into heaven, how is there supposed to be any movement forward? If

God stays up there and Lucifer stays down here, how can they even talk? One has to leave their place of comfort and power in order to have true reconciliation.

Sixth, Forest encourages us to refuse to take an eye for an eye. God holds Lucifer accountable for every evil thing that happens in the world and punishes him accordingly. Maybe if God showed a little less law and more grace, Lucifer might prove that he is able to be reconciled.

Seventh, Forest encourages us to seek nonviolent alternatives. God keeps talking about throwing Lucifer into the lake of fire. Has there not been enough violence? God needs to figure out a good way to interact nonviolently with Lucifer.

Eighth, Forest encourages a posture of holy disobedience. God doesn't have to approve of Lucifer's actions in order to love him. Sometimes, the best way to love someone is to keep them from doing more harm. God's responsibility is to love Lucifer regardless.

Ninth, Forest encourages a life of recognizing Jesus. I think of Jesus as the best that is possible. Sometimes, even God has to be reminded of his best self. In order to love Lucifer, God is going to have to utilize his best self to recognize Lucifer's best self.

If my intuition is any indication, I believe that Jim Forest might just have set two mortal enemies on the track to reconciliation. *Loving Our Enemies* is a challenging book for living out a challenging commandment in a challenging time. In the midst of a world that is struggling with so much with hate, I endorse love and therefore, I endorse the book

Amen.

The Rev. Dr. Jeff Hood is a Baptist pastor, theologian and activist living and working in Texas. The author of six books, Dr. Hood serves on the National Council of FOR. With deep soul, Dr. Hood sprinkles mysticisms and prophesies at revjeffhood.com

March 27, 2015

Lenten Reflections from the Executed: #521 Donald Newbury / February 4, 2015

*These reflections are taken from pieces of the last words of the last 40 persons executed in Texas.

"That each new indignity defeats only the body."

Donald Newbury knew that the indignity of execution could only defeat the body. For Newbury, the soul is always free for those who allow it to be. No matter the indignity of your circumstance, have you unchained your soul?

I invite you to pray the last words of Donald Newbury:

"That each new indignity defeats only the body."

Amen.

March 27, 2015

Lenten Reflections from the Executed: #522 Manuel Vasquez / March 11, 2015

*These reflections are taken from pieces of the last words of the last 40 persons executed in Texas.

"Thank you Lord for your mercy and unconditional love."

Who can describe love greater than any love imaginable? Who can comprehend love that is without end? Manuel Vasquez knew that the mercy and love of God never failed or ceased. Do you know?

I invite you to pray the last words of Manuel Vasquez :

"Thank you Lord for your mercy and unconditional love."

Amen.

March 28, 2015

Beware of the Palm Waivers

The people of Jerusalem waived their palms madly to celebrate the entry of Jesus into their town. Less than seven days later, Jesus was tortured and executed in the same place. Though Palm Sunday is a time to celebrate, I can never get past the fact that the same palm waivers either participated in or did nothing to stop the execution of Jesus. The lesson of the juxtaposition should be one of caution.

Emily and I don't have a tremendous amount of close friends. We are too skeptical for that. Truth be known, we have experienced far too many showdowns where no one showed up to help. We have known many palm waivers who stand on the sidelines waving palms at us in the moments of triumph and who run for the hills when times get difficult. In our ministry, we have learned to love generously and trust cautiously.

How did so many people praise Jesus and either participate or do nothing when he was executed less than a week later? While certainly a complex question, I think one should never underestimate the desire that humans have to praise and be praised by institutions. The people decided that power was more important than love.

We live in a day and age where everyone wants to talk about power. The palm waivers thought that Jesus was about power and they wanted to be on the winning team. When everyone realized that he was about love, the execution went pretty smoothly. Thousands of years later, people largely remain the same.

Love is always going to be far more dangerous than power.

Beware of the palm waivers who might try to convince you otherwise.

Amen.

March 30, 2015

Killing Jesus and Saving the Church: A Holy Week Manifesto

I don't really like going to church. There are some ministers who love the mystery and majesty of it all no matter what. Not me. I am so tired of the modern presentation of Jesus that I have mentally and spiritually dropped out. Week after week, church leaders use their pulpits to demand more money and more people. One would think that the Gospel of Jesus was, "Go ye unto all the world and be as cheesy as possible while collecting as much money as possible...and lo, I am with you as long as you work to become a megachurch." There is no theological depth to a modern Jesus that is peddled about like a used car. Unfortunately, the modern Jesus won't even get you halfway to your house without leaving you broke down and begging for help on the side of the road. Regardless of the consequences, spiritually lazy and ignorant churches are addicted to the meaninglessness of the modern Jesus. How can we expect to save a diseased and dying church with blind devotion to the modern Jesus? I have an idea.

"Crucify him! Crucify him!" Though these words were chanted at an awful time, I would suggest that this language can be interpreted metaphorically to help us kill the modern or fake Jesus that is destroying our churches. When you hear that following the modern Jesus is about constant church growth, you should be chanting, "Crucify him! Crucify him!" When churches tell you that the modern Jesus is not political or concerned about social justice, you should be chanting, "Crucify him! Crucify him!" When you are told that following the modern Jesus is about giving more and more money to the church, you should be chanting, "Crucify him! Crucify him!" In order to save the church, real Christians should be leading the charge to kill the modern Jesus. Thankfully, followers of the real Jesus are not a people who believe in death without resurrection.

I can just hear the mourning. What happened to the modern Jesus who let me be racist, sexist, classist and homophobic with no problem? What happened to the modern Jesus who let me be rich and not care about my neighbor? What happened to the modern Jesus who never challenged me? For those who wanted a modern Jesus that was just a selfish and hateful as they are, the time for mourning will be long. For those whose hearts longed for a resurrection of love in the person of the real Jesus, it will finally be time to go to church and meet him.

This Holy Week, followers of the real Jesus must be a people who work for both death and resurrection.

Amen.

March 31, 2015

24 Hours at the Cross: A Holy Week Confrontation with Execution in Texas

While churches always have a plethora of odd smells, there is one that is particularly memorable. Smelling like a mix of mold and mildew, I have always imagined it to be the results of inactive butts marinating in the pews for years and years. When I arrived for the prayer breakfast on abolishing the death penalty, the smell reminded me that we were probably just going talk without really saying much of anything. In the midst of the hollow words, I started to pray that Jesus would show up. With a small commotion, I noticed everyone looking at the door. Turning, I saw a Buddhist monk walking in.

One after one, people shared their stories over breakfast. Truth be known, I knew which story I wanted to hear. When the time came, Tashi Nyami tilted his head back and recalled the moment when he and his mentor walked up on a group of guys mercilessly beating a single guy. Before Tashi could collect his thoughts about what to do, his mentor spoke up and yelled out, "Wouldn't it be more fun to beat up a couple of Buddhist monks?" Embarrassed, the guys stopped the beating and ran away. Tashi reminded us that the pursuit of love and justice always requires us to place our bodies into the conversation. I have never had a story stick to me like this one did. Tashi drew me to the cross and helped me to realize that bodies can still make a difference.

For many years, I have worked against the death penalty. From lobbying to walks to vigils to fasts, I have sought to place my body into the conversation. People consistently ask me, "Why do you care so much?" My gut reply is always the same, "I am a follower of Jesus committed to his teaching of loving your neighbor as your self...and I know I can't love my neighbor and let them be killed." Throughout Lent, I have studied and prayed over the last words of persons executed in Texas. Through it all, I have consistently been reminded that a society can't kill people to teach people to stop killing people. We have got to stop this evil cycle of violence. I believe that love is the only antidote there is. At the cross, Jesus showed us that the fullness of love is found in giving your life so that others might live. If Christians would give their lives to love, there would be no death penalty. How much longer will we have to wait for Christians pick up their crosses and demand an end to executions? I can't wait on anyone else. I'm taking my cross to Huntsville.

At the Walls Unit, the red bricks are piled high and the infrastructure resembles a fortress. Behind the wire and concrete is the place where person after person has been executed in Texas. During Holy Week, I knew I needed to carry my cross down and share the love of God. I cannot let hate and violence continue without question. For the follower of Jesus, the biggest questions are always in the form of a cross. On Maundy Thursday at 3pm, I will begin a 24-hour vigil holding a 12-foot cross. Throughout my time there, I will remember the victims of this evil process and pray for an end to the death penalty. On Good Friday at 3pm, I will end the vigil by celebrating communion with other clergy. Wherever you are, I invite you to participate in person or in prayer. Together, we can embrace the love of God and stop the killing.

Amen.

April 4, 2015

Jesus is Dead! : An Easter Case for a Theological Resurrection

Throughout my ministry, I have heard awful stories of pain, abuse and suffering. Though the stories are many and varied, there is one that sticks out above all others. During a time of group counseling around spiritual abuse, an older gentleman revealed that his youth group pinned him down and probed his ass with a crucifix to show him how painful being gay was. When I ponder this story and the countless horror stories from the church, I am left with but one conclusion...the prevailing Jesus in our churches is dead.

For those who would quibble with such a message, I would like to offer a few examples. Progressive United Methodist ministers will stand before congregations and declare their love for queer people, but the overwhelming majority won't love them enough to sacrifice their pensions to perform their weddings. When your money matters more than people...you are a minister of a dead Jesus that offers dead theology to a dead world. Catholic, conservative and evangelical churches will talk about the blood of Jesus being the substitutionary atonement for our sins that satisfies the wrath of God. Unfortunately, substitutionary ideas of the atonement continue to lead to countless atrocities throughout the world. When your theology can be used as an excuse for the death penalty...you are a purveyor of a dead Jesus and not one that brings life into the world. Throughout the United Church of Christ and other liberal denominations, people will want to talk about liberating identities and communities. Throughout all the grouping, the soul of the individual will be slaughtered in a wave of goodwill and talk of justice. All of these churches will be shouting "He is Risen!," but the truth is that the church remains the greatest protector and promulgator of homophobia, racism, hate, inaction, violence and a whole host of other truly evil things. The truth of the matter is that Jesus is still dead and suffocating on our shit.

In the midst of our frightening theologies of resurrection, we have raised a Jesus that loves the same people that we love and hates the same people that we hate. This Jesus is just as abusive and dishonest as we are. What are we to do?

We do not have to be given over to death. There is hope. The process begins with the regeneration of Jesus. We must speak life into our ideas of Jesus. We must believe that Jesus is more important than any institutional or denominational pressures that would hold us back. We must believe that theologies of death are just that and replace them with a theology of life. We must believe that individuals matter more than our grouping of them. We must trade hate for love...for love is the only substance that can regenerate Jesus. In the midst of all of the dead Jesuses walking around like zombies, we must start the process of sanctification and take the time to clear our churches of ideas and theologies that represent death. People must matter more than money. God must matter more than institutions. Individuals must matter more than our dishonest groupings. Jesus must be cleansed and raised to newness of life. After the regeneration and sanctification of Jesus, we must take the difficult step of killing our safe Jesuses and claim the deification of the real risen Jesus. While I have great hope in the ability of this process to bring about a theological resurrection of Jesus, I know that most people and churches would prefer to worship safe dead Jesuses and leave the real thing in the grave.

Amen.

April 6, 2015

The Safety of a Dead Jesus: A Plea for Exclusion

*Easter Message Delivered in Denton, Texas

Let's begin with the excluded God. What does it mean for God to be left out? My mind immediately conjures up a situation at the church I attend, the Cathedral of Hope United Church of Christ. Our church was founded to be the ultimate space of inclusion for LGBT people and those that love them. Presently, the church's idea of liberation is based around your ability to fit within certain identities. This is not a phenomenon unique to our church. For the past 40 years, identity-based churches have become the leaders of progressive Christianity. You have the gay church, black church, latino/a church and many others. These spaces exist to liberate the populations they serve. I am beginning to be firmly convicted that our ideas of liberation and inclusion have created a new exclusion. For illustration purposes, let me return to the Cathedral of Hope United Church of Christ.

We are a congregation that has existed to promote the inclusion of LGBT people. Over the last few weeks, I have noticed that a row of chairs in the back of the sanctuary where homeless LGBT people usually sit has been removed. While I can't speak to the precise reason why this row of chairs has been removed, I can say that a congregation that has consistently been about the inclusion of LGBT people has now marginalized some of the most vulnerable people in their midst. I am beginning to realize that inclusion has now become code for an ability to exclude whoever we want to exclude...or at least to interact with them on our terms.

Inclusion has become the highest priority in our modern culture. The Gospel of Jesus is not about inclusion...it is about exclusion. Following Jesus is about being included in the excluded. Whenever we institutionalize inclusion, we often find out that the institutionalization of inclusion most often leads to exclusion. When you are included you are excluded in the realm of God. Jesus said, "What you have done to the least of these you have done to me." I was hungry. I was thirsty. I was sick. I was in prison. Jesus was excluded and continues to be excluded in our exclusions. It is interesting that Jesus doesn't say, "What you have done to the included you have done to me."

We are at an interesting time in history. We are months away from marriage equality. We are having more nuanced conversations about race, class, sexuality, gender and a whole host of other things than we have ever had before. As the world shifts and some people gain more rights and access, how will we treat those who are excluded? If what I have seen throughout my life is any example, the suffering will be left to suffer and the excluded will continue to be excluded. Let me break it down in Easter terms...for most people, Jesus will remain dead.

Friends, a dead Jesus is a safe Jesus. For most churches and the people within them, a dead Jesus is far easier to manage than a Jesus that is alive. With regard to the message of Jesus, safe spaces are always going to be dead spaces. Jesus calls us to interact with the excluded or those who the world would say are not very safe. Dangerous faith is a faith that can declare that Jesus is alive. A safe faith would just leave Jesus in the grave.

When I think about living out a dangerous faith... I think about the courage that it takes for a woman to hold the hand of her girlfriend in homophobic spaces throughout this nation. I think about those who are struggling against police brutality in the midst of overwhelming racism. I think about those Christians in the Middle East who are daring to follow Jesus in the midst of certain death. I think about the Muslims who are pushing back against Islamaphobia in this nation. I think about the poor, homeless and dispossesed people of this world demanding better. I could go on and on...but there is something divine about having the courage to live dangerously and simply be who you are. Those who live dangerously will always be excluded...but Jesus will always be right there with you.

I think we need to quit talking about inclusion and safe spaces. If you are black and gay, you will not achieve equality based on the constructs of inclusion and safe spaces. If you are poor and transgender, you will not achieve equality based on the constructs of inclusion and safe spaces. If you are disabled and a woman, you will not achieve equality based on the constructs of inclusion and safe spaces. We have to create a movement of love and justice that liberates people based on who they are and not where they can fit. A dead Jesus makes people fit. An alive Jesus liberates people from their individual location...no matter where they are.

We will be able to say that Jesus is truly risen when we begin to work to create a world where people can feel alive in their individuality and find community in their exclusion.

Amen.

April 7, 2015

Let Judas Be Your Prayer Partner.

Stepping through the green wet grass, I picked up egg after egg. Stuffing the brightly colored pieces of plastic into the trash, I was reminded of how quickly we trash what we deem useless. I started to think about the message of Jesus. In the midst of my prayers concerning reimagining leftover resurrection trash, one name kept coming to mind...Judas.

Though the gospel writers totally destroy Judas, Jesus still seems to love him very much. After he made the terrible mistake of betrayal, Judas was so remorseful that he begged the authorities to stop the murder of Jesus and when they didn't he committed suicide. As for the rest of the disciples, they just hid in their closets and let the authorities kill Jesus without much of a fuss at all. Who loved Jesus more...the one who gave his life out of his love or the ones who hid?

I believe that Judas might have loved Jesus more than anyone else. After his death, I have no doubt that Jesus lovingly embraced Judas for all eternity. While I certainly don't encourage suicide under any circumstance, I think we would be wise to give our lives to Jesus with the same intensity and love that Judas did. Perhaps, now is the time to let Judas be your prayer partner.

Amen.

April 7, 2015

The White Jesus is a Serial Killer

You see them lurking in the hallways of church after church. In the same tired old faded colors, it is hard to miss the blond hair, blue eyes and white skin. I have even seen them in hospitals. Growing up, I was terrified of one representation that stared ominously at the viewer. The old white Jesus paintings hang in space after space as a sign that white Christians remain in power. Southerners are particularly afflicted by this phenomenon. There are millions of these paintings dotting the landscape of the South. Not to be outdone, BIOLA University has a huge mural of a white Jesus on campus. These depictions of Jesus are inherently racist and problematic for a variety of reasons, but I think the biggest issue is that the depictions feed a superiority complex that leads white Christians to freely assault and often kill black people. I believe the white Jesus is a serial killer. Don't believe me? Lets turn our attention to South Carolina.

Last Saturday morning, Michael Slager pulled over Walter Scott. After a struggle, Slager shot and killed a fleeing and unarmed Scott. In those moments, the consequences of the white Jesus surfaced. For his whole life, Slager was shown images of a white Jesus that taught him that he was superior to black people like Scott. When those who are supposed to submit don't submit, followers of the white Jesus often access lethal force to enforce orthodox adherence to whiteness. Now, Scott is dead and the white Jesus is to blame. How many more victims will the white Jesus claim? From Eric Garner to Jason Harrison to Ruben Garcia, there doesn't seem to be an end in sight.

White Christians keep saying they want to help. I think a good place to begin is to burn the paintings, smash the stained-glass windows, paint over the murals and trash all the books and movies depicting a white Jesus. The real Jesus was a brown man who declared, "Love your neighbor as your self." One cannot love their neighbor and keep sharing racist images that lead to their destruction.

Amen.

April 8, 2015

A Prayer for Michael Slager: The North Charleston Killer*

*"...love our enemies and pray for those who persecute us." -Matthew 5:44

Oh Lord our God, it is hard to pray for anyone that would shoot a man in the back. Walter Scott didn't deserve to die. While I wonder why you didn't step in to stop this atrocity, I will leave that for another day. Today, I only know that another black man lies dead in the streets of this nation and another cop pulled the trigger. In this instance, the North Charleston killer is Michael Slager. While I am deeply angry, you taught us that the only path to peace is through love. I know that the strongest activism that I can pursue is to pray for my enemies. With this deeply engrained in my spirit, I pray...

God, I pray for the health and wellness of Michael Slager. While sitting in jail, I pray that Slager will know both your grace and your correction. I pray for Slager's wife and their unborn child. I pray that Slager's wife will know your love in this incredibly difficult time. As for the yet unborn child, I pray that the child will be a great champion of social justice and lead a mighty reformation of love in their generation. I pray for Slager's other two children. May they both know and rest in your eternal presence. I pray that they will know that there is no safer place to be than in the palm of your hand. Though their lives are changed forever, I know that all of the Slagers are your children.

I have most of my time in prayer for the family of Walter Scott and I would be remiss to not pray for a few things in particular for them in this short prayer for Slager. I pray that you will grant them justice without delay. I pray that they will know your love and your love will guide them through the tragedy of this hour. In your divine providence, I pray that you will grant them the ability to forgive Michael Slager. I pray that your forgiveness will be so strong that it will draw these two families together. I pray that the Slagers and the Scotts will grow to love each other so much that they will learn to work together and become the greatest champions of racial reconciliation our society has ever known. Oh God, we need a miracle such as this!

God, I know that you are capable of things beyond our wildest imaginations. I pray for justice, reconciliation, mercy and love to flow like a raging river and come over all of us. From the North Charleston killer named Michael Slager to the rest of us, now is the time for all of us to open our hearts to a future free of violence and racism. Make it so God...make it so.

Amen.

April 9, 2015

Texans Kill Recklessly: The Execution of Kent Sprouse

For many years, Texans have worked tirelessly to litigate the case, guard the offender and secure the drugs. Now the moment is here, Kent Sprouse will be executed this evening at 6pm. From beginning to end, the cost of executing Sprouse will be millions of dollars (http://www.deathpenaltyinfo.org/costs-death-penalty). Apart from the moral contradiction of a state full of Christians executing someone, there is a huge moral problem with spending millions of dollars to kill someone when it is far cheaper to keep them in prison for the rest of their lives. Imagine what schools, hospitals, firefighters, law enforcement and many others could do with all the remaining money? If Texans worked as hard to create a state worth living in as we do executing people, they would live in paradise. As it stands, the death penalty is killing Texas morally and financially. We must do better.

Amen.

April 14, 2015

The Orgasms of God

I posed a question to a group of people the other day, "Has God ever had an orgasm?" Everybody gets excited when you start talking about orgasms. The replies were wildly diverse. Slowly, a common theme emerged. I found that almost everyone believed there was a stark separation between God and sex. For most, it was almost as if God created sex to tempt us to be dirty. One person even went so far as to push that sex was a result of sin and wasn't created by God at all. I quickly realized why he was the most ornery person in the room. Regardless, these answers made me realize that most people have a fundamental misunderstanding of a core part of who God is.

God is a sexual being. How can one be so sure? We are created in the very image of God and our sexuality is a core component of who we are. How can we be created in the image of God and God not be a sexual being? When we engage in sexual activity, I believe we are emulating the very creative process that God engages in. Whether we are aiming to create new life or simply seeking to make love, sex is a profoundly creative process that is unique each time despite commonalities. If God is not a sexual being, then are sexuality is a key component of who we are that is not made in the image of God and therefore unredeemable. I simply cannot believe such nonsense.

Orgasms are spaces of profound pleasure linked to a moment of physical and spiritual creation. We are the great orgasms of God. In creating us, God is constantly feeling the pleasure of physical and spiritual creation. This is why I don't believe that masturbation is a sin. In and of God's singular person, God is engaging the process of pleasurable creation. Masturbation and sex are emulations of God. Possessing all possible orientations and genders, God engages the entire spectrum of sexual and creative processes. The bigness and wideness of the love of God's love is immeasurable. When I look around at all of creation, I am in awe of the production of God. Thanks be to the God in whose many orgasms we live and have our being.

Amen.

April 15, 2015

The Invincible Love of the Garzas

Once a month, I make the trip down to Livingston. The roads are long and lonely. Upon arrival, I go through numerous checkpoints and searches. When I finally get to the cold and sterile visitation room, I sit down in front of the thick plate glass window and wait. In the ensuing between moments, I always look around and wonder about the backgrounds and motivations of the other visitors on Texas' Death Row. Sometimes, I am brave enough to strike up a conversation with those around me. I met Larissa Garza and her young daughter during one of those short interactions. Though I enjoyed the brief conversation very much, the words had to end when my visit commenced. Regardless of the brevity of my encounter with the Garzas, I was touched.

For many months after our initial meeting in numerous encounters in the visitation room, I witnessed the love that Larissa Garza shared with her husband Manuel.

Posing for pictures, kissing through the glass and gazing intimately at each other, I saw the Garzas share something very beautiful in a hopeless place. For a long time, I wondered why anyone would ever want to be married to someone on death row. Most of the people down there are violent killers. In the midst of a struggle in 2001, Manuel took the gun of San Antonio police officer Rocky Riojas and shot him in the head. Though Manuel committed a heinous crime, there is something divine about a love that can push through to fruition despite the worst of deeds.

In her love for Manuel, Larissa showed me what the love of God does. Despite our worst moments, God finds us and chooses to love us anyways. The problem with the death penalty is that it assumes that love must end based on actions. God doesn't work like that and neither did Larissa. Last night, we killed Larissa's husband. Though Manuel is dead, I have no question that we did not execute the love of the Garzas. In my prayers, I imagined the intimacy of those last moments the Garzas shared and I know they were beautiful. I pray that such beauty will come to pass for the entire world.

In our murderous rampage that is the death penalty, we cannot kill love. For, God is love and love will never die.

Amen.

April 16, 2015

The Darkness: A Meditation

In the stillness of the night, you know me. The mist reminds me. Though the mind might wander, you remain steady in the nothing that is everything. The absence of light paints a glorious portrait of mystery. The crickets speak the word. In the echoes of yesterday and tomorrow, you speak of today. The still waters create a symphony of unknowing. The trees protect me. I long to stay here forever with you. The darkness is your home. You are God.

Amen.

April 17, 2015

From the Southern Baptist Theological Seminary to Queer

"What man doesn't wonder about what it would be like to have sex with a man?" While dining at Cracker Barrel late one night, I asked the question of a friend. Before I could even to begin to muse about my own question, Don Fulton looked at me in my eyes and declared, "I'm gay." In the revelation of the moment, we found a joint love of God that we had never experienced before. In the darkness of the night, we were both afraid. Anyone who was a student at the Southern Baptist Theological Seminary knew the consequences of questioning the demanded sexual orthodoxy, but there was something emboldening about knowing that I was no longer alone.

While trying to make it, Don and I supported each other. Consistent questions and sheer determination were our only other allies. Life is both difficult and tragic when you hold such a secret that can destroy the life that you think you want. Though we heard Jesus knocking at the door of our closets, we only cracked it far enough to engage each other. In time, we graduated and learned to open wider the door.

The years have grown us. Through various schoolings and jobs, Don and I have learned to love and respect each other no matter the choices we make. Presently, Don serves as a Captain in the Chaplain Corp of the United States Army. I serve on the National Council of the Fellowship of Reconciliation, the largest consortium of pacifists in the United States. Don often remains fairly traditional in his theology. I write queer theology and get called radical from every end of the spectrum. Don has rejected the concept of heterosexual marriage for his life. I fell in love with a woman and have five children. We are different...and yet we remain the carriers of a unique common history. When we get together, we have learned to lovingly both push each other and stand with each other in love. When I survey the landscape of my life, I can say without hesitation that my friendship with Don is one of the queerest relationships that I have.

Early this morning, Don looked at me and pondered, "Can you believe we are here?" I had to think for a second. When compared to other denominations, the Alliance of Baptists is a progressive place. Unfortunately, Christian denominations are woefully unprogressive and inadequate to address the various crises of our world. "On some level, I wish we were going to something a little wilder," I responded. "Maybe us two queers are it," Don replied.

Amen.

April 21, 2015

A Systematic Theology of Love

GOD is LOVE & LOVE is GOD. Love created us in Love's image. We are created to be Love. In the beginning, we were Love. Unfortunately, we decided that Love was not enough. In our desire to control Love, we lost our way. We have been searching for Love ever since. In the person of Jesus, Love became flesh and dwelt amongst us. Truly, Love so loved the world that Love gave Love's only begotten Love that whosoever believes in Love will never perish but have everlasting life. Love came to show us that Love is the way, Love is the truth and Love is the light. In our ignorant self-destructive tendencies, we tried to kill Love and we failed. Thankfully, Love will never die. In the resurrection of Love is our hope. The spirit of Love works among us to take us back to the place that we are from...a place called Love.
Amen.

April 23, 2015

The Root of Police Brutality is Fear

"At the root of all war is fear, not so much the fear that men have of one another as the fear they have of everything." In the midst of desperate times, Thomas Merton wrote these words in a 1962 essay entitled, "The Root of War is Fear." Decades later, these words once again ring true in our own desperation. For an increasingly prolonged period, police brutality has dominated the news and caused everyone to question whether anyone is safe. The death of Freddie Gray is just the latest example. Prognosticators and pundits spend hours upon hours describing our problems and prescribing solutions. In our desperation to say or do something, we have ultimately not said or done much of anything to address the root of the problem. Our attention has been focused on the symptoms without attention to the cause. The complexity of our problems should not mask the simplicity of the solution. We are a people who are desperately afraid of everything. The root cause of police brutality rests solely in our own fear.

Fear of our neighbors causes us to constantly prepare for and perpetrate war. For the last decade, the United States has engaged in endless conflict. We believe that our fear gives us the right to destroy the lives of innocent people all over the world so that we might feel safe. We feel like the deaths of innocent civilians is a small price to pay for achieving the higher goal of a sense of safety. Though the safety is not real, we feel better when guns are firing and bombs are exploding. Too often, we fail to ponder the cost of our fear. The war mentality that we develop always comes home. The military hardware that was used overseas ends up in the hands of law enforcement. In our desperate desire for safety, we arm our police and prepare them for war. Our police carry the same fears that we do. We prepare them to be afraid of our neighbors just like we are. Every person a law enforcement officer comes in contact with is a potential threat. When officers are taught that danger is everywhere, we should not be surprised when they eliminate what they are afraid of. With constant access to lethal force, perceived fears become realized deaths. The bodies will continue to pile up until we do something about the pandemic of fear that has overtaken us.

We are also afraid of what is within our own persons. In a society of shadows, we are so afraid to be real. We know there are always consequences to expressing who we really are and what we really think. Carrying the dishonesty of false living, we put our defenses up against the world and our blinded by our self. We believe that our sole purpose in life is to show the world what we think the world wants to see. In our attempt to fit, we forget what is real and what is false. We become confused. If we cannot trust our self, we know that we cannot trust those around us. Our fears become compounded and we respond by arming ourselves. The resultant deaths in our streets are only a reflection of the deaths that are constantly taking place in the individual souls of the citizens of this nation. Police brutality begins with the fear within.

If we are to make any progress beyond our rhetoric, outrage and partial measures, we must work to put fear aside. Continued cultivation of our own fears will only cause more police brutality. The exorcism that we all need can only be performed by each of us on our own person.

Amen.

April 23, 2015

Guns Don't Belong at Church

Recently, I read a story that the evangelical megachurch Briarwood Presbyterian in Birmingham, Alabama is petitioning the state for its own police department. For a second, I couldn't believe what I was reading. The thought of a church or any other private institution being able to found and govern a police department is really problematic. Can you imagine the power that churches and private institutions would have to enforce their own moral judgments? Would those who don't pay their tithes get escorted off the premises in handcuffs? While I will stop there, I can think of many more scary scenarios. The article brought me back once again to a firm belief that guns don't belong in church.

'No guns in church' seems like a pretty obvious rule to me. Unfortunately, it is a rule that is not being followed all over the country. While the Briarwood example is extreme, know that there are guns in both liberal and conservative churches all over. In an age when safety is much more important than the actual message of Jesus, churches hire armed security all the time. Don't believe me? I attend and work out of the Cathedral of Hope United Church of Christ, the largest predominately gay and lesbian church in the world. We regularly have armed security patrolling the premises. Many other churches do the exact same thing. I find it incredibly alarming. On more than one occasion, I have walked into church and thought about the possibility of one of my young children dying on the front steps of our church due to the misfire of a weapon. I believe that the potential of such a tragedy is too high a price to pay for a false sense of security.

Can you imagine Jesus preaching with his disciples around him packing handguns for protection? I can't. If you can't, I suggest you challenge your church to get the guns off the premises. I am trying.

Amen.

April 24, 2015

The Blood of a Black Man in Dallas

Over a hundred times, the family of Jason Harrison reached out to Dallas police for help getting him to Parkland Memorial Hospital. Suffering from severe mental illness, Jason was often out of his mind. On June 14 of last year, police arrived at the Harrison residence. The body camera of one of the officers captured what happened next. Jason's mother Shirley came to the door and declared, "Oh, he's just off the chain. You can hear him, talking about chopping up people." When asked whom she was talking about, Shirley replied, "My son, bipolar, schizo." Seconds later, Jason appeared at the door with a small screwdriver and was told by officers to put it down. Refusing, Jason made a movement toward the officers. Less than five seconds after the initial encounter, Dallas police pumped five lethal bullets into Jason's body. As Jason's blood rolled down the driveway, the officers can be heard nervously trying to figure out what to do next. There seems to be little remorse or grief for what has happened. I guess we can't blame the officers...as they were just acting out what we know to be true...the spilt blood of a black man is nothing to get too upset about here in Dallas.

One of the police incident reports reveal that Shirley Harrison exclaimed shortly after the shooting, "They could have just shot him in the leg." Why would they have shot him in the leg? Police view a problematic black man in Dallas as something to be exterminated not helped. Yesterday, the Dallas County District Attorney's office announced that there would be no indictment in the case. For now, the blood of black men will continue to roll down driveways, streets and sidewalks with impunity. However, God is not mocked. The judgment is coming. Those police who continue to spill the blood of black men will be held accountable...for black blood matters just as much as any other blood to God.

Amen.

April 27, 2015

The God Who Riots

Jesus couldn't get the horrific images of police brutality out of his mind. Walking downtown, Jesus was tired of seeing people assaulted and killed. Enraged, Jesus destroyed a police car and other properties. When officers started to show up in riot gear, Jesus gathered his friends together and confronted them. "Get out! Get Out! Get out!" they kept screaming in unison. Though everyone kept calling them agitators and thugs, Jesus and his friends refused to back down in their quest for justice. Anyone who doesn't believe Jesus is capable of such things simply hasn't read John 2 and Mark 11. Throughout these stories, Jesus cuts up for the sake of justice. Overturning tables and swinging a whip, Jesus destroys the tools of oppression and drives the oppressors out. Followers of Jesus are brought face to face with a God who riots. In the aftermath of the lynching of Freddie Gray and in the midst of the fires of Baltimore, one should not assume that Jesus is on the side of law and order. He's not. God is always most present on the side of justice. You can't cheer on Jesus in the temple and condemn the rioters in the streets. Jesus shows us that we serve a God who is willing to destroy the tools of oppression and drive the oppressor out of the city. Let's pray this is what is happening in Baltimore.

Amen.

April 28, 2015

The Charlatans

There are only a few moments in my life that I have unintentionally projected liquid out of my mouth. Today, I had one such moment. This afternoon, I was watching a press conference when I witnessed a pastor jump in front of the microphone and function as if he was speaking for Jesus and the church on marriage equality. This wouldn't have been a big deal if I didn't have prior knowledge that this particular pastor refuses to do same-sex weddings for fear of losing his position and pension. Though I can't predict the future, I have every reason to believe that this particular pastor will not perform same-sex weddings until his denomination says it is acceptable...regardless of what the Supreme Court of the United States decides. This does not sound like moral conviction to me. Those who have consistently failed to stand up for all of their neighbors on the issue of marriage in the past should not be the ones speaking for Jesus or the church on the issue of marriage in the present. If you haven't had the courage to perform a same-sex marriage before now, please repent and step away from the microphone.

Amen.

April 28, 2015
Lines

The violence in Baltimore represents the failure of identity politics on a catastrophic scale. For decades, the people in Baltimore were told if they elected the right black people then their problems would be solved. Now, we have black elected officials referring to the children of the community as "thugs." The lines that many assumed would save them are the very lines that caused this crisis in the first place. We have a black president that cares so much about black people that he continues to protect the economic system that causes so many of them to remain in poverty. We have a black mayor in Baltimore who presided over a police department that harassed black people and killed Freddie Gray in the first place. Who are the real thugs? For the sake of justice, we have to begin to erase lines that are keeping us from each other. We can do so much better together.

Amen.

April 29, 2015

Testimony on Texas HB 1527: A Bill to Abolish the Death Penalty

Thank you. My name is Rev. Dr. Jeff Hood. I am the Minister of Social Justice for Hope for Peace and Justice...which is the social justice ministry of a consortium of churches in the Dallas area...and I sit on the Board of the Texas Coalition to Abolish the Death Penalty. I am here to speak in support of House Bill 1527.

I am here to talk with you a little bit about Jesus. Y'all ok with that? I am also very tired. I am the father of five children under the age of three. We have two sets of twins and a single. This morning in Denton, I woke up early at my home and expected no one to be up. Peeking around the corner, I encountered my redheaded three-year-old son named Phillip. Since I knew I was heading down here, I thought I would engage Phillip on the death penalty. I asked Phillip, "What should I tell these folks in Austin about the death penalty? Why is our family opposed to the death penalty? We are Christians..." Without hesitation, Phillip replied, "We don't want to kill people." My three-year-old son is wise enough to know that the death penalty is a basic violation of human conscience...but even more for my family and I...we know that the death penalty is more specifically a violation of the Christian conscience.

So let's talk about Jesus... Jesus was present at two potential executions. The first execution was a woman who was caught in the very act of committing a capital offense. As this woman was about to be executed, Jesus stepped between her and her executioners. So, Jesus stopped the first possible execution he ever encountered. The second execution Jesus was at was his own. Unless you believe that Jesus should have been executed, the execution of Jesus is what could have happened to our dear brother Anthony Graves...the execution of an innocent man.

Jesus lived his life in a way that shows us that executing people is wrong. Therefore, for those who follow Jesus...the death penalty is a fundamental violation of Christian conscience. We love to talk about religious liberty in this state. I mean I feel like all I hear out of Austin these days is talk of religious liberty. Well, the death penalty is a violation of the religious liberty of Christians all over this state. This practice of execution is turning us Christians into killers. You can't follow Jesus and kill people. I can't follow Jesus and be for life...and consistently be implicated in our dreadful system of executions.

Jesus commanded us, "Love your neighbor as your self." Folks, you cannot love your neighbor as your self and kill people...period. We have got to stop our addiction to killing.

Everybody wants to talk about an eye for an eye and a tooth for a tooth...if we followed this practice, all of you would be blind and toothless...as would all of us. We don't live in such a way and it is foolish to keep talking in such a way.

I invite you to consider what Phillip told me this morning, "We don't want to kill people." I don't want to kill people. You don't want to kill people. We don't want to kill people. That is a very human statement...but it is also the Gospel.

Amen.

May 2, 2015

The Color of Evil

Scared, Jesus ran away. When evil was on top of him, Jesus refused to fight back. The officers were rough. I guess they didn't realize who he was or didn't care. Jesus screamed. Looking up, the color of evil was blue and white. Though he had committed no crime, Jesus was arrested and led away. Unable to breathe, Jesus was going down quick. The officers threw Jesus into the back of the wagon. Screaming for help, Jesus fell out of his seat. When the wagon stopped, Jesus thought that maybe help was coming. After the door opened, Jesus was placed back into the seat. Jesus pleaded for a medic. Looking up as the door shut, Jesus saw that the color of evil was blue and black. Once again, Jesus collapsed into the floor and lost consciousness. The last color of evil that Jesus saw was blue and black. After Jesus lost consciousness, the color of evil that consistently failed to get Jesus help over and over again was black, white and blue. Once medical help finally arrived, Jesus was in cardiac arrest. Upon reaching the hospital, there was little anyone could do. Jesus died on April 19.

While there are many who would push back against reference to Freddie Gray as Jesus, I don't know what else to call him. In Matthew 25, Jesus said, "What you have done to the least of these you have done to me." The incarnation of Jesus is a consistent event. Jesus is constantly binding his person to the marginalized and oppressed amongst us. Freddie Gray is the epitome of marginalization and oppression. This man was completely innocent and then was dead. I have no doubt that Jesus was there the entire time. If you think that Jesus is one race, let me assure you that Jesus is wherever oppression and marginalization is. I also have no doubt that Jesus stands against evil no matter what color it is.

While there is no question that we live in a society plagued by systemic and internalized racism, I am not interested in talking about police brutality in ways that let officers of color off the hook for their roles in these horrible crimes. With three black and three white police officers involved in the murder of Freddie Gray, the consistent color of evil in this situation is blue. Using language to marginalize and oppress, President Obama and Baltimore Mayor Rawlings-Blake consistently called protestors, "thugs." Actually, I think the real thugs or violent criminals in this country are the police officers who carry guns everywhere they go and kill with impunity. Together, we can resist the color of evil. We can bring together a rainbow coalition of people to defeat a police brutality that is as broad and diverse as the officers who perpetuate it. I believe that a Jesus who is as diverse and colorful as we are stands with us.

Amen.

May 2, 2015

When did Jesus Become God?

If Jesus got down from the cross, would we still call him God? Does the cross make Jesus God or was Jesus God before then? I think the answer lies in the fact that God is Love in perfection. Jesus cannot be God until he becomes the perfection of Love. When Jesus died on the cross, he showed us what perfect Love looks like. If Jesus got down from the cross, I believe we would call him a great prophet but not God. With this in mind, I think Jesus becomes God on the cross. In those moments, Jesus displays a love that is queerer than any love the world had or has ever known. We follow Jesus to the cross and seek to love queerly so that we might eventually become Love too. In becoming God, Jesus showed us the way.

Amen.

May 3, 2015

When Violent Bigots Meet

This is not about Islam. I know too many Muslims to fall for that trick. This is about the consequences of unrestrained bigotry. Pamela Geller and the American Freedom Defense Initiative are bigots in every sense of the word. Today in Garland,

Texas, the bigots hosted a "Muhammad Art Exhibit and Cartoon Contest" as a means of insulting Islam and promulgating hate. Two other violent bigots responded to hate with hate and pulled up guns blazing. Now, both shooters are dead and one security officer was injured. Geller and her hate group will now argue that Islam is every bit as violent as they claimed it was. When violent bigots meet...evil triumphs, lives are destroyed and nobody wins. Bigotry cannot drive out bigotry...only love can do that.

Amen.

May 4, 2015

Liberation Will Only Come Through Revolution

In the wake of the flames of the streets of Baltimore, Christians of all stripes have incessantly talked about the need for liberation. It often goes something like this, "Let's seek God for liberation in our time...." While these words are wonderful on their face, they don't speak to the depth of the crisis that our nation faces. Liberation is impossible in this nation without revolution. There has to be a total transformation of the way that we think and engage with each other. White churches can't keep all of their wealth and expect real liberation for persons of color. There has to be real sacrifice and change. Words alone simply will not cut it. We must work to revolutionize the hearts and minds of our neighbors. While change is possible, it simply will not happen until people come out of their prayer closets and get into the world. We can dismantle racist institutions and systems...but we are going to have to pray with our feet.

Amen.

May 5, 2015

The Wayward Movement of the Movement

I'm sick. I can feel it deep down in my stomach. The comments are eating at me. For the third time in less than a week, I heard a respected activist make a problematic remark. Now, I'm not talking about anything that was misconstrued. I am talking about blatantly problematic remarks. There was the black activist who casually declared, "No Homo!" There was the feminist who spoke of keeping Muslims out of her neighborhood. There was the immigration activist who spoke of transgender persons as Frankensteins. Though I didn't let these comments pass by unnoticed or unchallenged, I am beginning to wonder if the subliminal goal of activism is to help groups gain enough power where they can talk shit one everyone else. What good is a social movement that only grants rights to some and creates another group of marginalizers and oppressors?

While I am tremendously proud of all the organizing efforts that are taking place all over the country, I don't think we have spent much time thinking about where we are going. I think this is partly due to the fact that many people are just trying to survive. Regardless of the reason, I look around and see many of the strategies of the 1960s being redeployed and repurposed. From Baltimore to Ferguson, much of the work and organizing that is going on...from the marches to the mass meetings to the teach-ins...seem to be a throwback. White liberals love this development...which tells me I need to be afraid of it. The Civil Rights Movement of the 1960s produced many tangible gains, but was probably most successful in paving the way for the continued economic oppression that has plagued black communities ever since. Our nation also left the 1960s more racially divided then ever before with no clear idea of how to come together. We have to remember that the same old strategies produce the same old results. Where are the innovators who are seeking to organize and create in ways that bring about revolution, liberation and reconciliation at the same time? We can do better than empty slogans and events that are simply a repurposing of the past that allows oppression and marginalization to continue.

Realizing that we have a shared past and future is the fundamental truth that is going to bring us together and move us forward. We have to understand that the liberation of the marginalized and oppressed can only come through the liberation of the marginalizer and oppressor. Do we not belong to each other? If we can't answer this question in the affirmative, we are already fucked.

Amen.

May 7, 2015

Would Jesus Call the Police?

Last Tuesday night, someone called the police and reported a homeless man with a dog harassing people in Venice Beach. A short time after police arrived, one of the responding officers shot unarmed Brendon Glenn dead. In the understatement of the year, Los Angeles Police Department Chief Charlie Beck described the shooting as "concerning." I would use the word "concerning" to describe a power outage. When talking about the shooting death of an unarmed man, the word "murder" seems much more appropriate.

The murder of Brendon Glenn is part of a national outbreak of police brutality. With each of these shootings, we are given more and more evidence that you simply can't trust the police to not kill someone. From Dallas to Aimes to Baltimore to North Charleston to Albuquerque to New York and everywhere in between, the stories of unrestrained violence are endless. We here the same excuses over and over... "He went for my gun." "I feared for my life." "I didn't have any other options." We now have enough evidence to know that these excuses were and are often bullshit.

Throughout the country, officers are largely shooting at will. The truth is stark... When you call the police, you don't know if you are calling help or an executioner.

Can you imagine how the person who alerted the police to Brendon Glenn feels? They thought they were helping their community and the police made them an accessory to murder. When police have such ready access to lethal force, I think that such a catastrophic result is always possible. With such ambiguity, I no longer believe that Jesus would call the police.

Amen.

May 7, 2015

We are not Christians...

With five children, I spend an excess amount of time saying silly things to them. Last week, I was joking around with my son Phillip and said, "We are Christians and Christians pick up their toys." Phillip replied emphatically, "We are not Christians!" Surprised by his sharp reply, I questioned, "What are we then?" Without hesitation, Phillip declared, "Dad, we are people." At the age of 3, Phillip is one of my greatest instructors of what it means to be human.

Amen.

May 9, 2015

Falling Fastly / A Mother's Day Ode to Emily

I never thought we would fall like this. Who would have dreamed it? When we met, love was all I could see in your eyes and I fell faster than I imagined possible. Falling is scary. Though it felt so out of control, I just kept returning to you. Remember when we talked about having a big family? We got so much more than we could have ever bargained for. When we found out about the first set of twins, the absurdity of your laughter pulverized my fear. I knew that your joy would carry us through. Though my anxiety was through the roof, you calmly delivered Jeff and Phillip. The radiance of your face was breathtaking. You loved them both so much. Unable to take my eyes off of you, I fell faster and faster.

I had no idea what to do with two babies. You always seemed to lead the way. Throughout those difficult months, we worked together and we made it. I pushed into you and together we pushed into the future. Surprise! Who would have thought that you would get pregnant again so fast? I didn't even feel like we had sex that much. When you told me that you wanted to have the baby in our living room, I thought you were nuts. Pushing aside all of my fears, you made it happen. I never thought a birthing tub could be so warm and inviting. It was such a privilege to hold you in that water as Quinley came. When you kissed him for the first time, I will never forget the way you lingered there with tears coming down your face. With each passing second, I fell faster and faster.

Three babies was tough. Pushing into each other, we just kept going. When it happened, we knew we got hit by lightening. Two sets of twins? How in the hell did this happen? Condoms are liars. We didn't spend much time thinking about it. We just did it. I talk when I am nervous. You told me to stop talking over and over again. You squeezed my hand and beautiful Lucas came. We kissed his cheeks together. Then, I kissed you. You got weaker and weaker. The blood on the ground terrified me. For the first time, I thought I was going to lose you. When Madeleine came, I was so worried. Though I wanted to hold my daughter, I couldn't let you go. When all was well, we held her together. Distress turned to beauty and it was as if the whole world stopped. Pushing against your face, I knew I was falling faster and faster all over again.

Our love is a weightless breathless plummet that only has swiftened with the birth of each of our children. Being with you is the great privilege of my life. From a slightly different angle, I know that Jeff, Phillip, Quinley, Lucas and Madeleine would say the same. We love you.

Amen.

May 10, 2015

Stand Down America!

Last Saturday in Hattiesburg, Mississippi, Police Officers Benjamin Deen and Liquori Tate were making a routine traffic stop when they were gunned down in a hail of bullets. There are many in this nation who heard about such a situation and believe that the two got what they deserved. After all, brutal police have been gunning innocent citizens down all over the country in recent months. I wrestled with similar thoughts until I heard an interview with Ronald Tate, Liquori's dad. "Take off the blue uniform! This was my son. This was my baby," Tate implored the audience. I was moved back to Jesus by his passionate words.

After some thought, I realized once again that our police officers are simply a reflection of us. They are violent because we are violent. They carry a whole host of prejudices and hates because we carry a whole host of prejudices and hates. They are afraid because we are afraid. If we want to know the source of police brutality, we have to look in the mirror.

Officers Deen and Tate carried guns because we gave them to them.

Growing up, I remember hearing over and over, "Guns always escalate any situation." The folks who shot Deen and Tate knew that they had guns and felt the need to shoot them before they got shot. If they hadn't had guns, I don't know that the impetus to shoot would have been as strong. By expecting our police to carry guns, we are creating the escalation over and over again. The police are always prepared for a gunfight. We shouldn't be surprised when they actually get one.

If we want to eliminate police shootings and the shootings of the police, we are going to have to ask all parties to get rid of their guns and stand down.

Amen.

May 14, 2015

The Church is Dying...Kill It.

According to the Pew Research Center, the Christian population in the United States has declined steadily from 78.4% to 70.6% since 2007. Throughout social media, prognosticators and pundits have raced to explain why the church is dying and how it can be saved. The frenzy of it all has been very informative for me. Everyone wants to freak out about the decline yet no one wants to analyze why this information makes us freak out in the first place.

Did Jesus ever identify as a Christian? Why would we expect followers of Jesus to identify as something that Jesus never identified as? There is an entire generation of followers of Jesus learning to identify as just that...followers of Jesus. Why are we so protective of the name Christian? I think the name Christian has to do with power. Christians have always been a recognized political and economic force in the world. We are desperate to maintain our influence. Jesus is not interested in such constructs. Jesus shit on our influence in order to bring about the realm of God. Drop the names and just take up the name above all names.

Why do we care so much about our buildings and institutions? Jesus tore down our constructions in order to bring about the realm of God. I think that people freak out about the decline of Christians because they want to protect the wealth of their churches. Jesus said to sell everything you have...yet we have churches sitting on millions and millions of dollars. If we lost everything, we might see Jesus clearer than we ever have.

Do we not believe that the Spirit of God is in the business of drawing in all people? Do we actually believe that God lost a few over the last couple of years? Leave the numbers alone and just make sure you are in the number.

There was a time when Peter got concerned about everyone else and Jesus shared some wise words in John 21:22:

"...what is that to you? Just follow me!"

The church is dying. Don't freak out. Kill it and we might actually learn to follow Jesus.

Amen.

http://www.pewresearch.org/fact-tank/2015/05/12/5-key-findings-u-s-religious-landscape/

May 15, 2015

Is it Safe?

"Aslan is a lion- the Lion, the great Lion." "Ooh" said Susan. "I'd thought he was a man. Is he-quite safe? I shall feel rather nervous about meeting a lion"..."Safe?" said

Mr Beaver ..."Who said anything about safe? 'Course he isn't safe. But he's good. He's the King, I tell you."

— C.S. Lewis, *The Lion, the Witch, and the Wardrobe*

Throughout my ministry, I have often wondered back to this scene from my favorite childhood books. During one of my talks in Houston, someone asked, "Is your queer theology safe?" My answer was swift and unrelenting, "In a world of constructed and demanded dualisms and dichotomies, there is nothing safe about a theology that dares question and deconstruct our categories for the sake of saving and liberating the individual." I don't care anything about being safe. I believe it is our safe spaces that have led us away from the dangerous love of God. Following Jesus is what I care about the most and I know where that path leads...to death by love. Why do we keep trying to sanitize the message of Jesus? Jesus is not safe but Jesus is better than anything that is. Jesus shows us that the work of liberation will always be dangerous...and if it ceases to be...then we should question whether it is liberation that we are truly working for...

Amen.

May 16, 2015

Noise in the Silence: Poetry from Southwestern University

The Quiet

noise

noise

noise

i feel it
i read it
i hear it
i know it

then it stops

i am lonely again

The Things Above

thud! the walls are closing in
help! there is no way out
stop! tomorrow is gone
leave! the judgment is here

look to the things above you say
what about all the destruction today

you say compassion they say condemnation
you say kindness they say hate
you say humility they say pride
you say gentleness they say force
you say patience they say now

coming again in glory
give me a break
where were you then
where are you know

where will you be

fires

murders

executions

earthquakes

rapes

famines

poverty

genocides

if you love us...

we can't wait forever
perhaps we need to take matters into our own hands

for now the things above will suffice
for then we need you

amen

Time

you are not real
now is then and then is now
watches are handcuffs
you will not imprison my soul
i will simply be
me

The Ascension

you left us
where did you go
we needed you
we are now orphans
why did you leave us
the spirit doesn't feel like your touch

I put down my pad and look to the colors of your incarnation.

Amen.

May 16, 2015

Communing with James Holmes

In Matthew 25, Jesus said, "I was in prison and you visited me *(or you didn't)*." Through these piercing words, Jesus declares that he is with and in those who are in prison regardless of their guilt or innocence. With the trial of mass murderer James Holmes underway in Colorado, Christians must decide if they believe the words of Jesus or not. Though Holmes' crimes were heinous, I believe what Jesus said. When we take communion today around the world, we will be communing with a man who killed 12 people and injured 70 more. We must somehow learn to thank God for the life of even Holmes...because without him we do not have access to Jesus.

Amen.

May 18, 2015

The Murder in Grapevine

The images haunt me. The sounds reverberate in my ears. The video plays over and over in my head.

While investigating a false burglar alarm, Grapevine Police Officer Robert Clark came across Rubén García sitting in his parked car. Perhaps due to some combination of his undocumented immigration status, intoxication and standard fear of the police, García fled. Officer Clark chased García for a few minutes. When García finally pulled over, he got out of the car and put his hands on his head. Screaming and shouting obscenities, Clark proved that he was terrified of this drunken man. Escalating the situation with every second, Clark kept screaming and threatening as García stumbled toward him asking to be arrested with his hands on his head. When García stumbled too close, Clark shot him twice. After he was determined to be unarmed, Rubén García received treatment and later died after being transported to the hospital.

The victims of police brutality are no longer just unarmed...they are stumbling and reaching for help and we kill them anyway.

Does anyone care that a Mexican father was senselessly murdered in Grapevine?

I can't sleep over it.
We have got to work to get this killer cop off the streets.

For those who still don't seem to get it, wait until Officer Robert Clark murders someone you love and then it might be a little clearer.

Amen.

May 18, 2015

A Word & Prayer at the Rally Protesting the Murder of Rubén García

"Good Evening. My name is the Rev. Dr. Jeff Hood. I serve as the Minister of Social Justice for Hope for Peace and Justice, the social justice ministry of the Cathedral of Hope United Church of Christ. I am here representing a rainbow people. When Grapevine Police Officer Robert Clark murdered Rubén García, we were reminded that police brutality can strike anyone at anytime. We must unite the rainbow of humanity to push back and get these killer cops off our streets. With all that we are, we stand with you. We will not quit until there is justice for Rubén and the countless others gunned down by murderous cops. I know that God is with us. Amen."

May 19, 2015

A Land of Nightmares

Nightmares follow me or maybe I follow them. I was tossing and turning in a foreign bed. The road is often unkind to me. Event after event leaves me weary. I saw Emily torn to shreds by the bullets of the police. I knew the consequences of standing with Jesus. How did this happen? I rushed to Emily's side and in the midst of her final breaths, I shot up and opened my eyes. The strange scent of a friend's home helped me to get my feet on the floor. The images were painful and fresh as I tried to move. The water of the shower simply would not wash the nightmare off. If you live in Texas, violence stalks you whether your eyes are open or not.

The rain pounded my windshield. I wanted to cry. Depression finds me at the cruelist times. Looking around on the walk in, I realized the church met in a really conservative space. When I pushed open the heavy doors, I could feel the weight of the decades of oppression. This house of horrors was complete with stained glass depictions of a white Jesus encircling the space. Though the people were warm and inviting, I couldn't get past the space. I arose and started to speak. I knew I couldn't tell them everything that I was feeling...no one would hear me...but I had to tell them enough. Those in power get to name the God. The stained glass windows of a white Jesus might as well have been guns trained on the worshipers to make sure that they didn't get too far out of line. We have one God in Texas and its name is violence.

The miles past slowly. My bladder filled to capacity and I resisted. I have an aversion to stopping. Pulling off the interstate, I noticed chaos. People running. Police swarming. Bikers being arrested. Motorcycles everywhere. I looked up at the location, Twin Peaks. On this day, violence against women turned into violence against each other. There was nothing I could do. Struggling to come to terms with what I saw, I got in my car and headed north. Calming down, I finally got the courage to look at my phone. Nine people dead and dozens injured. Two hundred arrested. I realized that I witnessed the aftermath of a massacre. I needed to pull over and get some relief. The bell dinged and I went straight for the juice. I love juice. When I got to the register, I just wanted to purchase my drink. The lady at the register smilingly remarked, "We have our Confederate flag bandanas buy one get one free...we are trying to make room for the new ones." Taking my juice, I walked out to the car in a daze. I am still there.

When you live in a place where violence is a religion, you just try to stay awake through the nightmare of it all.

God damn Texas and save us.

Amen.

May 20, 2015

Welcoming Christian Parks and Conversing the Queer

*This is the initial conversation between my summer intern Christian Parks and I. Christian is a Mennonite and a senior at Eastern Mennonite University. Identifying as queer, I met Christian a few months back when he was censored and not allowed to direct the play *Corpus Christi* at his school.

J: Christian, I feel so blessed that you are here. You are one of the queerer individuals I have ever met and I am so excited to be spending the summer with you. What made you want to do an internship with such a rogue minister as myself?

C: In my journey with the Christ, I have found myself in a place hungry for hope - hungry for new life in the Gospel. When we first met, Jeff, you made a comment that gripped my soul and peaked my curiosity, you told me "God is queering the world and saving it from the sin of normativity." This statement hasn't left my mind and has encouraged me to take a step of faith and join you this summer as we offer this message of Christ's liberating Gospel to all that we meet.

J: In recent days, new collective awareness of the many injustices in our land has created a heightened desire for social justice that is sweeping through our land. As a variety of people are raised to greater levels of consciousness, I believe that the time is right to help people understand that liberation comes through the individual at the intersections of their existence. Christian, I believe that you are committed to living out your queerness and working to help others find their own paths of liberation.

C: We are a world hungry for authenticity, a Jesus-like authenticity. We are constantly bombarded with illusions that oppress our consciousness and our spirits.

I hear the Church crying out, "No More." I hear my Queer family, my brown-skinned family yelling for the world to recognize our Divinity. This summer is for them. This summer is for me to learn the skills to be a queerer in this fallen, normative world. I just want to live as Jesus lived...liberating the people. Right now, I am thankful that I get to spend the summer following a rogue pastor. Together, I know we will blur many categories and set the captives free.

J: Christian, I am excited about this moment. I believe that beauty grows when we push against the lines that hold colors in. The mixing of colors reveal the colorful reality of what God created us to be. May the beauty of it all never stop growing.

Amen.

May 21, 2015

Jeff & Phillip.

My sons. God formed you to be perfect in the queerness of your being. Even though you have now traveled three years since your formation, perfection is still there. Learn to live into your being. For, in the queerness of your being is your perfection...and the perfection of the God who created you. In this journey called life, God is within you. Your stunning hunger for knowledge is from God. Don't let anyone tell you where you can explore and where you can't. Knowledge is everywhere. Your beautiful love for everyone is from God. Don't let the world teach you a bunch of useless categories that complicate and divide. Love the splendor of all spectrums. Your energy is from God. When you start to get tired, keep pushing and don't stop. You will learn to run and not grow weary. You are now three...so be three...but as you grow...don't forget to zealously keep searching and loving for as long as you have breath. I will love you forever.

Dad.

May 23, 2015

The United States Flag at the Front of the Church is Blasphemous

A United States soldier processed the flag of the United States of America in to our sanctuary as we stood at attention singing "God Bless America." The veterans in our midst were honored as we sang the "Star Spangled Banner." The "Battle Hymn of the Republic" proceeded the pastor's fiery sermon on the coming destruction of our beloved nation if we "...did not turn from our wicked ways." Somehow gays, abortion and popular culture always made it into these services...but that is another story. The service concluded with an invitation to salvation as the congregation sang "God of Our Fathers." To say that the services of my Baptist youth were precariously wrapped in nationalism is an understatement...we believed that God's military was the United States military. Despite the fact that we did so much else that was problematic, my mind remains focused on the United States flag on that gold stand up on the altar.

In many Memorial Day services throughout our nation, some of those who have fallen victim to our thirst for violence and power will be honored and celebrated. We will remember the soldiers and attempt to reconcile their sacrifice with our faith. Unfortunately, there will be little conversation about peace and preventing the deaths of any one else. There will be no conversation of the millions and millions of people who have died as a result of our failed foreign policies and military interventions. The words of Jesus will be forgotten amidst the words of patriotism and nationalism.

No one will recite Jesus' words in Matthew 26:52, "...those who live by the sword will die by the sword." Matthew 5:44 and Jesus' reminder to "love our enemies and pray for those who persecute us" will not make an appearance. Least of all will we remember the millions and millions of people who have died in places with names like Hiroshima, Hanoi, Waziristan, Nagasaki, Kabul and Baghdad in the infernos created by our bombs...those "least of these" dead because we failed to see Jesus in their midst. No these words won't be remembered... and I know most congregations won't be talking beyond the soldiers who have died and will miss the opportunity to have a conversation about the wider call of Jesus to peace and justice.

My mind wonders back to that flag though. To put the United States flag on the altar of a church is to insinuate that somehow the United States has a claim to the grace of God that other nations and peoples do not. To put the United States flag at the front blurs that glorious declaration "For God so loved the world..." Can you imagine what someone from another country thinks when they see that United States flag up front at our churches? There is no nationality barrier to the altar of God. Jesus does not love the United States more than any other nation...to put a flag at the front and bless the atrocities committed by an incredibly powerful people in the name of Jesus is blasphemous.

A real conversation about the non-violent love of Jesus and our purpose as followers can only happen when we take down the United States flags in our sanctuaries that stand in the way. If we want to truly honor slain soldiers we will stop perpetuating the nationalism that killed them. So let's toss out all the flags and have a real Memorial Day next year...one that memorializes and celebrates a time when we began to emulate Jesus' love for all people and put to death the nationalism that fooled us into thinking that violence can bring about peace.

Amen.

May 25, 2015

On the Nature of God

J: Christian, I am glad to be returning to this space of formal theological conversation with you. Lately, we have consistently talked about who or what God is. The nature of God has proven to be a topic we return to over and over again. I thought that we could spend some time there tonight.

C: So, what do you think God is?

J: I first must say...I think God is going to be beyond whatever thoughts we can construct. God is always the God beyond God. With our finitude affirmed, I think God is in a constant state of being and becoming. God's being is love. God's becoming is love. God's love expands with our expansion. The love of God is constantly growing. God is the neverending story of love. What do you think Christian?

C: I love "God is in a constant state of becoming." God is breath; a matter in which we can never fully understand yet we can process it, we can experience it. God is an active process that is ebbing and flowing in and out of creation. This process is one full of nothing but authentic, self-less love. God is power, a force encompassed in ability. I think most importantly though God is a means of becoming. If God is constantly becoming, what does this mean for us?

J: One of the core components of the way that I construct queer theology is a strong dose of eschatology. We have to recognize that we are in a state of becoming before we can most fully learn to live into that becoming. The journey toward queerness is a process of holiness or of becoming more and more like God. We do evil to our self and others when we go against that process. We were created to be a unique brand of love and when we try to become anything else we become a unique brand of hate.

There is nothing queer about just breathing...there is something very queer about truly living.

C: God in process offers us a journey. The journey is one towards fullness - fullness in authenticity. God already in a state of becoming, we are invited in on a journey in progress. God has and will always continue to be love and yet we have to be caught up on how, when, and why. God proves to us that we are each love in our own fullness, still though we must be constantly assured of this fact. Our assurance comes by authenticity, by way of becoming a whole and connected self just like God.

J: Thanks be to God.

Amen.

May 25, 2015

The Self-Righteousness of Christians

Injustices that make us feel righteous are always our favorites. Over the last week, I watched Christians get practically giddy over the downfall of The Duggars. I have wondered if people realize that the evils that Josh Duggar committed had victims? In post after post and blog after blog, I watched Christians express their pain at what The Duggars said in the past about a whole host of issues. Now, Christians feel more righteous with the discovery that Josh Duggar committed these evil acts. So now what? Are we in a better place to deal with the evils that are committed against women and children in Christian spaces? I don't think so. I am worried that our own feelings of righteousness have kept us and will keep us from helping the ones most vulnerable.

If we are to be believed as followers of Jesus...our self-righteousness can't be our chief concern.

Amen.

May 28, 2015

My Confession: I'm an Evangelical

"I believe Jesus rose from the dead and inhabits my being right now." When asked about my thoughts on Jesus, I answered as clearly as I could. The room grew quiet. "Are you an evangelical?" someone asked. After some thought, I replied just as clearly as I did the first time, "I guess I am."

For many years, I have run from the evangelical world. Truth be known, anyone who watches the news sees that there is plenty to run from. After graduating from the Southern Baptist Theological Seminary in 2009, I was so hurt that I wanted to leave forever. Six years later, I realize that I am not willing to cede my personal relationship with the resurrected Jesus to anyone. I embrace the miracles and divinity of Jesus with all that I am. On issues of social justice, I believe that Jesus queerly crossed lines of identity and set the captives free. I don't believe that Jesus came to save groups of people...on the contrary...I believe that Jesus came to save us all. I believe in Jesus. If that makes me an evangelical, then so be it. That is my confession. In an age of brutality and oppression, I believe that the very love and person of Jesus is exactly the liberation the world needs.

I doubt I would be the radical theologian and activist that I am without the evangelical in me constantly yearning for more than the world is presently offering.

Amen.

May 30, 2015

A Man Named King

Lightning crawled across the sky. The thunder roared. Rain warned of impending flood. Through the cleansing drama of it all, Jackson remained as dirty as ever. Filled with the secrets of past transgressions, you never know what filthy hate might resurrect next. Even in the midst of the blight, one can find beauty if they are willing to work for it. Echoes of the woman caught in adultery filled my ears. Jesus got down in the dirt to save her. Without the dirt, there would be no salvation for the oppressed or the oppressor. Jesus toils in the dirt to bring about the salvation of others. Rev. Ed King functions similarly.

Walking through the rain and into the restaurant, my eyes immediately went to his jaw. The scaring and disfiguration is a visual reminder of his sacrifice. In what he refers to as an assassination attempt, Rev. King was permanently disfigured when his car was rammed over 50 years ago. When we sat down, I situated the kids with a show on my phone and started to tell Christian about my friend. From describing Rev. King's presence and role in Montgomery to the Freedom Rides to Jackson to Freedom Summer to numerous Democratic National Conventions to a wild and vast assortment of other social justice battles, I went on and on. After I finished, Christian asked, "What made you leave your comfort and do all of this?" Without delay and in his slow deep drawl, Rev. King answered, "I just tried to be a Christian."

Amen.

May 31. 2015

The Magic of Our Moment

*Derived from a sermon delivered at Tupelo Unitarian Universalist Congregation on May 31, 2015

Have you ever fallen in love? I think people call it falling because you feel so out of control. While it can be very scary, there is something in you that simply won't let go and desires to just keep on falling. In such a state, there is something full and complete about simply being with the one that you love. It's magic.

I know I am speaking to a tremendously learned congregation this morning. Have you ever wondered if you have learned so much that you have forgotten how to feel? For clarification purposes, I'm not knocking knowledge. I have seven degrees. I love school too much. With that said, I have learned enough to know that magic don't come from thinking...magic comes from feeling.

There was a moment in the life of Jesus where he or she (we can talk about that after the service) stepped into a situation full of emotion and allowed the entirety of his person to feel and be felt. The Pharisees caught a woman in the very act of adultery. Does this mean they were close enough to see the penis entering the vagina or was there some other combination of sexual organs interacting? Regardless, we are left with a clear impression that the Pharisees were the religious peeping toms of their day. What happened to the other partner? I think we can be certain that another injustice occurred when this woman was expected to take the full punishment for the situation. After being drug around, the woman was thrown at Jesus' feet. The Pharisees picked up rocks and prepared to stone her. Instead of calling for help or running away, Jesus felt deeper into the situation.

Placing his body on the ground next to the woman, Jesus was prepared to give his life to her. Everyone wants to talk about what Jesus wrote in the dirt, I am more interested in the fact that Jesus got dirty. Looking up, Jesus told the Pharisees, "Whoever is without sin can throw the first stone." What if the stones had started flying? Jesus was prepared to die. Due to the magic of his witness, the Pharisees slowly walked away. Jesus felt his way in the situation and saved a life.

The magic of our moment is our ability to give our lives to this moment. We can transcend our protectionism and love our neighbors as our selves. In the midst of overwhelming racism, classism, poverty, sexism and a whole host of other evils, we can choose to be like Jesus and give our lives to each other. There is no queerer construct than loving your neighbor as your self. You can do it. You can be the magic the world is desperate for. You will have to let go. You will have to fall. You will have to get dirty. I could try to name all that will be required of you...but these requirements are but minor inconveniences when compared to the overwhelming beauty of saving lives. Embrace the magic and let the magic embrace you.

Amen.

June 1, 2015

The Premeditated Murder of Lester Bowers

Does God care about those we execute? While I think we all know the answer to such a question, we better hope not. If God cares, we deserve to be damned. These executions are the work of evil in a pure form...premeditated murder. Lester Bower is the next victim.

While there are serious doubts as to his guilt, I am not in a position to weigh all the evidence or facts of Bower's case. I can only speak to the fact that Texas has mediated on how it is going to kill Bowers for over three decades. Does premeditated murder make you uncomfortable? It does me. We can't do this again.

Join me in praying for the salvation of murderers here in Texas...us.

Amen.

June 1, 2015

On Jesus

*a theological conversation between Christian and I on the lake in North Georgia

J: Who or what do you think Jesus is Christian?

C: On one level, Jesus is an embodiment of an active, participatory and liberating love. On another level (and maybe there are no levels) Jesus was human like you and I. Through community and trust, Jesus found liberation within and without. The answers are simple.

J: Like all of us, I believe that Jesus was born queer in the image of a God who is queer. In time, Jesus completely lived into the queerness of God and ultimately became God. In living into the queer perfection that is God, Jesus became an example to all of humanity of what it means to truly be queer. I believe that Jesus experienced what it means to be fully human and fully God in every possible way. With the fullness of the experiences of Jesus affirmed, I believe that Jesus experienced the entire spectrum of genders and sexualities. I believe the masculine language we use to describe Jesus is the most problematic and misleading of our failings to understand the fullness of Jesus. In the fullness of humanity and God,

Jesus transcended the categories to live into God and provides example to us on how to do the same. What do you think Christian?

C: We can see this transcendence throughout the Gospel narratives. Jesus went places, talked to folks and rebelled against folks that were supposed to be off limits. Jesus proved to us that the way to live is to live as if the Kingdom or Queendom or whatever else of God is already here - to be queer. Jesus laid out the path of liberation...we are to stand with the marginalized, get beat up with the oppressed and push back against the tyrants. Over and over again, I find a call to authenticity in love, which gives all the power to transcend, even death. Jesus not only affirms fullness, Jesus also proclaims that God is here so that "all may have life, a life of wholeness and abundance."

J: Through the power of the resurrection, Jesus is in us. Jesus changes as much as we change. Jesus is as queer as the entirety of all of us. I know of no greater beauty...I know of no greater God. I have absolutely no doubt that Jesus is with us in our journey my friend.

C: In the eternal resurrected presence of Jesus, we know that a way has been prepared for us. No matter what may come we can take courage in that resurrection power. We can take courage in our queerness. For we know that we are enough to follow Jesus, we are enough to live into the Queer.

J: Thanks be to the diversity and beauty of the God who dwelt and dwells among us.

Amen.

June 4, 2015

Suicidal Theology

"You have to get married. I have to get married. If I don't get married this time then I will never get married. You have to get married. I have to get married. Stop. This isn't the person I want to be with. It doesn't matter. Do you love me? I have chosen her for you. Do you want to go to hell? Get married immediately! If you hadn't seen her naked you could move on...but now you have to get married immediately. I love you and want what is best for you. You are a filthy creature and have no idea where you would be without me."

Informed by my suicidal theology, the conversations between God and I cycled so rapidly in my mind that I struggled to grasp reality. I was very sick and slipping faster and faster into depression. I grasped for God. Unfortunately, the God I grasped for pushed me deeper and deeper into despair.

The Southern Baptist Theological Seminary was not a helpful place for those struggling with diseases of the mind. Believing that sin was the cause of most mental illness, people kept telling me to cling to Jesus and pray my way through what was happening. I tried and it almost killed me.

When I heard earlier this week that Sugar Land Baptist Church pastor and former President of the Baptist General Convention of Texas Rev. Phil Lineberger committed suicide, I couldn't help but wonder if it was our suicidal theology that killed him. We valorize suffering to the point that seeking help is considered weak. Jesus valiantly went to the cross and so should we. There is beauty in suffering. Dark nights of the soul are where we find God. The Psalmist was as depressed as anyone and was a person after God's own heart. I have heard all of these suicidal theological constructs my entire life. I know they are lethal for some. We have to do better.

If we keep theologizing suffering as divine, we will continue to lose people to suicide. Would Jesus have gone to the cross if he had been on antidepressants? I don't know. I do know that suffering is not the main point of our faith. Jesus is. If following God makes you suicidal, I encourage you to follow something else and you will find Jesus there. Suicidal theology needs to die not us.

Amen.

June 5, 2015

Encounters with a Monster

Over the last few months, I have had numerous interactions with a monster. When we first talked about the injustice of video visitation at the Denton County Jail in the midst of our respective brands of activism, I had no idea who he was or what he had done. Texas made sure I found out.

When he was 12, Josh Gravens touched sexual body parts with his little sister (age 8) twice. When Gravens' mother found out, she called the local fundamentalist Christian counselor. Under mandatory reporting laws, the counselor called police. Gravens was sentenced to multiple years of incarceration for his crime. Before he went to prison, Gravens fundamentalist family performed an exorcism on him. Over a decade and a half later, Gravens has started a family of his own, become a fulltime advocate for criminal justice reform, been recognized with a prestigious George Soros Justice Fellowship and boasts a large network of supporters that includes his little sister. Still on the sex offender registry, Gravens is required to regularly contact local officials. Following a series of confusing encounters with the Dallas Police Department, Gravens is facing 25 years to life for accusations that he failed to register on time. Josh Gravens is the type of monster our government thinks we need protection from.

We create monsters and believe they have no humanity in them. "When this ordeal started, it was as if Jesus and my humanity were taken from me and I was on my own...I still feel like I am trying to get them back," Josh Gravens remarked. Our tendency to monsterize people is highly problematic. Based on our fear, we make lifetime sex offenders out of children and ruin their lives. When will we learn that our society will not change until we recognize the humanity in those we call monster and seek their restoration. Jesus stood with the societal monsters of his day. I choose to stand with Josh Gravens.

Amen.

June 7, 2015

Back to the Future: A Call for Queerness

*Delivered at Metropolitan Community Church of the Rockies in Denver, Colorado on June 7, 2015

There was a time when all was well. We call it "Eden." Do you remember? We have spent all of human existence yearning to go back there...back to the future. There are times when we know we are particularly far from such a space.

A few years ago, my uncle committed suicide. I will never forget my dad calling me and telling me to go tell my grandparents that their son was dead. When I entered the house, my grandmother knew something was wrong. After breaking the news, my grandmother demanded, "a word from the Lord." I have never felt pain like that. Stumbling through my Bible, I landed on John 14..."Do not let your hearts be troubled. Believe in God; believe in me. In my Father's house there are many mansions, If it were not so, would I have told you that I go to prepare a place for you?" When the disciples sensed that they were far from were they wanted to be, Jesus told them that there was a place...a place back to perfection. In our moment of crises, we could hear the words of Jesus calling us into the future. I believe you can too.

I know that this church has faced difficult hours...declining attendance and a whole host of other struggles...can you hear Jesus calling you into the future? You have been an LGBT space and God is calling you to be a queer space. The categories are a relic of the past...you have to be a space that celebrates all individuals and allows them to be exactly who God has created them to be. A queer space for queer people!

Centuries after Jesus walked, a young prophet climbed the steps of the Lincoln Memorial and told the world about his dream. Dr. Martin Luther King, Jr.'s address to the March on Washington encourages all who hear it to dream about a future where all people are free. How can you be a part of setting people free? We have spent so much time asking people for their identities that we are now in a space where such categories serve as prison. This morning, I invite you to step out of the identities that have built this church and live into the queer space that God has always called you to be. People should walk out of this space and declare, "Free at last! Free at last! Thank God Almighty I am Free at Last!"

Let's go back to the future...

Don't be afraid! Stand up for love! Stand up for justice! Be the queers that God has created you to be!

AND FINALLY
HAVE NO FEAR, GOD IS QUEER!!!
Amen.

June 8, 2015

The Competent Soul Understands Racism

I don't trust people or institutions to connect me to God. I believe that the journey to God is ours alone. There is only one force that can manifest generosity, love and justice in our lives...God. The soul alone is competent in matters of God or righteousness. I first learned about the doctrine of *soul competency* in the writings of Southern Baptist theologian Dr. E.Y. Mullins. Since encountering the doctrine at the Southern Baptist Theological Seminary, I have clung to a deep abiding belief that real justice is possible only when the soul recognizes injustice through the power of God and responds in righteousness. I do not believe that we can teach our way to a better future.

Generosity cannot be taught. Generosity comes from God alone and must be birthed and embraced. Love cannot be taught. Love comes from God alone and must be incarnated and experienced. Justice cannot be taught. Justice comes from God alone and must be manifested and lived. If we live out the deep righteous inclinations of our souls, true equality and beloved community is not only possible...but will manifest as a present reality. We have the power to do better.

When I first saw the video of police brutality outside of a pool party in McKinney, Texas, I was struck at the core of my soul. I wondered how anyone could watch this video and not realize that racism is a problem in our nation. To deny racism is a problem is to deny the God that created us. There is no amount of teaching that can bring someone to God....only God can do that. There is no amount of teaching that will be able to change the denial of racism...only God can do that. I believe that the soul alone is competent to understand racism. Let us pray for souls stuck in denial.

Amen.

June 9, 2015

Our Magician: The Holy Spirit

C: What is the purpose of the Holy Spirit?

J: The magical Holy Spirit is the great queerer. Blurring our identities, the Holy Spirit guides us into deeper being. In deeper spaces of being, we learn to be exactly who and what God has created us to be. I believe that the Holy Spirit is working throughout the world to draw us together in the queerness of our collective beings. Do you believe that there is magic working within you?

C: The magic working within me allows for a triune connection. For me, the Holy Spirit is the breath of God that was breathed into creation. As we connect with our breath we better connect with God and in connecting with God we better connect with others. Each of these pieces are intimately connected. Without all three pieces, we aren't fully participating in the magic God offers our souls and our world. The magic of the Spirit is transcendent love that hopes, believes, and cares. Do you believe we've forgotten the magic?

J: I think most of us wouldn't know the magic of the Holy Spirit if it slapped us in the face. We are so busy trying to be safer and safer in the creation and maintenance of categories and identities. Unfortunately, God does not call us to safety. Freedom is dangerous and the Holy Spirit invites us to exist in the freedom of a God who created us to be wild. We must give up our desire to control everyone and everything and cling to the magic. In the magic of our creation and destiny is the very queerness of holiness or our place in God.

C: I could not agree more. We have lost openness to the magic. We spend so much time policing and controlling everyone else that we don't realize that we are squashing the queerness of the Holy Spirit in each other. Our attempts to control kill anything that is queer. I just want to be able to embrace the queer magic of being me.

J: Me too, my brother...me too...

Amen.

June 12, 2015

The Racial Ambiguity of Jesus

How far would you go? How far would you go for liberation? How far would you go to save lives? Followers of Jesus are called to go all the way. How could anyone go that far? Jesus shows the way.

"I was hungry..."

"I was thirsty..."

"I was a stranger..."

"I was in prison..."

In naming a variety of oppressions, Jesus illustrates that responding to oppression is about becoming something. In the incarnation with oppression, Jesus even goes so far as to say, "What you have done to the least of these you have done to me." How do we follow Jesus? How do we incarnate our persons with the oppressed? Jesus shows us that the path to liberation is about becoming something...namely the oppressed.

The story of Spokane, Washington NAACP President Rachel Dolezal is very complicated. From growing up with two white parents to having four black siblings to attending Howard University to teaching Africana Studies to her present position, Dolezal seems to have navigated a path of becoming more and more connected to the black community until she got to a point where most people believed she was black. Many believe that Dolezal intentionally misrepresented her race in order to advance her career. While I can't speak directly to her character, I have wondered if there is benefit in admiring her for placing her body into the struggle for liberation in ways not often seen from people of any race? While there might be much Satan in this story (Isn't there always?), I also sense some pieces of Jesus in Rachel Dolezal's various struggles for liberation.

Through a consistent incarnation with the least, Jesus becomes black and every other race in order to liberate. Are we too not called to constant efforts for liberation? No matter what our color, the only pathway to liberation is by becoming liberation for others...perhaps that too is our only hope at salvation.

Amen.

June 12, 2015

The Greatest Commandment: A Parable on Not Treating God Like Shit

Jesus was giving a talk at a local hotspot when a couple of pastors showed up. Unable to stomach the words they were hearing, the pastors demanded, "This all sounds like new age mumbo jumbo. What are you really saying? What is the core of your message?" Slowly moving toward the questioners, Jesus replied, "Those of you who think you are religious especially need to listen up. God is God. We are to love God with all that we are. You can't love God and treat your neighbor like shit. God is in us. How can you love the God within you and hate the God in your neighbor? God is not shit. Love your neighbor. There are no words greater than these." One of the pastors got it and replied, "You are right. I feel and know it deep within me. Love is the way. Love is the truth. Love is the only path to life." Singling out the pastor, Jesus replied, "You are drawing close to the realm of God." The room was silent.

Amen.

June 13, 2015

Daring to Love Strangers

The lifeless body hung by a rope. Tears streamed down my face. I couldn't believe I was crying. I thought I was watching the execution of a murderous tyrant. I tuned in to celebrate. Why was I crying? Everything in my cultural context told me that I was supposed to be overjoyed at the execution of Saddam Hussein. I wasn't. I couldn't figure out what was going on. Something happened to me. After a few more moments of tears hitting my keyboard, the feeling hit me like a slap in the face. I loved him.

While I could spend pages upon pages writing about all of the evil that Saddam Hussein is responsible for, I learned in the moment of his execution that evil can never drive out evil. Murder is wrong no matter who the perpetrator is. Although I arrived at a clearer understanding of the ethical nature of the situation, I still didn't know what happened to me. How did love overcome the evil within? I mourned for a moment and then explored my feelings.

In those days, I was still rabidly conservative. I was ready to cheer on the USA. Somehow in the midst of my nationalism, my heart opened. While I don't know if I opened it or if God did, I know that the opening of my heart was the first step to loving a stranger. Though I had loved strangers before, this was the first time I felt such love in such a pronounced way. While I wanted to shut the feelings down, I knew that I would be shutting down a piece of myself if I did. On some level, the realization that my feelings made me intimately connected to Saddam Hussein was salvific. While I am sure that this is an extreme example for most, we must remember that love for any stranger is always going to be strange.

We live in a society that teaches all of us from the earliest of ages that a stranger equals danger. With such an understanding, we should not be surprised that we have a fundamental inability to trust each other. With trust gone, we are all left to our own destructive protectionisms. Our fears consistently cause us to run way from each other. Despite our best efforts to find safety, the othering of strangers is only causing us more danger. Running to each other is our only hope. When we learn to feel deeply with each other, we discover that the stranger holds a piece of us and we them. In such a realization, we learn to feel together and discover that in each other is our future.

May today be the day that we open our hearts...begin to feel...and discover the salvation that is found in acting strangely with strangers.

Amen.

June 16, 2015

The Southern Baptist Convention is So Gay

Conversations around southern dinner tables are always colorful. One Sunday, I remember sitting with my family to talk about the sudden departure of one of the leaders of our Southern Baptist church. I didn't understand what was being said at first. Throughout the course of dinner, I slowly began to realize that he got banished because he liked men. I had a feeling he wasn't alone.

I experienced attraction to men in high school. I thought about going to talk to my youth minister about the multiple manifestations of my sexuality. When I heard him joke around about cutting your penis off if your gay, I knew I wouldn't be making that appointment. I still wonder about his sexuality from time to time.

During college, I was involved in large Southern Baptist church ministries. I was always suspect and weary of those who protested the loudest. Some years later, I now know that most of them were just putting on their own brands of closeted shows.

I attended the most prestigious seminary in the Southern Baptist Convention, The Southern Baptist Theological Seminary. During my time there, my Southern Baptist pastor and mentor came out to me on his deathbed. I also knew plenty of students who were closeted and many of them presently serve Southern Baptist churches. One of my closest friends consistently talked about getting hit on by a member of the Board of Trustees in the seminary gym. If you wanted to stay closeted at our school, there were plenty of people very willing to keep your secrets. Looking back, I truly believe that I now know more closeted Southern Baptist pastors than I do straight ones.

Over the years, I have listened to sexuality rumors swirl around some of the most prominent pastors in the Southern Baptist Convention. I have no doubt that many are true. I also remain in relationship with numerous Southern Baptist bloggers and writers that remain closeted. With Southern Baptist Convention President Ronnie Floyd's latest pronouncement that the Southern Baptist Convention is declaring "spiritual warfare" on gay marriage, I have to wonder if he has examined his own soul or even looked around the room. Make no mistake Brother Ronnie, queens run the pulpits and the convention.

Amen.

June 17, 2015

Response to the Tragedy at Mother Emanuel AME Church

"Tragedy amplifies our desperate desire to hear a word from God. In the midst of suffocating times, sojourners gathered last night and placed their ears to the sky. As a testament to their love, the group welcomed a stranger. When the shots rang out, the nine souls of Mother Emanuel AME Church heard the beautiful comforting of words of God, 'Let not your hearts be troubled...'" As we hear the echoes of last night, may we not forget that God is preparing a place for us beyond all that holds us back. If we are willing, racism and violence can die today. Listen. Can you hear the words of God calling us to make it so?"

June 19, 2015

"I Forgive You" : Words from the Dallas Mother Emanuel AME Church Vigil

Many years ago, I received a phone call that no one would ever want to receive. My father informed me that my uncle had committed suicide. His next request was unfathomable. I need you to go and tell your grandparents before they find out from someone else. When I walked into the house, my grandparents knew that something was wrong. I managed to get out that my uncle had shot himself and my grandmother immediately demanded "a word from the Lord." I opened her Bible and scrambled to find something. I managed to find my way to the words of John 14, "Let not your hearts be troubled. Believe in God, believe also in me. For in my Father's house..."

Upon driving into Clemson, South Carolina early Thursday morning, I heard on the radio that something horrible had happened in Charleston. When I got into the hotel room, I began to realize the extent of the tragedy. Nine dead at the Mother Emanuel AME Church. I returned to the words of John 14, "Let not your hearts be troubled. Believe in God, beli eve also in me. For in my Father's house..." Unfortunately, these words didn't seem to bring the comfort they once did. When I thought about the evil that has overtaken our society, I found it hard to believe in a future. I prayed for a word from the Lord and waited.

Earlier today...just when I thought that God had not heard my prayer...I tuned into the bond proceedings for Dylann Roof taking place in a South Carolina courtroom. While there was much emotion in the room, one phrase stood out above all others. The daughter of Mother Emanuel AME Matriarch Ethel Lance stood up and shouted out, "I Forgive You!" In the magic of that moment, a word from the Lord thundered through the devastation.

We are a people who have no other means bur forgiveness to change the world. Forgiveness is a queer concept that takes power away from the offending party and invites them into right relationship. We have no future apart from forgiveness. Let that sink in. Let it sit.

Make no mistake...we are called to usher in the realm of God through one phrase, "I Forgive You."

Amen.

June 21, 2015

Forecasting the Future: Repenting of Racism and Daring to Go in Love

Less than a week ago, a young man entered a bible study at Mother Emanuel AME Church in Charleston, South Carolina. For over an hour, the group communed around the word of God. In that hour, the people of Mother Emanuel illustrated the love of God in their warm embrace of the stranger in their midst. When Dylann Roof opened fire, he declared, "I have to do this." I have stayed with that phrase ever since I heard it. Why would anyone feel like they have to kill anyone based on the color of their skin?

Our constructions of identity have led to heinous consequences. People think they have to hate people because they are outside of their identified group. We will either learn to love each other in spite of our differences or perish together as fools. The choice is ours this morning. Will we decide to love beyond the lines that we have drawn around us? Will we stand with Dylann Roof in the defense of constructed identities or with God in the liberation of the world?

In John 14, the disciples were worried about the future. In the midst of difficult hours, Jesus declared, "Let not your hearts be troubled..." Listen to me now, "Let not your hearts be troubled...Believe in God, believe also in me...For in my Father's house there are many mansions..." I believe that God is preparing a magical place of celebration. I believe that it is big enough and wide enough to hold the beautiful diversity that is each and every one of us. Do not get stuck. Press on toward that day when we shall all be one. In the midst of this great tragedy..."Let not your heart be troubled..."

You are a church founded on identity. You were forged in the fires of the LGBT movement. Is God calling you further still? Is now not the time to examine your hearts and purge your spirits of racism? We cannot be free until we are all free. If you don't know how to shake all the shit that is keeping you from your neighbors...listen for the word of God. The disciples were confused about the way as well...then Jesus said, "I am the way...I am the truth...I am the life." This passage takes us even further. God is love...Jesus is the incarnation of God...therefore we can say with certainty, "Love is the way...Love is the truth...Love is the life." Today, I am asking you to make a decision. Do you believe that love is the way? Do you believe that the LGBT movement is powerful enough to liberate everyone? Do you believe that the future can be now?

I invite you to repent of your racism...let's fall in love with each other...and simply be...a queer people united in difference.

Let not your heart be troubled...believe...and be the future.

Amen.

June 21, 2015

Pushing into the Flames: Rev. Charles Moore and the Struggle Against Racism

The moisture forming in my eyes caused the screen to grow blurry. The emotion was so heavy that I was having difficulty comprehending the words. On June 23, 2014 around 5:30pm in Grand Saline, Texas, Rev. Charles Moore walked to the front of his car in the middle of a Dollar General parking lot and placed a burning match to his head. Within seconds, Moore's body was engulfed in flames. Despite the efforts of bystanders, Moore died. Upon inspection of the writings he left behind, Moore's family realized that his self-immolation was a protest against racism. Soon after I read the initial article, I called him a martyr and started praying to Moore. In the year since, I haven't stopped. In the midst of difficult struggles for racial justice, I have heard God speak from the bespectacled image of Moore burning over and over.

Not long after I discovered his story, I wrote a piece about Moore's death. Having studied self-immolations in my graduate studies at the University of Alabama, I knew people would try to write him off and call him insane. The problem with such thinking is that it neglects the fact that most self-immolations are highly logical acts of protest. I didn't think Moore was insane then and I don't now. In my piece, I begged people not to turn their heads from Moore's sacrifice. Sadly, I feel like most people did. Within the last year, among a plethora of other offences...police brutality has been on the rise, undocumented immigrants are constantly mistreated and brutalized, children of color are brutalized at swimming pools and just last week Mother Emanuel AME Church was shot up by a virulent racist in Charleston, South Carolina. Even in Moore's own United Methodist Church, people seem to be most comfortable with partial steps that don't speak to the racism and segregation that dominate most church spaces. Over the last year, I have constantly wondered if Moore died in vain.

A few weeks after his death, I attended Moore's funeral. There weren't many people there. Throughout the service, I watched minister after minister try to carefully navigate the events. By following Jesus to death, Moore backed them against the wall. How was any minister supposed to talk about giving your life to Jesus now? My quiet revelation that I admired Moore was met with suspicion and jeers. Regardless of all that was going on, I couldn't take my eyes off of the image of Moore. Out of the excess of his love for God, Moore stepped into the flames. I refused to turn my head.

Months later, I sat alone in a cell at the Dallas County Jail. Earlier, I spoke at a rally against police brutality and helped lead marchers down the streets of Dallas. Now, I was alone. For hours, I just sat there. The demons started whispering. I began to doubt. When I closed my eyes, I saw the burning image and felt the call to simply keep following Jesus. For the remaining hours of my incarceration, I was bolstered by Moore's presence.

From many accounts, Charles Moore was a cantankerous man. While I don't know if our personalities would have meshed in life, I do know that his witness in death has saved my life and activism. I am strengthened in the knowledge that a modern pastor went all the way in the fight against racism. Jesus calls us to give our lives in service to others. I remain impressed that Moore was brave enough to follow the call of God all the way until the end.

Overwhelmed at the assault of a young black girl at a swimming pool in McKinney, Texas last month, I decided to venture out to the spot where Charles Moore self-immolated. I needed a word from God. Driving through the night, I was struck at the desolation of everything. When I pulled into the Dollar General parking lot, I located the exact spot where Moore self-immolated. I saw the burning image of Moore once more. I felt the presence of God in the orange glow. The light of Moore's sacrifice still guides me. I can't look away. I know that there is always more for me to give in the struggle against racism. When I wonder how much will be required, I just close my eyes. In the darkness, I still see the whip of Moore's flames calling me onward.

Amen.

June 24, 2015

The Fire at the Upstairs Lounge: The Worst LGBT Massacre in US History Occurred 42 Years Ago Today

On June 24, 1973, an arsonist attacked the Upstairs Lounge in New Orleans, Louisiana. The space was full of members of the local Metropolitan Community Church gathered to celebrate the last night of Pride Weekend. When the fire broke out, the bars on the windows kept most people from escaping. As onlookers made jokes, MCC Pastor Rev. Bill Larson burned to death hanging out of a small opening screaming, "Oh, God, no!" When the flames subsided, 32 people were dead. No one was ever charged with the massacre.

When viewed in the light of the shooting at the Mother Emanuel AME Church, the anniversary of the massacre at the Upstairs Lounge reminds us that the path of Jesus passes through both New Orleans and Charleston. As we remember, may we not forget the words of Jesus, "Follow me."

Amen.

June 25, 2015

The Intern Monologues: The Church

*This is the fifth intentional conversation between my summer intern Christian Parks and I.

J: Why is the construct of the church relevant?

C: The church is relevant because it is the most diverse construct we have in our world. The gospel of Jesus is a unifying message...no matter language, tradition or creed. Our homogenous spaces suffocate us and the church offers a model for breathing in our diverse oneness. Do you think the church is really the church?

J: Hell no. The church in the United States is dying due to our fundamental inability to see the suffocating nature of institutionalism. Our segregated classist spaces of worship have very little resemblance to what Jesus called us to be. We exist to protect the normative nature of power not to represent the gospel of love in our broken world. We were called to go to the nations...and we spend all of our time drunk on nationalism. We were called to be with the poor...and we think that our monthly feeding ministries are enough. We were called to be with the outcast...and we think that spaces full of means are the mark of success. We have failed. There is only one way out...to get saved and be the church. I have a firm primary belief that the church exists most fully in the streets. How do we get there?

C: We must repent of our ists and isms that cause us to treat our neighbors like our trash. We must remember that Jesus teaches us courage in the face of fear. We must be willing to take faithful steps out of our doors and into the streets. Our control must be no more. Our lives must be changed. Our fullness must be embodied. We must love. Do you think it is possible?

J: While the true universal church will always be present, the institutional church can't survive in present form. How can the church in the United States experience resurrection when it clings so much to life? I don't believe in resurrection without death. Instead of growth consultants, our churches need more undertakers. You ready to be an undertaker Brother Christian?

C: Hell yes. I believe in resurrection. I trust Jesus to make all things new. I know that this truly is our moment.

J: Thanks be!

June 27, 2015

"With Friends Like These, Who Needs Enemies? : A List of Christian Denominations that Discriminate against LGBTQ Persons."

With celebration of the Supreme Court of the United States' recent marriage equality decision sweeping the nation, I thought now would be a good time to examine where Christian denominations are at on LGBTQ issues. When I decided to compile a list of denominations that discriminate (based primarily on ordination, marriage and a variety of other indicators of inclusion), I knew that my efforts would not be an exact science. The list I compiled is based on an amalgamation of researched information and personal knowledge. This list is not a complete or perfect list. While some might question the usefulness of this list (or even if some of the groups I include should be on here), I simply wanted to illustrate that the vast majority of denominations in our nation are still homophobic, transphobic and queerphobic. Though much progress has been made, most of the church landscape in the United States is still a terrifying and violent place for LGBTQ persons. With friends like these, who needs enemies?

The Seventh-Day Adventist Church
The Southern Baptist Convention
American Baptist Churches, USA
The Cooperative Baptist Fellowship
The United Methodist Church
National Baptist Convention, USA
Reformed Church in America
The Eastern Orthodox Church
The Roman Catholic Church
The Lutheran Church - Missouri Synod
The Wisconsin Evangelical Lutheran Synod
Most Pentecostal Denominations
Most Anabaptist Denominations
Most Evangelical Denominations
Presbyterian Church in America
Evangelical Presbyterian Church
Associate Reformed Presbyterian Church
Orthodox Presbyterian Church
Friends United Meeting
Friends Evangelical Church
General Church of the New Jerusalem
Vineyard Churches, USA

The African Methodist Episcopal Church
The Christian Methodist Episcopal Church
The African Methodist Episcopal Church - Zion
Most Methodist Denominations
The Church of the Nazarene
Church of God in Christ
The Church of Jesus Christ of Latter Day Saints
Progressive National Baptist Convention
Jehovah's Witnesses
Most Baptist Denominations
Most Churches of Christ

Parts of the Community of Christ
Parts of the Episcopal Church
Parts of the Presbyterian Church USA
Parts of the United Church of Christ
Parts of the Disciples of Christ

June 28. 2015

The Intern Monologues: Baptism

C: Early in this journey I had the opportunity to witness you baptize your youngest twins, Madeline and Lucas. As a Baptist preacher, why infant baptism?

J: I believe that nothing can separate us from the love of God. I baptize my children as an outward sign of an inward grace. An inward grace that comes by being created in the image of God...such grace continues to flow through the veins of Jesus and down into the baptismal waters. I don't believe that the love of God expressed through Jesus will ever let Madeleine and Lucas go. Since they cannot reject God, I feel no need to wait on them to make any decision. The love of God will never leave them. Baptism is about belonging to God and each other. Can you unpack this idea of belonging?

C: I remember in the Gospels when Jesus was preparing for the Sabbath meal he was stopped and made aware that his mother was at the door waiting for him. Jesus responded by declaring to all present that they are his mother, father and brothers. Each and every person gathered at the table had a claim to being a part of God's family. No one greater than another and no one left out. This is the great symbol of Baptism that love meets us where we are, as we are and beckons us into the family. We are reminded that love reaches even us as the waters of grace washes us clean and makes us anew. What is the power of Baptism today?

J: Baptism is an outward sign of cleansing. When we baptize children, we are expressing a hope that our past sins might be cleansed from the child as we connect them to Christ. When we baptize adults, the individual is expressing a hope that their sins might be forgiven as they connect to Christ. Baptism might be the greatest moment of eschatological hope we practice. I think we keep the waters stirred because we know that our salvation lies in the cleansing. Baptism is about hope and hope will always be as powerful today as it was yesterday. Would you agree Brother Christian?

C: Yes, our hope lies in our constant willingness to be cleansed by love. Baptism reminds us that love truly has the power to make all things new.

J: Let hope reign.

Amen.

June 28, 2015

Don't Stay at the Table Too Long

* Derived from a Sermon Delivered at New Heart Community Church in La Mirada, California on June 28, 2015

Justice starts in our beginnings. Too often we run from beginnings. Even when we think about the creation myth in Genesis, we run from the snake, the bite and the ejection to the incarnation of God in Jesus. Just give me Jesus. Just give me Jesus. Evangelicals love to talk like that. Just give me Jesus. Unfortunately, I don't think most people understand the consequences of asking for just Jesus.

I am a child of the South. I grew up in a big Southern Baptist Church. Throughout my early years, I had a love/hate relationship with Jesus. I loved the Jesus that called for the little children. I hated the Jesus that was going to throw many people I loved into hell. Our church loved hell more than they did Jesus. I think our pastors thought that enough talk about hell would scare the hell out of everyone. These tactics had the opposite effect on me. The more we talked about hell...the more frightened I got. I couldn't understand how the God of Hell could be the same as the God of Eden...who was all about collective being and love. Regardless of my doubts about the message, I still believed enough of what was being taught to be constantly scared. In the midst of constant talk of being left behind after the rapture or going to hell, I was desperate to find and accept the real Jesus. I was so desperate that I prayed for salvation hundreds if not thousands of times...but a Jesus that actually loved me seemed like a distant figment of my imagination.

In high school, I decided that scripture was going to be the answer to all of my doubts. Evangelicals tell people all the time to just go to scripture...all the answers are found in scripture. Do you know if people were dumb enough to follow that advice...they would go crazy? We all know that scripture is full of some of the weirdest commandments that you could ever imagine...especially in Leviticus. Nevertheless, I took the advice "all the answers are to be found in scripture" quite literally. I started reading and reading and reading and reading...I knew that all the answers to all of my questions would be found in the Bible. There was even a pastor I followed who would hold up a Bible and say, "The Bible is the way, the Bible is the truth and the Bible is the life...no one comes to the Father apart from what is revealed in this Bible." I wanted a strong relationship with Jesus so badly...but this book called the Bible always seemed to get in the way. This passage here or this passage there...someone's interpretation here or someone's interpretation there...this theology here or this theology there...ultimately, I couldn't find the answers in the Bible.

When I got to college, I found the first theology that I had ever encountered that really did claim to have all the answers...Calvinism. When I became a Calvinist, I started to believe that God predetermined everything. Blessings and abundance became a sign of God's favor. I was doing pretty good...so I decided that God must be on my side. When I looked around and saw marginalized and oppressed people, I was certain that God was not on their side. Suffering was a sign of God's disfavor. Theologies centered on the blessings of God can take us to some really warped places. For the first 22 years of my life, I made the major theological mistakes of placing all of my trust in the book and then in the blessing.

When I decided to go to seminary, I knew that I had to go to the summit of Southern Baptist education...The Southern Baptist Theological Seminary. When I got to school, there were answers everywhere. I couldn't get the answers into my brain fast enough. I loved it. I learned that masturbation was sin. I learned that God hated anyone who had sex before they got married. I learned that the United States was God's favored nation. I learned that women shouldn't even hold a Bible much less teach out of one. I learned that the scripture was clear about stoning gay and lesbian people...but we have enough grace not to practice that now. Through it all, I learned some pretty twisted stuff. The problem was that all this exegetical and theological knowledge led me further away from Jesus.

Evangelicals love to talk about being born again and getting saved. Well, let me tell you where these things most fully happened to me. I was about a year or so into my theological education when I got a phone call from Georgia. My dear mentor and Southern Baptist pastor was dying of lung cancer. I raced to visit him. When I arrived at his house, I was greeted by his wife and family and went into his bedroom. The hospital bed was daunting. I grabbed his extended cold wet hand and he said, "I'm gay and I always have been." Here was a man who represented the incarnation of Jesus for me and all of a sudden I had to deal with the fact that Jesus was now gay. My life was changed forever. Slowly over the next few years, I realized that Jesus was and is most fully found in those that we marginalize and oppress. I could not lean on the Bible, the blessings or the knowledge for the answers...the incarnation of Jesus in the least of these was and is the only way.

There was a time when a group of religious leaders with an abundance of scriptural understanding, blessings and knowledge found a woman in the very act of committing adultery. These pastors threw the woman in the dirt at the feet of Jesus and demanded she be stoned. In this moment, we find the fullness of the Gospel in the actions of Jesus. Instead of inviting the pastors to sit down and talk things over...Jesus got down in the dirt with the woman. In this moment, the pastors have their stones raised in the air and are ready to kill. We too live in a time where people have their stones raised all over our country and are ready to kill. What does Jesus do? Instead of debating, Jesus gets down in the dirt and is ready to die with the woman. If the stones had started flying, we would have had an early execution. The path of Jesus is not about talking...it is about boldly placing your body into the fight against oppression and marginalization.

I know that you call this church a third way space and that you are a space centered on talking about controversial topics...but I want to remind you about the one who said that he was and is the way. I know that you are all about bringing people to the table for conversation...but let me assure you that the woman would have been dead if Jesus would have tried to bring the pastors to the table for conversation. I know that you are a space concerned about staying at the table and remaining in conversation...but don't stay at the table too long.

People continue to abuse and mistreat LGBTQ people all over our nation...don't stay at the table too long.

Nine people were murdered while studying their Bibles in Charleston for no other reason than they were black...don't stay at the table too long.

Five black churches have been burned to the ground over the last week...don't stay at the table too long.

Sexism steals the dreams and lives of young women on a regular basis...don't stay at the table too long.

Suffocating and stifling poverty is growing worse and worse...don't stay at the table too long.

LGBTQ persons in Texas can be fired tomorrow for celebrating the marriage equality decision last Friday...don't stay at the table too long.

Trans persons of color are being murdered throughout the nation...don't stay at the table too long.

The police are killing anyone who dare cling to their rights...don't stay at the table too long.

I could go on and on...but I guess that you get the point that our God is marching on...Jesus stands with those who are suffering while you are talking...don't stay at the table too long.

Will you stand with Jesus or will you continue to talk about what that might look like?

When people are being abused, assaulted, marginalized, oppressed and killed...we need action not words...

Don't stay at the table too long...

Amen.

June 30, 2015

The Irrelevance of Denominations and the Relevance of the Church in the Ongoing Struggle for Marriage Equality in the South

Raised in Georgia, educated in four southern states and presently living in Texas, I am an undeniable product of the South. When I joined in the celebration of the marriage equality ruling of the Supreme Court of the United States last Friday from my speaking tour (currently in California), I worried how the implementation of the decision would go in the region I have always called home. After a few days of news coverage, most of my fears have come true. In state after state, elected officials are standing in the way of marriage licenses for same-sex couples. Where are the people of God?

Following the ruling, denominational reaction ranged from outright disdain to caution. Only a few denominations offered outright support and most of them have very few churches in the South. Even some of the more progressive denominations sought first to assure their people that no one would be forced to be a part of the same-sex wedding. With national denominational reaction so timid, how can we expect their local affiliates to do anything that might disturb the peace that has been entrusted to them? The irrelevance of denominations in the ongoing struggle for marriage equality in the South is palpable. Thankfully, denominations are never the arbiters of who or what constitutes the church.

In our present moment, I have no doubt that the church is fully realized in the people of God who are giving their lives to making marriage equality a reality for all people in the South. The true church is standing with those who dare push against the forces of darkness that are promoting bigotry and homophobia from elected positions. If individuals tried to wait on denominations to give them permission, most would be waiting for the rest of their lives. The church is in you and you can embody the relevance of the church. Stand with your LGBTQ neighbors. Become part of your LGBTQ neighbors. Become your LGBTQ neighbors. The time is now. God is in this moment. God is in this movement. Don't let God pass you by. Stand up for justice! Stand up for love! Stand up for the South!

Amen.

July 6, 2015

The Intern Monologues: Communion

J: What do you think happens during communion?

C: Communion is the place where we fully encounter the other. We are reminded the way of Jesus is broken and shared among us all. What do you think?

J: I believe the elements become God as we ingest them together. We are all made in the image of a God that is queer. We are queer. When all of us queers commune together...we start looking like God. The elements bring us closer to each other and closer to God. The actual queer body and blood of Jesus appear in our actual queer body and blood as we draw nearer to be a reflection of the queerest one of all. Do you think communion is salvific?

C: Our salvation is found in the collective encounter with God and ourselves. Gathering together, eating together, listening to God and each other offers us new ways of living into our liberation where our salvation is found. Liberation is salvation. We are co-liberators as we create the bountiful face and experience of the Queer God. What does the communion experience offer our world?

J: Communion is a collection of queerness or a visual representation of God in our world. I believe that we grow in our knowledge of God through growth gained in our knowledge of our self during the communion process. Communion offers the world a relationship with God and the other. Do you think that any of our churches are practicing communion with any of these thoughts in mind?

C: Most everything in the current manifestation of the church is stuck in theories as if their hands and feet are detached from the mind. We crave authentic relationships and miss the mark with our stagnant purity ethics. Communion has the power to meet us as we are in all that we are. Sadly, the church continues to miss the invitation.

J: You fundamentally cannot commune with anyone or anything until you are ready to love your self. The church consistently teaches people to hate who they are. There will be no real communion until there is real love for the self. The future of the church hinges on the liberation of individual souls from the chains of normative ways of doing and being. We can do more to commune with the God within...if we are to survive...we must.

Amen.

July 7, 2015

Ruminations from the Cross

I did not kill

I tried to heal

I was not fake

I can't escape

I have tried to scream

I'm on your team

You do not listen

Because God put me in this position

I am dying

I will

I will not

I will

Dreams turned to nightmares so quickly

Then back to dreams

For I am the now and the not yet

Forever and ever

Amen

July 9, 2015

Confession Not Deflection

After hearing an acquaintance make two racist remarks, I insinuated that his remarks were problematic. I didn't respond in violently. I simply tried to steer my acquaintance in a better direction. Instead of acknowledging any error, my acquaintance kept making deflecting comments. "Aren't we all just a little racist?" I tried again. "Yeah, but we are all racist you know." The circular conversation was exhausting. When confronted with troubling behavior, I have found that this is the new line of defense for many people. With all of the problems that we face, followers of Jesus have a particular duty to confess their sins. There can be no repentance or recovery with a circular pattern of deflection. Progress comes from confession not deflection. I am a recovering racist and probably always will be. What about you?

Amen.

July 12, 2015

Raw Theology at Be Loved

The Be Loved Community is full of surprisingly raw theology. Rev. Amy Cantrell founded and leads the ministry that feeds hundreds of people each week at a small house near downtown Asheville, North Carolina. I was thankful for the invitation to be in such a space. Though I delivered a sermon, I felt like it was the people who preached to me.

One of the dear brothers in the group leaned over and whispered to me, "If it smells like shit, tastes like shit and feels like shit...then it is probably shit." I was reminded that God gives us the ability to smell, taste and feel for a purpose. If we want to keep out of the shit, we have to trust our senses.

The Queen Mother of the group overheard someone complaining about the lack of meat in the meal and she responded, "The only meat I'm concerned about is meeting

Jesus." In the face of so many distractions, we have to remember to keep our minds on the ultimate things.

Pastor Amy let it rip and shouted out, "There are no barriers to God. The less walls you create the closer you are to God." Too often, we try to manage souls. We all have unlimited access to God.

You keep out of the shit by trusting your senses.

The ultimate things deserve our ultimate attention.

There are no barriers to God.

Thank you Be Loved.

Amen.

July 13, 2015

Dr. Robert Jeffress Deports Jesus: A Cautionary Tale

Miracles weren't supposed to happen on nights like that. Gunshots filled the air. Violence was everywhere. Already feeling the contractions, Maria was desperate to find refuge. Just when Maria thought she wasn't going to make it one more step, a woman opened the door of her shack and invited her in. Within the hour, Maria gave birth to a son and named him Jesus. When José made it to Maria, they knew they had to get Jesus to a safer location. After some hesitancy, the family decided to cross the border.

Over and over, Maria and José wondered if they would make it. The scorching desert burned their skin and stole their hydration. Just when they thought they were as good as dead, they stumbled on a highway. A generous man pulled over and drove the family to Dallas. After some hard months, Maria and José were able to afford an apartment. Desperate for spiritual nurture, the family started to attend the First Baptist Church of Dallas.

Over the years, Jesus grew in his knowledge of God. In high school, Jesus made an appointment with his pastor to discuss his call to ministry. Coming off a heated interview, Dr. Robert Jeffress was shocked to learn that Jesus didn't have proper immigration papers. Unable to go back on his strong statements, Dr. Jeffress asked his secretary to call ICE. I guess he couldn't see the savior of the world sitting in front of him.

In an interview with Fox News last week, Dr. Robert Jeffress insinuated that churches should assist in the deportation of undocumented immigrants. How far from the Gospel of Jesus can a minister get? Does the love of Jesus only extend to our borders? In Matthew 25, Jesus declares that he embodies the stranger. Please don't follow Dr. Jeffress and blind your eyes to Jesus.

Amen.

July 16, 2015

The Intern Monologues: Eden

J: Do you remember a place called Eden?

C: Growing up in a context where the Bible was considered infallible, inspired, and fully authoritative, I remember beginning every Vacation Bible School (VBS) with the story found in Genesis. Where did you first come in contact with Eden?

J: I don't feel like it has ever left us. I feel it in my fingertips. I know it in my soul. The entirety of my being yearns to return to a place called Eden. I think we all do. Why does it seem so far away?

C: Eden is here. This is God's created world. Yet we continually attempt to locate Eden outside of who we are and what we have. I believe the magic of Eden lies in the mind as a state of being. Eden is the place where hearts and God are one. Fear distracts us from participating in God's abundance. When we are one with God, love frees us into abundance. Why do you want to return?

J: We are already on the way. I believe Eden represents the queerest we can be both as individuals and the world. Eden is our home. Eden is the place where we and God are one. Our hearts will be restless until they rest in God...in that place called Eden. Why do you think we left?

C: We are cultured consumed, not by love for ourselves and others. We are consumed by the search for a safe God, a Santa-Clause-type God. A God that requires nothing yet gives everything we want. We are lost on the search, afraid of the God of Love that requires us to live bodly into our queerness. What is our hope?

J: Eden is our hope. The fullness of love and justice are there. The propensity for Eden is in each one of us. If we are to find it in our world we must first find it in ourselves. Do you think we can make it back there?

C: Jesus has showed us the way. We must courageously take the risk to follow.

J: Love is the way. Love is the Truth. Love is the light. Thanks be to God.

Amen.

July 16, 2015

The Vagina of Jesus

"How dare you insinuate Jesus had a vagina!" The woman was livid. In my talk, I stumbled on the most disturbing idea she'd ever been presented with. With church doctrine and dogma over the centuries in mind, the thought of Jesus having a vagina didn't seem too out there for me. Since the earliest days of the church, haven't Christians believed that Jesus was fully human and fully divine in every sense of the words?

"So you believe that Jesus was transgender?" "What would be so bad about that?" I mused aloud. While I can't know for sure, I feel like some combination between a vagina and penis was probably what the most perfect representative of all sexes and genders to ever exist was working with. Regardless, the woman continued, "I know for a fact that Jesus was a man!" In deep anticipation of a strong argument, I waited for her next sentence. "We all know that God has a penis and Jesus is God." "What happens when God gets an erection?" I asked. I couldn't help but make an absurd remark. The idea of anyone being certain that God has a penis and a penis alone was too much for me. Feeling the need to wrap up the conversation, I paused and asked her a question, "How did the penis feel when you reached up Jesus' skirt and grabbed it?" I don't know anyone who ever saw or touched the sexual organs of Jesus. Flabbergasted, the woman walked out.

"God created humanity in God's own image, in the divine image God created them, male and female God created them." With regard to our connection to God, I believe there is no more powerful of a verse of scripture than Genesis 1:27. The scriptures declare that God created the first persons to be male and female. In Eden, I believe the first persons had both sexual organs and functioned at unique spaces on the gender spectrum. The scriptures declare that the entireties of our beings are created in the very image of God. With the creation of male and female, how could

God not have both sexual organs? The first persons were intimately connected to God. Throughout the early church, there was a constant theological desire to connect Jesus with the first persons. If Jesus was like the first persons, then it makes since that Jesus would have a vagina and a penis.

Regardless of whether you believe these theological arguments or not, Jesus declares that the incarnation is not a singular event. In Matthew 25:40, Jesus says, "What you have done to the least of these...you have done to me." In placing Jesus' very being with the least of these, Jesus becomes the least of these. Throughout Matthew 25, Jesus says that the person of Jesus will inhabit the hungry, the thirsty, those who are strangers, the naked, the sick and those who are in prison. I think we can be certain that persons with vaginas are regularly a part of each of these categories. With that affirmed and sealed for eternity, we can also be sure that Jesus has a vagina.

I believe that the vagina of Jesus is a miraculous occurrence. We should work to smash the patriarchal understandings of Jesus for broader conceptions that create greater access to the person of Jesus. If this essay offends you...I encourage you to get saved from your addiction to erectile theology.

Amen.

July 16, 2015

Statement on Prayer Vigil for Undocumented Immigrants

"The First Baptist Church of Dallas has long been a home of intolerance. Dr. Robert Jeffress is proudly carrying on the family tradition. In his recent statements about immigration on Fox News, Jeffress showed that he follows the Jesus of his imagination and not the Bible. For in the Bible, Jesus and his family fled without any papers to Egypt to avoid persecution. For in the Bible, Jesus tells us to love all of our neighbor as we would our self. For in the Bible, Jesus tells us to welcome the stranger. Does Jeffress stand with Jesus or not? If he would encourage the deportation of persons without papers, I have no doubt that Jeffress would stand against and deport Jesus too. If these evil statements were being made in ignorance on a blog somewhere, I wouldn't be responding. However, these statements are being made by the pastor of one of the largest churches in our nation. In sharing hate, Jeffress is poisoning our faith. Xenophobia has absolutely nothing to do with the Gospel of Jesus Christ. As a fellow Southern Baptist pastor, I am demanding that Jeffress stop the insanity.

I have chosen to stand with my documented and undocumented friends and neighbors in front of First Baptist Dallas. In my standing, I am praying for Jeffress' repentance. I believe that light is more powerful than darkness. So, I am holding Jeffress in the light of God. I believe that love is stronger than hate. So, I have chosen to love Jeffress. I am doing all of these things so that undocumented immigrants will know that they will never stand alone."

July 17, 2015

The Vision

Blindness/Can you see me?

Fear/Can you see me?

Pain/Can you see me?

Terror/Can you see me?

Death/Can you see me?

Consciousness/Can you see me?

Hope/Can you see me?

Vitality/Can you see me?

Life/Can you see me?

For thine is the way and the truth...///and the life?

Amen.

July 18, 2015

Pain: A Visit and Conversation with the Rev. Dr. Garth Baker-Fletcher

* This interaction is derived from a recent conversation that I had with the Rev. Dr. Garth Baker-Fletcher at a rehabilitation facility where he is recovering from hip surgery. A retired professor, Baker-Fletcher is the author of *Somebodyness: Martin Luther King, Jr. and the Theory of Dignity* (1993), *Xodus: An African-American Male Journey* (1996), *My Sister, My Brother* (with his wife Karen) (1997), *Black Religion After the Million Man March* (1998), *Dirty Hands: Christian Ethics in a Morally Ambiguous World* (2000) & *Bible Witness in Black Churches* (2009). A cherished friend, I affectionately call him Brother Garth.

J: Brother Garth thank you for this time. How do you define pain?

G: I am going to string some defining words together for you. Pain is a shocking, singular, grading, raw, fierce, determined, frightening and empowering experience. How would you define it?

J: Pain is a jolting and dislodging experience that we always want to get out of. We always want to find the way to make it stop. How do you deal with constant pain?

G: I have had lupus since I was a child. The medicine they gave me to treat the lupus destroyed the ball joint in my hip. Literally, I have surgery after surgery to fix this hip implant (it looks like a tadpole). My daughter has always called me handicapable. I've always pushed back against being in a wheelchair. Regardless, I had ten surgeries in the first ten years that I had this implant and I've had to just stop counting since then. The pain was jolting and dismembering at first and has since become a chronic event that keeps me away from the business of life. Being in regular pain and in the hospital is an isolating experience. I often feel very alone. People make the assumption that they can't comfort you and therefore they stay away. The sense of solitude is an additional corresponding painful sickness.

J: The spiritual pain seems as raw as the physical pain.

G: There is no question about it Brother Jeff. You have develop a spirituality capable of pushing back. You have to dare to believe in a God that has the strength and fortitude to carry you through. Do you think there is such a thing as social pain?

J: The pull of the normative is strong. Our sickness is that we expect everyone to be like everyone else. We create categories and force people to fit. If you are black then you need to act black. If you are gay then you need to act gay. If you are white then you need to act white. The categories become a prison that does not allow for individual expression. Our uniform expectations are the weapons that we use to inflict social pain on others. Do we not understand that queerness is a gift from God? Living into our spirit we are able to combat the sickness of uniformity. There is nothing more painful than living in a society that expects you to be something other than you. So what we do is we get on a pain management regiment. Our spiritual life is our only form of pain management. To be born is to suffer. We have to find a way to survive despite the pain. Unfortunately, we have developed this sense that everything is supposed to be safe and pain free. We are delussional. The only way we can live honestly is by pushing into the danger of life with an eschatological hope that God will meet us in the end.

G: I have had five surgeries in the last year. I am now in a position of chronic pain. Over and over I have experienced the shock of pain. I feel this is very connected to our social sicknesses. Those who exist outside our normativities are faced with shocking pain over and over. Violence is a regular occurrence because the antinormative is the greatest threat to normativity. At 59, I have finally come to the conclusion that I am disabled. To be disabled in this society is to be on the outside. The only way the disabled person gets to come back in on the inside is if you conform to the expectations of the society. Normativism is the meta-ism. All other oppressions flow out of a concept of normal. I will probably be in pain the rest of my life. Our society teaches us that pain is something we have to get over. What happens when you're not going to get over it?

J: What happens if we start to view disability as a higher level of ability? It seems to me that those who are learning how to live through pain on the level that you are...are almost superhuman. I think about my dear friend Rev. Justin Hancock. From a motorized wheelchair, Justin does more in one day than most people accomplish in a lifetime. Disabled persons seem to be functioning at a higher level of spiritual ability.

G: When I started experiencing the othering of disability in my younger years, everyone assumed that I just needed to be healed. I have had no more painful of experiences than people trying to heal me. As I have grown older, I have realized that often I am the one that needs to be doing the healing.

J: Have you ever thought of yourself as superhuman?

G: I had a dream one time along those lines. When I was a teenager, I dreamed that I carried all the pain that I had on my back. I was so strong. I looked like a superhero. I had muscles everywhere. When I looked at the rest of the world, all the people looked like stick figures. I have thought about that dream ever since. In the mystical nature of that experience, I realized that going through this pain was a gift that I could give the world. I think there is a sense that the disabled are spiritually superhuman. I think you have some of that.

J: In my own suffering with bipolar disorder, I have to come to a place where I saw my mental disability as a mental ability.

G: We have that connection as well. In the words of some of the disability theorists, maybe we should call ourselves differently-abled.

J: I still don't think that gets at the spiritual point we are making...that disability is a higher spiritual level of ability.

G: On some level, I agree with you. Although, I think we are on the right track. We have got to lead an uprising against these normative terms and ideas that have oppressed our ability to truly see and experience our self and each other for so long.

Amen.

July 20, 2015

The Christian Politics of Respectability

The phone buzzed. The text from a dear friend said it all, "I'm done." For the second time in the last few months, a friend was fired from a ministry position for their social justice work. To make matters worse, both of these ministers are persons of color and one is gay. Though the stories are different, each represents the consequences of our Christian politics of respectability.

Standing up at the council meeting, my friend questioned, "How can we have a taskforce for LGBT inclusion that doesn't have any LGBT people on it?" This was the beginning of the end. The social justice work my friend did with persons with disabilities was respectable. Challenging a system that continue to oppress one of the most marginalized and oppressed populations in our churches was not. When my friend reached out to the apartment complex across the street from the church, everyone was excited about having greater Latina/o participation in worship until they realized that the church was incapable of responding to their physical needs. Political statements about immigration were acceptable until someone sought asylum in the church. Standing with black people was ok until cities started going up in flames. On and on my friend was encouraged to follow Jesus in ministry...that is until he did. The meeting made things real. "The Bishop thinks you are too involved in issues of social justice," the fellow minister said. The phone call was even more ominous. When the hammer came down in the council meeting, the reason was clear. So as to not look like they were treating a person of color poorly, the council decided to give my friend a few months severance.

To be gay in affirming churches is to be expected to perform in certain ways. So as not to upset anyone, you should seek to be as normative as possible. Understanding the consequences of stepping out of line, my friend worked in one of the denomination's most difficult assignments. This is typical. Marginalized and oppressed populations are expected to succeed in ministry from the bottom. Some make it...most don't. Though active for many years in issues of social justice, my friend largely held the denominational line on issues of social justice. Unfortunately, even the denominational line is much further than what most in the denomination want to go in practice. With person of color after person of color being gunned down in the streets, my friend felt that the silence of the denomination made it complicit in the crimes. As a person of color, my friend was accustomed to persons of color being used by the system...but the relative silence of the Bishop was deafening. I consistently pushed my friend to go further. Though upset, my friend felt the need to hold the denominational line. The phone call was ominous. A private meeting was usually not good. "Jesus has nothing to do with social justice," the Bishop replied. When the Bishop declined to appoint my friend to another church after her appointment expired, the result was a firing. I couldn't understand. My friend was as cautious as anyone I knew. Though an injustice had occurred, the denomination escaped unscathed...a person of color just fired a person of color.

Though my friends tried, I don't even think Jesus could function within our Christian politics of respectability. Why do we ask ministers to follow Jesus and fire them when they do? I am beginning to realize that our denominations are woefully inadequate to respond to the great crises of our time. I think it is time to just follow Jesus.

Amen.

July 20, 2015

Words from the Prayer Vigil for Undocumented Immigrants

We are gathered in this space because we believe that something can be accomplished by gathering. We choose to love in this space because we believe that something can be accomplished by loving. We believe that there is more to life than the maintenance of constructed lines that do nothing more than protect our shit. We are here because we know that we serve a God without borders. On some levels, we unite tonight to be evangelists to Dr. Robert Jeffress and the people of First Baptist Dallas. We know that God can't be found through hate and we are here to share such a truth.

Do you know the story of the early years of Jesus? Do you remember how the parents of Jesus had to flee to another land in the face of grave political violence? What kind of immigration documents do you think Jesus had?

Borders only exist to protect our shit.

How Christian does it sound to spend so much effort maintaining them?

Amen.

July 20, 2015

The Apocalypse

Growing up, our church loved to talk about the end of the world. From pew to pew, everyone believed that they would be saved from the destruction to come. I didn't know for sure. I had doubt. Downtown, a man held a sign high into the air, "The End is Near." I was terrified. I thought I was going to get left behind. When we got back home, piles of clothes haunted me. Every time I saw the assortment of fabrics, I just knew that God called my parents to heaven and they left their clothes. On more than one occasion, my mom found me thrusting her clothes into the air screaming, "Why did you leave me?" With a long history of being haunted by bad eschatology or discussion of ultimate things, I am the last person one would expect to be arguing for expansion of the conversation. However, I believe our greatest contemporary affliction is a failure to discuss ultimate things. Currently, we speak in sound bites about temporary ineffective solutions with no idea of what love perfected looks like. Sometimes in the midst of our yearning for love, an apocalypse of greater revelation finds us.

Like much of the nation, my eyes have been trained on South Carolina for many weeks now. The murder of churchgoers at Mother Emmanuel AME Church in Charleston shook me to my core. How could God allow folks to be murdered in their place of worship? I began to doubt that anything other than chaos was possible. When South Carolina took down the Confederate Flag, I experienced a little bit of hope. Was it possible that a better way was creeping through the bullshit? Reality struck back. The violent images of white supremacists marching and taunting black people were beyond disturbing. Downtown Columbia looked like Nazi Berlin. Just when I thought that hope was lost, I experienced the Apocalypse.

Photographer Rob Godfrey's image found me. Within the small frame, came the apocalyptic revelation of God. While marching for hate, an older white racist clad in a swastika-adorned black shirt (advertising the supremacist National Socialist Movement) started experiencing symptoms of a heat stroke. In the hour of the racist's distress, a black police officer named Leroy Smith showed him love. The photograph shows Officer Smith helping the white racist to safety. In the hours of our lives where we are as evil as the white racist, Jesus leads us to love. I don't think Jesus will ever stop. Officer Smith refused to allow evil to block love. God does the same.

The Apocalypse is the moment of greatest revelation. Is love not the greatest revelation? In this photograph, I see the inbreaking of God into the world. Love is the Apocalypse. In my youth, I never would have imagined that God was black.

Amen.

July 21, 2015

The Intern Monologues: Death

C: What is death?

J: Death is a lie. The resurrection of Jesus is the ultimate definition of death. Like a lingering sickness, death afflicts us until we succumb to it and realize that ultimately the full manifestation of the sickness is the healing. Our healing is found in our resurrection. However, there is no such thing as resurrection without death. I feel very comfortable standing with the Apostle Paul on this one, "Where is death's sting?" How does one talk about the temporary sting of death in the face of the resurrection?

C: I believe we take courage and walk through death much like the caterpillar. For a season we find the caterpillar growing in life. That season ends with a journey to its cocoon - a death. This death though is merely a stop on the way to transformation. The caterpillar dissolves into nothing and emerges as a butterfly. I also agree with Paul. Death is a transformation "from glory to glory." Where can we find the courage to enter death?

J: From plastic surgery to vitamin supplements to the latest fad diet, we are a people addicted to denying death. We think we can live forever. We spend our lives convincing ourselves that we are never going to die. Regardless of how you shake it, we are all perpetually dying. The path of Jesus is about choosing life in the midst of overwhelming evidence that death is the end. Courage is the belief that death is not the end. How do we combat the psychological deaths that are afflicting marginalized and oppressed people all over the world?

C: I believe the resurrected Jesus is the fullness of love. Jesus shows us that when we die to love we are transformed into love. Love is the only power of resurrection. In resurrection, love is the balm for the afflicted. We must learn to practice resurrection. It is only after we have died to love that we can we fully love. In dying to love...privileges fade, identities dissolve and fear departs. We are empowered to live into the queerest of our being and repair the world in the process. What does it look like to die to love?

J: I don't know that one can die to love. God is love. Love created us and it is love that sustains us. Love is always with us. We must die to the evil within us and live more fully into the love that will never leave us nor forsake us. How do you die to the evil within?

C: I have committed to loving each piece of who I am. In a world that tells me black isn't enough, I embrace my heritage. When the world says Queer is an abomination, I celebrate the ways I love and who I love. I purge the evil and allow love to fully live within me. How does love renew you?

J: Love calls all of us to perpetual resurrection.

Amen.

July 22, 2015

Healing: A Visit and Conversation with the Rev. Dr. Garth Baker-Fletcher

* This interaction is derived from a recent conversation that I had with the Rev. Dr. Garth Baker-Fletcher at a rehabilitation facility where he is recovering from hip surgery. A retired professor, Baker-Fletcher is the author of *Somebodyness: Martin Luther King, Jr. and the Theory of Dignity* (1993), *Xodus: An African-American Male Journey* (1996), *My Sister, My Brother* (with his wife Karen) (1997), *Black Religion After the Million Man March* (1998), *Dirty Hands: Christian Ethics in a Morally*

Ambiguous World (2000) & *Bible Witness in Black Churches* (2009). A cherished friend, I affectionately call him Brother Garth.

J: What do you think about the healings that Jesus performed?

G: I struggle with the fact that ideas of punishment/evil and disability are so closely connected in the stories of Jesus. I choose to believe that this was a problem with the authors and not the actors. Our ideas of disability are always connected to healing and this is a major problem. Most often in churches, I think we use disabled persons for our own benefit.

J: I call it disability pornography. We roll disabled persons in so that everyone will feel good based on their presence. Then, when disabled persons start to stretch us...we roll them out or claim that we don't have the means to accommodate them. I find it horrific.

G: Have you ever thought of sitting with disability as a means of sustenance?

J: I have. I believe that disabled persons bring a higher level of spirituality to church spaces. I think we need to stop trying to heal disabled persons who walk through the door and realize that we are the ones who are healed by their presence.

G: We are called to a higher level of being. Jesus is healing people to make them clean. You have to remember that this was a time when you couldn't even go into the Temple without being healed.

J: I would argue that the ideas of cleanliness are part of the problem. We are dirty. There is no space on earth that is clean. Ideas of healing make a claim at perfection that I feel is highly problematic. We need to quit trying to normatize everything and become comfortable with that which is queer.

G: We have to think about eschatology. The disabled are going to be in heaven. God is going to judge us for how we have treated these folks.

J: The queer always judges the normative and transforms it. We have to transform our thinking about who or what God is. I think there will be wheelchairs in heaven. Maybe God will even inhabit one. Who knows? Maybe God is blind. Maybe God is lame. I often think it is our ideas of ability that are the real disability.

G: I think we will all be healed. I think the lame will walk. I think the blind will see. I don't think the wheelchairs will be there. With that said, I think we will still have the wounds. Remember, Jesus still hand the wounds when Thomas wanted to put his hands in there.

J: I think our culture is like Thomas. We are looking at persons with disabilities unsure of what to do and we cannot be made whole until we are willing (or even invited) to place our hands in the wounds. Disabled persons bring to us the incarnated Christ.

G: Yet...we are the ones still doubting whether disabled persons can be resurrected. We want them to prove that they have been healed. The truth is standing in front of us.

J: I think that God is permanently disabled. God is blinded or restricted by love. I think this is what makes us call such an entity God. I don't want God to be healed of such blindness or restriction.

G: God is with us. God feels. God experiences. God is disabled because we are disabled. God doesn't need to be healed.

J: We are the ones who need to be healed from our false dichotomies. I feel like ability is an illusion. Nobody is abled. Despite the links to which our culture goes to deny death, everyone is dying or afflicted by death. Why do we feel the need to categorize ability and disability?

G: We are addicted to normatizing and shunning anything that is different.

J: We need to be healed.

G: That's where God comes in.

Amen.

July 23, 2015

Speak Their Names!

I struggled to garner the courage to write this piece. I am a part of a progressive world that teaches people to stay in their place or face the consequences. The difficulty of such constructions is that there are times when we all need to speak. I am a follower of Jesus and that means I am called to stand with the oppressed and marginalized irrespective of their identity.

For the last week, I have been immersed and emotionally distraught in the cause of Sandra Bland. I wept when I saw the arrest video. In the pit of my gut, I knew racism murdered her. At a rally last week, I reminded the gathered of the words of Jesus, "I was in prison and you didn't visit me." I wondered aloud, "Who was there to save Sandra from these racists? Who was there to visit her?" I asked the crowd to make a covenant to never be silent or inactive in the face of oppression. Tonight, I laid in my bed pondering those words.

There is not a day that goes by that I don't think about the haunting last words of Eric Garner, "I can't breathe." I am reminded when God tells Ezekiel, "Prophesy to the breathe." I have sought to do my best. Tonight, I heard those haunting words again. This time they came from the mouth of a white man. After attending a concert with his wife in North Mississippi, Troy Goode was acting erratically. Someone called the police. When officers showed up, an unarmed Goode ran. Upon apprehension, Goode was hogtied and placed face down on a stretcher. No one cared to listen to the last words that Goode said on this earth, "I can't breathe."

We live in a police state. While I have no question that the aggression exhibited by officers all over the country overwhelmingly affects persons of color, I also know that no one is safe. A father of an infant son, Goode was murdered in one of the most racist states in our county. We are going to choose to believe that we are in this struggle against evil together or there will continue to be victims. The evil of police brutality will not stop until it comes face to face with the overwhelming power of love united. We have a choice. Do we say the name of a white man murdered by the police? I think so and I believe our future depends on it.

Jesus said that his person would be with the "least of these." I know that Jesus was on that stretcher as Troy Goode choked to death and in that cell as Sandra Bland did the same. Will we say their names?

Amen.

July 23, 2015

The Intern Monologues: Injustice

J: What is injustice?

C: Injustice is oppression. Oppression is violence created to keep us in isolation from each other. Injustice hinders us from living into the beloved community where all have the opportunity to be in their fullness. What do you think?

J: Injustice is the incorrect ordering of God's creation. Where does injustice come from?

C: Injustice stems from the belief in scarcity. Scarcity is the belief that the beloved community will never fully welcome us in. In scarcity, fear is born. We fear that our story won't matter; we fear that we will be made extinct. We cling to life tightly; any other narrative threatens our wellness and personhood. Injustice is created in the fight to hold tightly to our narratives in a world of abundant diversity. Where does injustice come from?

J: Our failure to love. How does injustice manifest?

C: When we hold an ideology of liberation for us and not for them, this is injustice. When narratives of oppression are filtered only through our lens...that is injustice. We see its destruction all around us. From the occupation in Palestine to police brutality to a booming prison industrial complex to a failing educational system, it is everywhere. We must understand that injustice crosses our constructed boxes. Injustice is a human condition. What is justice?

J: Loving your neighbor as you love yourself. What do you think?

C: Creating enough room for love to flourish in its varied richness. What do we do with injustice?

J: We fight it. We place our bodies between the marginalizer and marginalized, the oppressor and the oppressed. We have to give our bodies to the struggle. Jesus showed us what love looks like in action.

Amen.

July 27, 2015

The Juxtaposition of Our Borders: A Queer Conversation on the Way to Immersion

*This is a conversation that took place on July 27, 2015 between Kristin Kelly (Educator), Christian Parks (Intern) and I on our journey to an immersion experience on the US/Mexico border focused on queer theology.

J: Who is God at the juxtaposition of our borders?

K: God is borderless. God is the immigrant coming to find new possibilities. God is embodied in the struggle of the journey. God dies with those who don't make it. God never denies wellness, opportunity and hope. How is an immigrant supposed to view God in the midst of consistent denial of access to our religious bodies?

C: Those who place their bodies on the line for freedom find God in more abundant ways. Those who create boundaries to the love of God forget God's abundant grace. There is much to be learned from the God of immigrants. What does Jesus teach us about immigrants?

J: I think the better question is what does Jesus not teach us. Sometimes I feel like the teachings of Jesus are used to glorify the suffering of the immigrant at the expense of the liberation of the immigrant. Our collective salvation depends on our willingness to cross borders and struggle together. Why do we feel we need maintain borders?

C: Our fear of the other consumes us. We are afraid of losing our comforts and our normality. Each border is a manifestation of our ideas of preservation. Why do you think we maintain our borders?

K: Borders allows us to maintain the space of normality and comfort. They also keep us separated from the other and allow us to dodge the complexities of difference. Our borders uphold our constructed statuses of power, politics and religion. Ultimately, we fear losing control. What's the role of the church in our current immigration crisis?

J: We have got to get rid of all this patriotic bullshit. When I walk into a church and see a US flag, I see that congregation lifting their arm slowly, extending their middle finger and saying "fuck you" to the borderless God. If our churches cannot be a sanctuary for all of God's children...then our churches have nothing to do with Jesus. What is the connection between our national borders and our racial borders?

K: Both borders are invisible structures of power created by fear and deeply embedded notions of supremacy. We need to talk about both borders separately and collectively as they create a system that honors some lives over others. The connection is the lost of lives. Should there be borders?

C: If we believe in a God beyond our imagination, borders should never exist. If we believe in a God of love, then all should have access to opportunity, resources and hope. Borders hinder our ability to love others and ourselves.

J: Now, if we can only get people to realize that you can't follow Jesus from behind the borders of our constructed closets.

Amen.

July 27, 2015

The God Beyond Borders: A Prayer at the Start of a Queer Immersion

* A prayer at the beginning of an immersion on the border of the United States and Mexico.

You are God. You are Dios. You are Allah. You are Jah. You are Adonai. You are the queerest of them all. You are the God beyond our borders. You are the God beyond God. You choose to join us here. You choose to be the God who is with us. You leave your family to seek a better life. You defy the laws of the lawless. You walk across borders. You die in the desert. You sit in detention. You are deported. You cross the border over and over. You are already here... You push through all boundaries to bind the cosmos together. No closets will survive your movement. You kick down the doors. No injustice will survive your movement. You set everything to right. No hate will survive your movement. You set all to love. Oh God beyond God...meet us here and make us queer. Amen.

July 27, 2015

Jesus' Flight from Peru

*This is a story used with permission and based on the experiences of an undocumented immigrant.

Jesus said, "I was a stranger and you didn't welcome me in..."

Unable to care for him, Jesus' parents left. What is a child to do with no parents? For a few years, Jesus found refuge with his grandparents. When they found out he was gay, their kindness ran out. Jesus went to the busiest street he could find and started to beg. Living in Lima's trash, he refused to die. Unsure who to tell about his sexuality, Jesus kept quiet.

The lady that offered him work and a place to stay saved his life. The dream slowly turned into a nightmare. When people started to find out that he was gay, Jesus was confronted with extreme persecution. Trying to go to school, he had to dodge the gangs who sought to eradicate all gays in Lima. After he got stabbed, Jesus got tossed out of his house. The lady felt like it was no longer safe for him to be there. Running out of options and only able to afford a small place, Jesus knew he had to flee. Before he could, the beatings turned into a daily occurrence. With his life in danger, Jesus prayed for God to save him. When he finally saved the money to get out, Jesus thought the United States would offer him safety.

Flying to Hermosillo, Jesus worked his way up to the border. The gangs and cartels tormented him the entire time. When he paid someone to take him across, he was put into a holding house along the border with no food or water for six days. With a gun pointed at his face, Jesus was forced to do things that he didn't want to do. As much as it hurt, he was more hurt by the things the children were forced to do. When he was moved to a holding house closer to the border, he could barely stand. Finally, the group was given a little bit of water and told to walk across the border. It wasn't long before the Border Patrol picked Jesus up. The pain only increased.

Having traveled thousands of miles for the right to love freely, Jesus was placed into a cold and lonely detention facility in Arizona. Depressed and feeling abandoned by God, Jesus prayed for help. Targeted for being gay, he could get no relief. At 22,

Jesus couldn't figure out how he ended up in this nightmare. It was tough to apply for asylum, Jesus cried out for help. The judge is known as tough on all people...especially LGBT persons. Will he be sent back to torture and maybe even death? Hitting his knees, Jesus prayed with all the strength he could muster, "Save this nation from the greed of its borders."

Jesus is named Rudy.

Amen.

July 28, 2015

Jesus Tore Shit Up

Traveling on the campus of the University of Cincinnati, Samuel Dubose saw the lights flashing behind him and pulled over. After numerous encounters with police, Dubose was trying to avert more trouble. When Officer Ray Tensing approached the car, Dubose handed him an open container of alcohol. The situation escalated into a physical altercation. When Dubose took his foot off the brake during the struggle, the car began to roll. Officer Tensing was knocked to the ground and fired the shot that killed Dubose. Throughout the encounter, Dubose was unarmed.

Though the body camera video of the incident has yet to be released, Chief Jeffrey Blackwell of the Cincinnati Police Department described it as, "...not good." Cincinnati City Manager Harry Black went even further, "...it's not a good situation...Someone has died that didn't necessarily need to die and I'll leave it at that." In numerous statements, officials have expressed fear about the release of the video and appealed for calm when it is finally released. Despite the fears, Dubose family attorney, Mark O'Mara, has called for the immediate release of the footage. If officials are already expressing fear of unrest before the video is released, one can safely assume the scenes are devastating.

Evil is perpetuated when people remain calm and do nothing. Faced with the glaring injustices of his day, Jesus rioted in the Temple. For those Christians addicted to order at the expense of justice, you are complicit in the ongoing slaughter. Overturning the tables, pushing out the oppressors and unleashing destruction, Jesus refused to allow the weapons of marginalization to operate any further. Christians allow them to continue uninterrupted. I am disgusted by the presentation of Jesus as an accomplice to the ongoing injustices of our day. Upon encountering injustice, followers of Jesus must love their neighbors by destroying the weapons of marginalization. In a nation as evil as ours, calm is a means of further oppression. When the video finally comes out, I want to remind everyone that Jesus tore shit up.

Amen.

July 28, 2015

Our Borders Can't Shutdown Communion

The terrain looked fuzzy. Heat has a way of altering our perceptions. The wall was enormous. The square poles made of scrap steel filled with concrete were placed one after the other for miles and miles. The dust grew thicker. People on the other side waved. The ropes used by migrants to scale the wall flowed in the breeze. Shoes littered the landscape. Roadrunners and jackrabbits ran freely back and forth through the barrier. The border between the United States and Mexico is a spiritual place.

Borders are always a product of evil. Anyone with a rudimentary knowledge of the message of Jesus or even basic goodwill can figure this out. You can't love your neighbor and put up a wall to protect your shit. You can't love yourself and wall yourself into a closet for perceived protection. The point of traveling out to the desert was not to speak against the evil of borders. One doesn't have to travel to Douglas, Arizona to do what they can do at home. The point was to commune with the dry bones.

I fell twice on the way up. The view was so stunning that I couldn't concentrate on the next step. The breeze mitigated the heat slightly. Looking out into the vastness of the desert, I thought about all of the bones of the migrants. I put on a dirty white robe. The same robe that I wore during my arrest protesting deportations at the White House last summer. I put on the colorful stole. The same stole made for me by a Guatemalan woman who lost family in this exact desert. I took out the bread and wine. I could feel them. The prayers grew stronger. I knew they were there. This is the body and blood of Jesus Christ and all of the migrants who died in this desert. In that moment, I knew our communion extended beyond the borders of time and space. We stood in communion with our friends on the other side remembering the lives lost seeking a better life. We stood in communion with the bones of migrants that filled miles and miles of desert.

Can these bones live?

They never died.

Amen.

July 29, 2015

Borderless: A Conversation on the Return Home from a Queer Immersion

*This is a conversation that took place on July 30, 2015 between Kristin Kelly, Christian Parks and I on our return home from an immersion experience on the US/Mexico border focused on queer theology.

K: How has your perspective of God changed?

J: Sitting on the hill overlooking the border, I saw people on the other side. Sometimes I had the chance to wave, sometimes I had the chance to make eye contact and once I had the chance to say hello. Those brief glimpses of the other side reminded me of the brief glimpses we get of God. I believe the incarnation of Jesus is in the oppressed and marginalized. On that hill...as I raised the bread and the cup...I knew that I was communing with those who mourned their loved ones on the other side of the wall. I knew that I was communing with the bones of migrants scattered throughout the desert. In such communion, I felt the majesty of God. I got to see a glimpse of the beloved community. So Christian, where do you feel that God is on the border?

C: While on a hike through the desert, I was visited by a butterfly. It was then I was reminded that God is the God of the journey. God travels with, gets dehydrated with, loses shoes with, gets caught in the rain with and even dies with each person on the journey. Kristin, where did you find God?

K: I found God while standing on a hilltop taking in the elements with a Latino, a Latina, White brothers and African-American brother. I recognized in that moment...as we broke bread and drank of the cup...that we do these things in remembrance not only of Christ...but also of every individual who takes the confusing and fearful journey crossing the border into the unknown. When we shouted, "Jesús Cristo, Presente!"...we were not only presenting Christ but also all those who have been lost. How has your perspective of borders changed?

J: I think the way that we perceive the borders of our identities is intimately connected to our national border. Borders of identity and nationality are inherently selfish and exist to shut others out. This trip has renewed in me a ferocious desire to cling to the God beyond borders. Christian, how do the problems of the borders in your own life help you to understand the problem with the national borders?

C: Constructed walls are a form of violence on my potential and ability to grow. I have found that our national borders constrict our nation's ability to evolve and progress. Borders stunt growth. In our restricted growth we never are able to see the fullness of God. Kristin, what potential is lost in your life and in our nation with our borders?

K: When we construct walls in our lives we are creating ways to keep people out. I have found in my own life that walls are constructed because of fear - fear of hurt and an ultimate fear of loss. Creating a wall between nations stunts the potential of building relationship. In losing that potential we encourage fear of otherness and we take away hope. Jeff, how do we deconstruct our borders?

J: We transcend them in our personal lives, we prophesy to that transcendence in our public lives and we don't let anybody turn us around. Borders keep us from God, our neighbor and our persons. We must refuse to allow the closet of borders to go unchecked. How do you plan on deconstructing the borders in your own life?

C: Learning to love myself, learning to love God and learning to love my neighbor. In love, our borders dissolve. In courage, our borders are dismantled. In queerness, our borders don't matter. How will you deconstruct your borders?

K: I plan to seek to embrace the divinity, not only in myself, but in each and every person I encounter. Deconstruction is a political, spiritual and even a physical act that calls me to be in full communion with God's creation. In order to deconstruct, I must first fully acknowledge and celebrate all that come to the table.

J: We give thanks for the Queer, the one and only borderless God.

Amen.

July 31, 2015

The Revelation in the Desert

When I was a child, I never thought my parents would leave me. I always felt God would. Fundamentalism and hopelessness are irreparably fused together. When I stumbled upon piles of clothes in our house, I knew for sure that God took my parents and left me. On multiple occasions, I wept.

We started the hike behind a house. The desert is treacherous. Over and over, I felt the thorns press into my flesh. Pushing through, I was amazed at how disorienting the terrain grew. I had to pull out my phone multiple times just to see which direction we were going. Less than a mile in, we stumbled upon something left behind. The first backpack we encountered was black, muddy and torn to shreds. The pack once carried the hopes and dreams of a migrant. Were they able to unpack it before they left?

The mud got between my toes. I constantly looked out for snakes. I couldn't imagine doing this journey in the dark. The pile of clothes sent me spiraling. Why was there this pile of clothes in the middle of the desert? Migrants believe that changing into nicer clothes will make them look less suspicious when they enter the city. A group of about ten changed and left these clothes behind. What happened to them after they changed?

I noticed a black item in the bushes. In order to reduce detection from the air, water bottles are painted black. Did someone take a last drink from this container?

The three crosses stood out. Items of remembrance encircled them. What were the last words the family said to each other? How could an entire family die this close to a house? Our greed killed them. How could we be so heartless?

The revelation hit me.

Jesus came in the form of these migrants.

We let love die in the desert.

We left God behind.

Amen.

August 1, 2015

I Believe in Thou.

Thou found me.
I didn't know you were looking.
Thou knew me.
I didn't know I could be known.
Thou pulled me.
I didn't know where to go.
Thou lifted me.

I didn't know that I was down.
Thou transformed me.
I didn't know I could change.
Thou loved me.
I didn't know I could be loved.
Thou held me.
I didn't know I could be held.
I & Thou.
Thou knew.
I didn't.
I do now.
I believe in Thou.

August 1, 2015

Joseph Sheldon Hutcheson Dies in the Custody of the Dallas Sheriff

Desperate for help, Joseph Sheldon Hutcheson parked his truck on the curb of the Lew Sterrett Justice Center in Dallas and ran inside. Upon entering, Hutcheson screamed, "Don't hurt me, I just need some help." The deputies tackled him. As Hutcheson screamed that he couldn't breathe, a witness described one deputy restraining Hutcheson with "a knee on *his* back" and another deputy restraining him "with a knee on *his* throat." Hutcheson's face turned from white to blue. Around 11:30am, Joseph Sheldon Hutcheson was pronounced dead. Of course, authorities responded to the tragedy by releasing Hutcheson's criminal background and speculation that they could see narcotics in his truck. Unfortunately the Dallas County Sheriff's Department forgot to answer one question... How does someone rush into a jail asking for help and end up being killed?

http://thescoopblog.dallasnews.com/2015/08/authorities-investigating-after-47-year-old-loses-consciousness-in-dallas-county-jail-lobby-dies.html/
August 4, 2015

Protect and Serve the Badge: The Dallas Sheriff's Department Lied

Desperate for help, Joseph Sheldon Hutcheson parked his truck on the curb of the Lew Sterrett Justice Center in Dallas and ran inside. Upon entering, Hutcheson screamed, "Don't hurt me, I just need some help." The deputies tackled him. As Hutcheson screamed that he couldn't breathe, a witness described one deputy restraining Hutcheson with "a knee on his back" and another deputy restraining him "with a knee on his throat." Hutcheson's face turned from white to blue. Around 11:30am, Joseph Sheldon Hutcheson was pronounced dead.

Immediately after these tragic events, the Dallas County Sheriff's Department released speculation that they could see drugs in Joseph Hutcheson's truck. Late yesterday, the Department admitted that there were no drugs. Over and over again throughout our nation, the police have killed someone and slandered their character by releasing their criminal background. On this occasion, the Sheriff's Department went further...they released slanderous speculation. Let's make something very clear, in the case of Joseph Hutcheson...we now know the Dallas County Sheriff's Department lied. Does the Department believe that they only exist to protect and serve the badge?

Let us all pray for an end to police brutality.

Amen.

Before

Drugs in Truck

http://thescoopblog.dallasnews.com/2015/08/authorities-investigating-after-47-year-old-loses-consciousness-in-dallas-county-jail-lobby-dies.html/

After

No Drugs in Truck

http://crimeblog.dallasnews.com/2015/08/dallas-sheriff-seeking-witnesses-in-jail-lobby-death-says-no-drugs-found-in-mans-car.html/

August 5, 2015

A Letter to Chairman Coleman on the Brutality of the Sheriff's Department in Dallas County

To the Honorable Garnet Coleman,

On August 1, 2015 around 10am, Joseph Hutcheson parked his truck on the curb at the Lew Sterrett Justice Center in Dallas County and hysterically ran inside. Upon entering, Hutcheson screamed, "Don't hurt me, I just need some help." The deputies tackled him. According to the *Dallas Morning* News, as Hutcheson screamed that he couldn't breathe, a witness described one deputy restraining Hutcheson with "a knee on his back" and another deputy restraining him "with a knee on his throat." Hutcheson's face turned from white to blue. Around 11:31am, Joseph Hutcheson was pronounced dead. To add insult to injury, authorities responded to public concern about the tragedy by releasing Hutcheson's criminal background and speculating that they could see narcotics in his truck.

We represent very different groups of Texans. Hope for Peace & Justice is a historically LGBTQ organization. The Next Generation Action Network is a historically black organization. We have chosen to stand together out of concern for the injustice that took place last week in Dallas County. How does someone rush into a jail asking for help and end up being killed? We write to you to ask this question because we do not have anyone else to turn to. We do not trust any of the authorities in Dallas County to answer this question honestly. In your power as a State Representative and Chairman of the Committee on County Affairs in the Texas Legislature, we are asking you to conduct a public hearing on police brutality here in Dallas. We want answers as to what happened to Joseph Hutcheson and many others who have fallen victim to overzealous policing. Our communities are frightened of law enforcement and we appeal to you to help us make things right.

Sincerely,

The Rev. Dr. Jeff Hood
Interim Executive Director
Hope for Peace & Justice

Minister Dominique Alexander
President
Next Generation Action Network

August 7, 2015

The Intern Monologues: Last Things with a Spiritual Son

*This is the last intentional conversation of Christian Parks' summer internship.

J: Christian, you have become a spiritual son to me this summer. In the words of Ruth, "Do not ask me to leave you..." I am so very thankful for our three months together. A deep abiding love has bubbled up. What are the last things you want to discuss on our drive to the airport?

C: First of all, I feel the same way. Thank you so much for your love. Over the last day, I have pondered what it means to live into your teaching that I am enough. What does it mean to be enough? I feel like I have learned that the love and energy within me is enough. As I leave, I am constantly reflecting on how to be enough. I need to be queerer. I know that is the only way to live enough. In queerness, I know that everything will be alright.

J: Define enough.

C: Enough is to simply be.

J: Define being.

C: Being is living into the spectrum and my unique spot on it. Being is believing that my spot is enough. I blur the categories in my own person. In all queerness, Jesus shows us how to do this.

J: Jesus shows us that one does not arrive at queerness without death. The Canaanite woman helped Jesus kill his racism and grow queerer. In dying on the cross, Jesus shows us queerness is about loving to the end and beyond. Loving your neighbor as yourself is the great path of queer death and resurrection. Being cannot happen without death. Death cannot happen without resurrection. Queerness survives death and blossoms in the resurrection. When I met you...I met you in a period of death. Eastern Mennonite had just killed your play. I felt like you were looking for a resurrection. I hope you found it.

C: I did and more. We can only resurrect others when we have been resurrected. I learned in the words of Ezekiel, how to "prophesy to the breathe." I learned how to call forth life. Death is dead for me. I now have a courageous and reconstructed faith. I am on the way of the queer. The path you have shown me will sustain me for the rest of my life.

J: I want you to remember that normativity has taken over all spaces. We must expect both the oppressed and the oppressor to have addictions to normative constructions of power and hate. There is no identity that speaks for justice. Only queerness can do that. The normative ideas of fitting in and pushing contrary persons out has to die in order for justice to be a possibility. God is calling us to make all things new...to make all things queer. We can't do that with the constructed identities we currently have.

C: We must beware of the suicide of identity. We can't fall into the trap of thinking that our identities are enough. We are enough and that is so much bigger than the limited nature of our identities. You have taught me how to live queerer. Thank you so much.

J: Thank you my son.

Amen.

August 7, 2015

Only the Queer Heals

I couldn't believe how green the grass was. With each step, I felt like I was touching air. The water spoke. The closer I got, the more I realized that I could see aquatic life for miles. The clearness was unimaginable. I swam. With each stroke, I knew that I was beloved. I reached the rocks and climbed. When I got to the top, I was overwhelmed with the beauty of it all. I didn't hesitate. I jumped.

Before I hit the water, an eternity passed. Time was no more. I simply was.

Somehow, I left the water and flew into the sky. The experience was more real than anything I ever experienced. I could see billions and billions of unique people living in love and justice. The tears of joy started to flow. I never thought such a thing could happen again. I didn't want to open my eyes. When I did, I knew where I had been...Eden.

Humans are afflicted with a chronic illness. We are homesick. Together, we spend every hour yearning for what was. It is in our genetic composition. We have untapped memories. If we are ever to be healed, we must find a way back...back to our future.

The God beyond god cannot be contained by normative constructions. God is the great blurrer of all of our categories. Who can describe love beyond love? How do you describe the sexuality of a God who created and is within all sexualities? Who can describe justice beyond justice? How do you describe the body of a God who creates and is within all bodies? Who can describe mercy beyond mercy? How do you describe the gender of a God who creates and is within all genders? These questions combine with many left unasked to illustrate the fascinating vastness and beauty of God. In simply being, God is queer.

What happened to God's image?

Queerness was in limitless supply. Categories were unfathomable. The people simply were. With each day, God was there. The electricity that flowed through each person created life beyond life. With the knowledge that I could never do it justice, I hesitate to even describe it any further. Imagine a world where everyone was the very image of God. They were a queer people able to live into all queerness. There was no need for healing. No one was sick.

Can you imagine the queer sex that was shared in Eden? Passion existed in absolute perfection. Can you imagine the food and wine? The table was always open. Can you imagine the joy? There was no scarcity. All was as it should be. People loved in unfathomable ways. Everything was queer.

Then, the normative became an option.

The day was the darkest ever known.

The people awoke with love and purpose. The sounds were a symphonic melody. Walking around in their imaginations, the people approached the great tree. There was something different about the fruit. They couldn't figure out what it was. God warned them.

The sound of a snake didn't startle them. How could it? Everyone and everything loved each other. When the snake spoke, the people listened. "Do you want a bite?" The people didn't know how to respond. "God is afraid that you will be all powerful." Unable to comprehend the danger of normativity, the people wondered. Everything changed with one bite.

Categories rushed in. The people sickened. Being was fleeting. Pain was unbelievable. Why would God put something in Eden to harm them? They never knew why. Embarrassed of their lack of queerness, the people fled. We have been sick with normativity ever since. What happened? We may never know. The only thing we know is that we have to get back.

Queerness is the way, the truth and the life.

God didn't know how in the hell it went down like it did. One second everyone was enjoying each other in Eden and the next second everyone was running out with their leaves on fire. Regardless of the cause, God knew the result. Normativity took over the planet. Humans were relegated to a life filled with categories. For many moons, God tried to get people to understand that queerness was the only path back. One cannot expect to be right relationship with the universe when they are not living into the image of God that they were created to be. War raged within and without. Most people didn't know if they were going to kill themselves or their neighbor first. The twin sicknesses of violence and hate were amongst the most normative constructions that developed. Deeply pained and realizing that humanity needed a path to healing, God prepared a rescue mission. At exactly the right moment, queerness exploded onto the earth once more.

The queerest of them all hit the hay covered in blood and amniotic fluid. While it was obvious that most of the people there didn't realize the magnitude of what they were witnessing, the random poor shepherds covered in sheep shit might have offered them a clue. This child would grow to push us beyond all of our categories to that most holy space of queer. Though he was God, the child grew and struggled with normativity just like anyone else. Suffering from the normative sickness of being human, Jesus needed healing too. The categories were just too powerful.

Jesus was a racist. The Canaanite woman cried out for help. Her daughter was afflicted with a demon and needed healing from God. Instead of help, Jesus declared that he was here for Israel only and called her a dog. There ain't a damn thing queer about racism. In this moment, Jesus was just like every other normative bigot. Refusing to let him go without a healing, the woman questioned his racism and challenged him to be better. This woman was not even supposed to be speaking to Jesus and she had the audacity to queerly tell it like it is. At that very second she spoke, a miracle happened...Jesus was healed from his racism and he healed her daughter. One has to first realize they are sick before they can heal. This queer woman boldly dared to heal Jesus of his racism. Only the queer could heal Jesus.

There once was a woman whose queerness was destroyed early and almost entirely. Throughout her life, she sought healing. From counseling to spiritual discernment to relationships to supplements, she tried it all. On a whim, she married a man who had been interested in her for a long time. "Maybe I might find healing in the security of marriage," she thought. Thinking that she would never marry, her parents were thrilled. Before long, her husband started to abuse her physically and emotionally. She was in unbearable pain. At the market one day, a man caught her eye. She couldn't shake the thought of him and fell in love. Praying for forgiveness, she responded to a note he passed her. Before long, the two were involved in an affair. Love was all they knew.

When her husband found out, rage overwhelmed him. Immediately, he went to his local Rabbi and demanded the punishment prescribed by law. The Pharisees realized that this was the opportunity they needed to show their strength as the keepers of normativity. For a week, the Pharisees spied on the woman and the man she was having an affair with. After watching the live pornography for a few minutes, the Pharisees stormed in. Ordering the man not to tell anyone, the men grabbed the woman and drug her through the street. The entire time, the woman kept feeling like her first chance at real love was going to be what ultimately killed her. "If only I had just been normative and done what I was supposed to do like everyone else..." she thought. When she was slung at the feet of Jesus and the Pharisees raised their rocks, she knew she was going to die.

If Jesus had not met a queer Canaanite woman a few months prior, he wouldn't have been ready for this situation. Dust rose from the ground. Breathing was heavy. Hate was winning. The woman caught in adultery begged him for help. Looking down, Jesus knew that the only way to help was to cross a boundary. When he looked up at the Pharisees, Jesus looked deeply into their eyes and lowered his body further into the dirt. Nothing needed to be said, everyone knew that Jesus was placing his body into the conversation. In placing his person between the rocks and the woman, Jesus showed how the queer heals...by offering the body for the sake of justice. The Canaanite prepared Jesus to place his body in the dirt with an adulterous woman by drawing him into the plight of the oppressed and marginalized. The queer heals through incarnational body exchanges and so must we.

"Love you neighbor as yourself." Have you ever considered what a queer concept love is? The wellness of your neighbor is dependent on your ability to love yourself. You have to understand yourself as a queer human being made in the image of a queer God before you can heal. Normativity cannot be banished without blurring the categories and lines of what is. Jesus had to learn to be different in order to make a difference. When Jesus was talking to the Canaanite woman, he was just as racist as everyone else. The Canaanite decided to love her neighbor as herself and pull Jesus out of his racism to a place of love. When Jesus met the adulterous woman, he was ready to pull her out of the normative oppression of the Pharisees that she was facing. By getting down in the dirt, Jesus declared that the normative force of hate had no power in the face of love. Difference makes a difference. Queerness makes thing queer. To be like God is to give your body to healing...there is nothing queerer.

"Is there any other way?" Jesus knew there was not. The only way to be queer is to give your body for the healing of others. Regardless of the pain, Jesus was prepared. The Canaanite and adulterous woman made sure of it. You have to present your body as a roadblock to racism. You have to give your body to save others. You have to be queer in order to heal. When Jesus was lifted high up on that cross, I know that he thought about the two women who made him God. Looking out into the distance, he must have remembered how the Canaanite taught him to love everyone. As the blood dropped into his eyes, the woman caught in adultery must have spoken to him about how he saved her. Before him, the gathered represented the normatizers that we all are. In giving his body, Jesus wanted to set us all free. To love queerly is to give the body. In immense pain, Jesus cried out, "Forgive them for they know not what they do!" We fail to understand the consequences of our normativity. In the greatest healing moment of all time, Jesus was most fully queer and therefore most fully God. We know the way back.

Queer love is the most powerful healer of all. We are called to be the healed healers that we were created to be. In giving his body, Jesus loved queerly. We are called to go and do likewise. The path back to queerness is to love the self enough to give the self away. Imprints of Eden are within us. Search deeply. We have to first be healed of all the categories that hold us back and then place our bodies on the line for the liberation of others. There is queerness within us. We once walked without categories. We were free. Do your remember? Let us return. In the face of the devastating categories that afflict us, God is calling us to grow queerer...for only the queer heals.

Amen.

August 10, 2015

The Indictment of the Institutional Church

"Can you imagine Jesus sitting on his ass while people are gunned down in the street? Why do we? Cowardice is the highest level of evil and it exists in abundance in the institutional church. By doing nothing as bodies drop, the institutional church might as well be firing the guns. We will either stand with Jesus in the streets or continue to have the blood of the brutalized dripping from our crosses."

August 10, 2015

Christian Did Not Die in Vain

"I don't struggle to understand where God is when unarmed bodies keep hitting the pavement. I know that God stands with the brutalized. The case of Christian Taylor is a reminder of where God is not. God condemns the brutalizers. We are here to be a voice of judgment. We are here to declare that Christian should not be dead. We are here to declare that the Arlington Police Department has a murderer in their midst. We are here to declare that we will not stop until there is justice. Stand strong. We will win...for God is on our side. Christian did not die in vain. We are going to make damn sure of that. Amen."

August 11, 2015

The Brutality We Ignore

Under the auspices of enforcing the law, they came to the door. Grabbing the unarmed man, they forced him down the hallway. With every step, the man pleaded for his life. Opening the door, they forced him down. After multiple shots, they declared, "We feared for our lives and had to kill him." The highest form of brutality is to kill a defenseless individual. In the next two days, Texas will do it twice. As our nation burns with anger over police brutality, why there is not similar outrage over executions?

With little fanfare or attention, racial minorities, poor people and the mentally ill are legally killed in disproportionate numbers. In many cases, there are big questions as to guilt or innocence. Each time, we are told that these persons should cause us to fear for our lives. The language and consequences of killing unarmed people are similar no matter the location.

When will we stand against all brutality? Over the next two days, Daniel Lopez and Tracy Beatty will be executed in Texas. Will we care? The integrity of our battle against police brutality depends on it.

Amen.

August 15, 2015

We Forgot Ms. Shade.

Less than a hundred feet from residences, local authorities discovered the badly decomposed body of a transgender woman of color. The Dallas Police Department put out a detailed description of the body and asked for help. For two weeks, no one seemed to know who this woman was. When the woman was finally identified as 22-year-old Shade Schuler, I realized that she belonged to no one...she was amongst the forgotten.

In the twilight, the heat was excruciating. With every breath, I sweated through my shirt. The jokes of children filled the air. I laughed too. When we stepped onto the hidden gravel road, things got real. I knew we were on holy ground. No one spoke much. Everyone just seemed to be concentrating on the next step. The smell lingered. The heat didn't stop. I worried that the bread and chalice would slip out of my hands. The screech startled me. Perhaps, the bird was warning us that we were nearing the point of no return. I assumed it was an old fire pit. When I saw the black spot was in the shape of a body, I knew better.

The presence of God was unmistakable. When Carmarion Anderson and I lifted up the elements to the heavens, there was electricity flowing in the air. We remembered the oppression she faced in life. We remembered her murder. In the transcendence of the moment, we knew that she never died. "This is the body and blood of Ms. Shade." Bending down to touch the spot, everything stopped and Jesus whispered softly in my ear, "What you have done to the least of these you have done to me..." I believed the words as much as I ever had.

The forgotten are not forgotten. They are simply forgotten by us. Our job is not to remember them. Our job is to stand with them. God will do the rest.

Who stood with Ms. Shade when she was alive?

Who stands with her now?

Amen.

August 16, 2015

Joseph Hutcheson and a Failure of Identity Politics

"Why???" The tearful words of James Hutcheson echoed loudly against the jail. Throughout last Friday's press conference, the events of August 1 kept running through my mind.

Desperate for help, Joseph Hutcheson parked his truck on the curb of the Lew Sterrett Justice Center in Dallas and ran inside. Upon entering, Hutcheson screamed, "Don't hurt me, I just need some help." The deputies tackled him. As Hutcheson screamed that he couldn't breathe, a witness described one deputy restraining Hutcheson with "a knee on his back" and another deputy restraining him "with a knee on his throat." Hutcheson's face turned from white to blue. Around 11:30am, Joseph Sheldon Hutcheson was pronounced dead.

How does someone ask for help and get a knee to the throat? Why would deputies attack someone who is unarmed? Why did the Sheriff's Department slander the character of someone they just killed? Why hasn't Sheriff Lupe Valdez reached out to the family? The questions were endless. In organizing the press conference, I wanted to make sure the voices of Joseph Hutcheson's family came through loud and clear.

"Why???" Through tears, family members pushed the primary question through over and over. During the press conference, the family revealed that authorities kept Joseph Hutcheson's neck organs after the autopsy, they had yet to be contacted by the Sheriff and numerous witnesses corroborated the claims that Hutcheson was a victim of police brutality. The cameras rolled as the truth spilled all over the pavement.

After viewing the news coverage, multiple people contacted me. Over and over, I was reminded of the harshest line I uttered at the press conference, "Sheriff Valdez either needs to work with the family of Joseph Hutcheson for justice or we need a new sheriff." In most police brutality cases, this type of language is standard. When the Sheriff is the first lesbian or Hispanic to hold the office, I guess we are supposed to sit back and allow the brutality of her department to go unchecked. I simply can't. My faith demands that I stand with the marginalized and oppressed regardless of their identity. When deputies give a fatal knee to the throat of a man asking for help, I can only call that what it is...evil.

Despite the calls to stop, I kept pushing. Joseph Hutcheson deserved all I could give. When the evening rally arrived, I worried that only a few people would show up. I started to realize that Joseph was already there. People started to come from every parking lot. When they assembled on the steps of the Frank Corley Courts Building, I had never seen this many white people at any police brutality action before. With every speech, the energy grew. By the time we started to march, everyone was chanting as loud as they could, "Joseph Hutcheson!" We paused where he parked his truck. We walked up the hill. We opened the doors to the lobby of the jail and walked in. Over and over we chanted, "Joseph Hutcheson! Joseph Hutcheson! Joseph Hutcheson!"

When deputies in riot gear came from around the corner, I knew the Sheriff's department just made Joseph Hutcheson the lead story on the evening news. I thought about thanking them. I guess I should have.

If I had listened to the purveyors of identity politics, two things would have never happened. First, all of the deputies involved in the death of Joseph Hutcheson were placed on restrictive duty. Second, the Sheriff released a statement extending her condolences to the family. What makes us think that a person's identity protects them from criticism when there is a body on the floor? We will either choose stand against police brutality in the many identities it comes or we will become purveyors of it.

While I am thankful for the overtures extended by Sheriff Lupe Valdez, I am ready for her to extend the tape the incident...so that we can help the authorities extend some indictments.

Amen.

August 19, 2015

Social Pain

J: Is pain redemptive?

G: Redemption means that you've been freed from your situation and made whole. Pain is a sort of liberation theology. We are made whole by pain.

J: Is it appropriate to hurt someone in order to bring about wholeness?

G: Of course not! How can anyone know that the pain they are giving will actually help someone?

J: I would disagree. The destruction of property is painful but sometimes necessary to prevent the destruction of the innocent. However painful it might be, I have no trouble destroying your gun in order to keep you from shooting someone.

G: While I agree with you, we must remember that the infliction of pain can quickly get out of control. How do you keep people from destroying everything?

J: Your thoughts are both challenging and stimulating. With that said, sometimes I think people say things are getting out of control when they were already out of control. Who gets to determine what is out of control?

G: Protests and rioting are the language of the voiceless. By the time people actually act, most of the time the injustice has been out of control for a long time. The response to social pain is often a signal that healing is needed and healing is needed now. I think you are seeing these responses and signals all over the country right now. People are rebelling against destructive structures. Many people in this nation have no sense of somebodyness. We need some pain relief.

J: On some level, I feel like a protest or riot is a marker or testament of health. When people push back against injustice, we are reminded that they are very much alive.

G: When I was teaching at our first school during the Rodney King Riots, people always criticized me for refusing to criticize the rioters. Christians kept demanding that everyone live in unity. I always felt like unity was a tool to silence not to liberate.

J: Unity on whose terms...right?

G: Exactly.

J: I think about our majority black cities where you have black on black oppression. The calls for unity in these settings is always centered on fidelity to race.

G: Dr. Martin Luther King, Jr. taught us that there are two types of peace. The presence of a negative peace is actually injustice. The presence of an actual peace is actual justice. Many communities in a variety of areas have submitted to a negative peace.

J: Do you think there is ever a point that we participate in oppressive structures so that we can have a say in what comes next? Many people excuse their participation in mainline denominations this way.

G: The mainline denominations love gradualism and the politics of respectability. I can see where you're going with that. Institutions are very dirty. So, how do we Christianize our processes? How do we make love in these dirty institutions? I think it has to do with respecting persons outside of our normativities. How do we bring about the inclusion of the abnormal? I think we must create and push for more inclusive institutions.

J: I think our best bet is to speak to individuals. We have to convince people that there is something better than what is and that they can begin to push towards it in this life. Hope is the antidote.

G: This society needs a stiff shot of hope.

Amen.

August 23, 2015

Running Toward Evil

Mornings are hard. I think my medicine gets low. Placing one foot in front of the other, I pushed toward the bathroom and took a pill. Immediately, I start feeling better. I always take the pill before I see my kids.

Though I speak on many panels, I was nervous about this one. Often, I find it difficult to talk about suffering from Bipolar Disorder in public. People can be very nasty. Regardless, I pushed ahead. The church is a long drive from our house. I was thinking the entire way. When I arrived, I was thankful for the encouraging embrace of my dear friend the minister. Before I knew it, the panel commenced.

"I believe in evil personified." Everyone in the room jumped a bit. While describing my experiences serving as a mental health chaplain in Fort Worth, I stumbled into a description of my belief in the personification of evil. Throughout the panel, I succinctly described what it was like to be a Christian suffering from Bipolar Disorder. Now, I was tasked with talking further about possession.

When people kept asking about my suspicions with regard to mental illness or possession in a number of mass shootings, I replied that we don't always know what's going on inside someone. Whatever these killers are suffering from, we know they're sick. Jesus said, "I was sick and you visited me." Looking into the audience, I asked, "How many times have you visited these sickest amongst us?"

A lady ran up to me after the panel and declared, "I think that Dylann Roof is pure evil." Immediately, I replied, "Well if you think he is that sick, I guess all of us who love Jesus should run toward him as fast as we can." The greater the sickness...the greater our love response should be.

Instead of trying to explain acts of evil, maybe we should just start running toward the perpetrator.

That's what Jesus does.

Amen.

August 24, 2015

The Homophobia of Sandra Bland

Words have consequences. We have all spoken words that we wished we hadn't. However, our words often reveal what is going on in our hearts. When Sandra Bland made a video on March 31, 2015 (http://blacktimetravel.com/watch-sandra-bland-says-being-gay-is-a-choice-being-black-is-not/) describing sexuality as a choice and belittling the oppression that queer people face, she had no way of knowing the evil that would eventually happen to her in Texas. How could she? Regardless, the video makes something very plain...Sandra Bland suffered from homophobia. This doesn't change her status as a martyr, but it does make her a bit more human. In the life of Sandra Bland, there was room for redemption. I know the source of such grace. For just one moment, I wish she could hear the queer people marching in the streets saying her name over and over. I think she would feel differently. In fact, I believe she does.

One of the consequences of our rush to make saints out of victims of police brutality is that we take away their humanity in the process. I don't believe the homophobia of Sandra Bland should be hidden. It was a part of her life. We are all humans with major flaws. In this fight against police brutality, we must continue to learn to bind our hearts together. Bland's words should fuse us more tightly together with the realization that we must stand for victims of police brutality no matter what they believe. That is the nature of love.

Amen.

August 26, 2015

Fighting for Joseph Hutcheson: The Battle for the Tape

Desperate for help, Joseph Hutcheson parked his truck on the curb of the Lew Sterrett Justice Center in Dallas and ran inside. Upon entering, Hutcheson screamed, "Don't hurt me, I just need some help." The deputies tackled him. As Hutcheson screamed that he couldn't breathe, a witness described one deputy restraining Hutcheson with "a knee on his back" and another deputy restraining him "with a knee on his throat." Hutcheson's face turned from white to blue. Around 11:30am, Joseph Sheldon Hutcheson was pronounced dead.

Through blogs, microphones and bullhorns, I have told the story over and over again. Immediately after learning of the incident, I wrote a blog entitled _Joseph Sheldon Hutcheson Dies in the Custody of the Dallas Sheriff_ where I first publicly asked the question, "How does someone rush into a jail asking for help and end up being killed?" It would not be long before the Dallas Sheriff had to admit that her department lied about there being narcotics in Hutcheson's truck. I wrote about this development in *Protect and Serve the Badge: The Dallas County Sheriff's Department Lied*.

On August 3, we held a huge rally that brought out a broad diversity of people. Person after person shouted into the bullhorn, "Say his name!" To which the crowd thundered back, "Joseph Hutcheson." We marched right up to the lobby where Hutcheson got a knee to the throat and shook the foundations of the place.

At the end of the first week, Dominique Alexander and I set up a small press conference to call for the release of the tape and an investigation of the Sheriff's Department by the Texas Legislature. We pushed and pushed.

The next morning, exactly one week after Hutcheson's death, I stood in the exact spot of the jail lobby where Hutcheson died, lowered my head and prayed.

After our actions, I thought for sure the Dallas Sheriff would make a statement of condolence or something. We didn't hear anything.

When Hutcheson's family contacted me and asked for my help, I didn't hesitate. We immediately set up a press conference and rally for the following Friday. The emotional press conference moved me deeply. Compounding pain upon pain, Nicole Hutcheson revealed that her husband's neck organs were not returned. The Hutcheson's pain and anguish couldn't be ignored. I prayed that God would grant swift justice to this family. For the first time, we got a direct response. The Sheriff argued that she couldn't release the tape until the investigation was finished. That wasn't enough for me.

The rally was electric. I had never seen so many white people show up to fight police brutality before. After the speeches, we marched right into the lobby to demand justice. The Sheriff responded by sending out deputies in riot gear. Facing them down and screaming her son's name, was Ruth Boatner in her wheelchair.

Throughout the day, Joseph Hutcheson was the top story on every major news outlet in Dallas.

We also learned that all six deputies involved in the incident were placed on restricted duty. I couldn't believe it took so long.

We waited another week for the tape. Nothing.

On August 22, we gathered for another prayer vigil. This time there were close to 30 people who joined me in my sojourn up to the spot, including the Hutcheson family. I wore my robe and led the procession. The Spirit was with us.

Just last Tuesday, I spoke before the Dallas County Commission to demand the tape. Clutching the podium, I could feel the anger rising within. Why was it taking all of this to see a tape that belonged to the people anyway? After the meeting, Eddie Hutcheson and I had a direct confrontation with the Sheriff. Again, she made the excuse of needing more time to investigate. I didn't buy it. I consistently kept asking for the tape.

Three days later.

I was just told part of the tape is about to be released.

Amen.

August 29, 2015

The Consequences of the Tape: Pursuing Justice for Joseph Hutcheson

For the last month, I have fought for the Sheriff of Dallas County to release the video of the death of Joseph Hutcheson in the lobby of the Dallas County Jail. I have watched it over and over again. Without question, this is an instance of police brutality. The deputies took Hutcheson to the ground, placed their knees on his back and throat and killed him. If Hutcheson had been given proper medical attention when he entered the jail, we would not be having this conversation.

I gave the following quote to the *Dallas Morning News*:

"We see someone come in seeking medical help and they are treated like a piece of trash. They should have gotten a medical team down there to help this man, but instead they act like this is the World Wrestling Federation. And it begs the question, do these deputies know how to respond to these incidents in any other way than violence?"

Starring at the screen, I repeatedly pondered, "Why didn't they just help him?" I think the answer is that they don't know how. The deputies only knew how to treat Hutcheson like a criminal. I bet the situation would have been different if it was someone they loved. Without question, the Dallas County Sheriff's Department needs extensive training in dealing with these medical situations. Right now, the people of Dallas County are not safe to get sick around these deputies.

Thanks to the presence of Dallas County Commissioner John Wiley Price at the press conference, we were reminded that the release of the tape was a political event. I found this development particularly disturbing. The Sheriff of Dallas County is elected to serve and protect the citizens of Dallas County. Unfortunately, the Sheriff only seemed interested in serving and protecting herself.

This investigation was flawed from the beginning. Remember the narcotics in Hutcheson's truck that were never really there? Bound by her own political realities, I believe the Sheriff is unable to fully and properly investigate this matter. I call on the Sheriff to step aside and bring in an outside agency to investigate this case.

For our own safety, the public also has the right to know the names of the deputies involved in the death of Hutcheson. While I am willing to wait for the investigation to be complete for administrative action on the other deputies, the deputy who put his knee on the neck of Hutcheson should be fired immediately.

While I think the tape was released to calm things down, I'm more frustrated now than I was before.

These are the consequences of the tape.

Amen.

September 1, 2015

Only the Queer Heals

I couldn't believe how green the grass was. With each step, I felt like I was touching air. The water spoke. The closer I got, the more I realized that I could see aquatic life for miles. The clearness was unimaginable. I swam. With each stroke, I knew that I was beloved. I reached the rocks and climbed. When I got to the top, I was overwhelmed with the beauty of it all. I didn't hesitate. I jumped.

Before I hit the water, an eternity passed. Time was no more. I simply was.

Somehow, I left the water and flew into the sky. The experience was more real than anything I ever experienced. I could see billions and billions of unique people living in love and justice. The tears of joy started to flow. I never thought such a thing could happen again. I didn't want to open my eyes. When I did, I knew where I had been...Eden.

Humans are afflicted with a chronic illness. We are homesick. Together, we spend every hour yearning for what was. It is in our genetic composition. We have untapped memories. If we are ever to be healed, we must find a way back...back to our future.

The God beyond god cannot be contained by normative constructions. God is the great blurrer of all of our categories. Who can describe love beyond love? How do you describe the sexuality of a God who created and is within all sexualities? Who can describe justice beyond justice? How do you describe the body of a God who creates and is within all bodies? Who can describe mercy beyond mercy? How do you describe the gender of a God who creates and is within all genders? These questions combine with many left unasked to illustrate the fascinating vastness and beauty of God. In simply being, God is queer.

What happened to God's image?

Queerness was in limitless supply. Categories were unfathomable. The people simply were. With each day, God was there. The electricity that flowed through each person created life beyond life. With the knowledge that I could never do it justice, I hesitate to even describe it any further. Imagine a world where everyone was the very image of God. They were a queer people able to live into all queerness. There was no need for healing. No one was sick.

Can you imagine the queer sex that was shared in Eden? Passion existed in absolute perfection. Can you imagine the food and wine? The table was always open. Can you imagine the joy? There was no scarcity. All was as it should be. People loved in unfathomable ways. Everything was queer.

Then, the normative became an option.

The day was the darkest ever known.

The people awoke with love and purpose. The sounds were a symphonic melody. Walking around in their imaginations, the people approached the great tree. There was something different about the fruit. They couldn't figure out what it was. God warned them.

The sound of a snake didn't startle them. How could it? Everyone and everything loved each other. When the snake spoke, the people listened. "Do you want a bite?" The people didn't know how to respond. "God is afraid that you will be all powerful." Unable to comprehend the danger of normativity, the people wondered. Everything changed with one bite.

Categories rushed in. The people sickened. Being was fleeting. Pain was unbelievable. Why would God put something in Eden to harm them? They never knew why. Embarrassed of their lack of queerness, the people fled. We have been sick with normativity ever since. What happened? We may never know. The only thing we know is that we have to get back.

Queerness is the way, the truth and the life.

God didn't know how in the hell it went down like it did. One second everyone was enjoying each other in Eden and the next second everyone was running out with their leaves on fire. Regardless of the cause, God knew the result. Normativity took over the planet. Humans were relegated to a life filled with categories. For many moons, God tried to get people to understand that queerness was the only path back. One cannot expect to be right relationship with the universe when they are not living into the image of God that they were created to be. War raged within and without. Most people didn't know if they were going to kill themselves or their neighbor first. The twin sicknesses of violence and hate were amongst the most normative constructions that developed. Deeply pained and realizing that humanity needed a path to healing, God prepared a rescue mission. At exactly the right moment, queerness exploded onto the earth once more.

The queerest of them all hit the hay covered in blood and amniotic fluid. While it was obvious that most of the people there didn't realize the magnitude of what they were witnessing, the random poor shepherds covered in sheep shit might have offered them a clue. This child would grow to push us beyond all of our categories to that most holy space of queer. Though he was God, the child grew and struggled with normativity just like anyone else. Suffering from the normative sickness of being human, Jesus needed healing too. The categories were just too powerful.

Jesus was a racist. The Canaanite woman cried out for help. Her daughter was afflicted with a demon and needed healing from God. Instead of help, Jesus declared that he was here for Israel only and called her a dog. There ain't a damn thing queer about racism. In this moment, Jesus was just like every other normative bigot. Refusing to let him go without a healing, the woman questioned his racism and challenged him to be better. This woman was not even supposed to be speaking to Jesus and she had the audacity to queerly tell it like it is. At that very second she spoke, a miracle happened...Jesus was healed from his racism and he healed her daughter. One has to first realize they are sick before they can heal. This queer woman boldly dared to heal Jesus of his racism. Only the queer could heal Jesus.

There once was a woman whose queerness was destroyed early and almost entirely. Throughout her life, she sought healing. From counseling to spiritual discernment to relationships to supplements, she tried it all. On a whim, she married a man who had been interested in her for a long time. "Maybe I might find healing in the security of marriage," she thought. Thinking that she would never marry, her parents were thrilled. Before long, her husband started to abuse her physically and emotionally. She was in unbearable pain. At the market one day, a man caught her eye. She couldn't shake the thought of him and fell in love. Praying for forgiveness, she responded to a note he passed her. Before long, the two were involved in an affair. Love was all they knew.

When her husband found out, rage overwhelmed him. Immediately, he went to his local Rabbi and demanded the punishment prescribed by law. The Pharisees realized that this was the opportunity they needed to show their strength as the keepers of normativity. For a week, the Pharisees spied on the woman and the man she was having an affair with. After watching the live pornography for a few minutes, the Pharisees stormed in. Ordering the man not to tell anyone, the men grabbed the woman and drug her through the street. The entire time, the woman kept feeling like her first chance at real love was going to be what ultimately killed her. "If only I had just been normative and done what I was supposed to do like everyone else..." she thought. When she was slung at the feet of Jesus and the Pharisees raised their rocks, she knew she was going to die.

If Jesus had not met a queer Canaanite woman a few months prior, he wouldn't have been ready for this situation. Dust rose from the ground. Breathing was heavy. Hate was winning. The woman caught in adultery begged him for help. Looking down, Jesus knew that the only way to help was to cross a boundary. When he looked up at the Pharisees, Jesus looked deeply into their eyes and lowered his body further into the dirt. Nothing needed to be said, everyone knew that Jesus was placing his body into the conversation. In placing his person between the rocks and the woman, Jesus showed how the queer heals...by offering the body for the sake of justice. The Canaanite prepared Jesus to place his body in the dirt with an adulterous woman by drawing him into the plight of the oppressed and marginalized. The queer heals through incarnational body exchanges and so must we.

"Love you neighbor as yourself." Have you ever considered what a queer concept love is? The wellness of your neighbor is dependent on your ability to love yourself. You have to understand yourself as a queer human being made in the image of a queer God before you can heal. Normativity cannot be banished without blurring the categories and lines of what is. Jesus had to learn to be different in order to make a difference. When Jesus was talking to the Canaanite woman, he was just as racist as everyone else. The Canaanite decided to love her neighbor as herself and pull Jesus out of his racism to a place of love. When Jesus met the adulterous woman, he was ready to pull her out of the normative oppression of the Pharisees that she was facing. By getting down in the dirt, Jesus declared that the normative force of hate had no power in the face of love. Difference makes a difference. Queerness makes thing queer. To be like God is to give your body to healing...there is nothing queerer.

"Is there any other way?" Jesus knew there was not. The only way to be queer is to give your body for the healing of others. Regardless of the pain, Jesus was prepared. The Canaanite and adulterous woman made sure of it. You have to present your body as a roadblock to racism. You have to give your body to save others. You have to be queer in order to heal. When Jesus was lifted high up on that cross, I know that he thought about the two women who made him God. Looking out into the distance, he must have remembered how the Canaanite taught him to love everyone. As the blood dropped into his eyes, the woman caught in adultery must have spoken to him about how he saved her. Before him, the gathered represented the normatizers that we all are. In giving his body, Jesus wanted to set us all free. To love queerly is to give the body. In immense pain, Jesus cried out, "Forgive them for they know not what they do!" We fail to understand the consequences of our normativity. In the greatest healing moment of all time, Jesus was most fully queer and therefore most fully God. We know the way back.

Queer love is the most powerful healer of all. We are called to be the healed healers that we were created to be. In giving his body, Jesus loved queerly. We are called to go and do likewise. The path back to queerness is to love the self enough to give the self away. Imprints of Eden are within us. Search deeply. We have to first be healed of all the categories that hold us back and then place our bodies on the line for the liberation of others. There is queerness within us. We once walked without categories. We were free. Do your remember? Let us return. In the face of the devastating categories that afflict us, God is calling us to grow queerer...for only the queer heals.

Amen.

September 2, 2015

When the Truth Became a Lie

Truth was until it was not. The mutation of truth was the greatest deception of all. The truth we all thought we were following became the exact opposite. The advocates of truth became protectors of the lie. When people started to realize what happened, it was too late. The lie made us nothing more than the categories we created. Death came quickly.

Amen.

September 8, 2015

Only Kim Davis Can Save Us

With a population of less than 24,000 people, Rowan County, Kentucky is an unlikely place to capture the attention of our nation. However, a titanic moral and legal battle erupted when two residents of the county seat of Morehead refused to be denied a marriage license. Now, James Yates and William Smith, Jr. are married and county clerk Kim Davis served time in jail for her refusal to issue licenses to same-sex couples. While I have a deep abiding belief that our government should not discriminate against anyone who desires to get married, I have found myself strangely drawn to Kim Davis.

"What the fuck is she wearing?" "I wish she would just crawl up in a hole and die." "Does she put shit in her hair?" "How many times has she been married?" The language has been intense. I promised myself that I wasn't going to write about Kim Davis. I refused to engage the circus. Honestly, I wasn't going to write a damn word until I started reading the comments. Ranging from offensive to rude to downright evil, I read word after word attacking Kim Davis in every imaginable way. When I paused to pray, I realized that Kim Davis was our salvation.

In Matthew 5:44, Jesus commanded, "...love your enemies and pray for those who persecute you..." We are commanded to love and pray for Kim Davis. In 1 John 4:8, the writer declares, "Whoever does not love does not know God, because God is love..." Those who do not love Kim Davis do not know God for God is love. In multiple places, Jesus says that amongst the greatest commandments is to "love our neighbor as ourselves." Our job is to love Kim Davis as our self. The only way that we can experience salvation is to give ourselves over to love for our enemies. Since Kim Davis has become the object of our scorn, she has also become the object of our salvation.

Amen.

September 10, 2015

Shame & Suicide: The Scandal of Southern Baptist Theology

"He's not in heaven...and you won't be either if you kill yourself." I will never forget the cruelness of the language. The suicide rocked our Southern Baptist church. We descended deeper into judgment...the only fuel of fundamentalism. Secretly, I think most people thought shame was the antidote for suicide. I was ten. Even then, I knew better.

"Do you believe that Jesus died on the cross for your sins?" Throughout my life, I have heard that question over and over again. We were commanded to be certain and to make sure others were certain. When we failed, the question always arose, "Do you really think you're a Christian?" Struggles with certainty fuel obedience. The cycle of shame is what keeps Southern Baptists going.

Millions of times... I asked Jesus for salvation incessantly growing up. I was never certain. The talk of fiery hell, eternal judgment and rapture made things worse. I thought about suicide often. I planned a few times. The shame made me cycle into deeper bouts of depression and lose touch with reality. Southern Baptist theology made me very sick.

"If you cheat in my class, I hope you die before leaving this classroom...because the church doesn't need anymore cheaters for ministers." From the moment I entered the Southern Baptist Theological Seminary, I heard statement after statement to pour shame upon shame. I thought this was how to follow Jesus. I spiraled out of control. Panic and mania were all that I knew. We were told to examine everything about our lives. I examined to the point of delusion. I stayed up almost every night wondering if this would be the night that I finally decided to pull the plug. In the midst of studying Southern Baptist theology, I was the sickest I'd ever been.

"Your uncle just committed suicide." I will never forget the devastation I felt in my gut. My uncle was a Southern Baptist minister. While he took his own life, I know that it is shame that actually killed him. In the midst of difficult hours, decades of bad Southern Baptist theology made him feel worthless to the point of death. Forced obedience cannot save lives...only grace can do that.

When I heard that Southern Baptist minister and New Orleans Baptist Theological Seminary professor John Gibson committed suicide after suffering from depression for many years and realizing that his name was revealed in connection to the Ashley Madison website, I knew what killed him...shame. Like many others I have known, Gibson died based on a Southern Baptist theology of condemnation that promotes depression and hopelessness. What makes millions of lustful and gluttonous Southern Baptists think they can shame people to death? ...a theology that is devoid of the love of Jesus.

Make no mistake, shame only increases the body count.

I pray that Southern Baptists get saved.

Amen.

September 11, 2015

"Beyond Identity: The Image of a Queer God"

-Preached at Christ Church Episcopal Cathedral in St. Louis, MO on Sept. 7, 2015

Spaces of intersectionality are spaces of divinity. Such spaces draw us nearer to the God that exists at the intersection of us all. Such thoughts conjure up important questions... Who is God? Who are we? These questions can only be answered fully at a place of intersection...in the beginning.

We always fail when we try to describe God. We are always pointing to something beyond description. In the words of the great theologian Brother Paul Tillich, "God is the God beyond God." Let me explain it like this... Do you love your partner or your child or anyone else that you have a special relationship with just like you love everyone else? There exists love beyond love...mercy beyond mercy...grace beyond grace...hope beyond hope...justice beyond justice...that existence is God. We get small glimpses of these things...but the God that is...is the God that is beyond our finite categories.

Too often we spend our lives normatizing everything we come in contact with. We try to make things fit. We try to make ourselves fit. We try to make God fit...but God has never fit and we were made in that God's image. We spend so much time making God into our image and forgetting that we were made in God's image. We were not made to fit. We were not made for categories. We were not made for identities. Just like God...we were not made to be defined. We were made to be something so much more than this...queer.

Queerness is about rejecting normativity and living into the beauty of our creation. Queerness is about being holy and undefined...just like God. We were not made to be explained. We were made to be queer. We have a Queer God who created us in God's queer image. So what in the hell happened?

Y'all remember Eden? That old snake slithered up and said, "If you eat of the tree, you will be made like God." The first sin is always to look for God somewhere other than within. You were created in the very image of God. If you want to know God, look at your own queer reflection. Stop looking everywhere else! Believe that God created you queerly and you are enough! There is no need to look anywhere else. Yet...we've been looking everywhere else for a very long time. Let's run to Jesus for the solution.

John 1:1, "In the beginning was the Word, the Word was with God and the Word was God." Let me assure you... "In the beginning was the Queer, the Queer was with God and the Queer was God." The Queer is the queerest of them all. The Queer is beyond categories and identities. The Queer is Jesus...but it wasn't always like that. Jesus had to grow in his queerness...so that he could show us how to grow into ours.

That old Syrophoenician woman had to teach Jesus a thing or two. You see...JESUS WAS A RACIST. Let's make it plain. Jesus was a racist. Jesus was approached by the Syrophoenician woman about healing her daughter and Jesus called her a dog. Does that ring any bells? Christ Church Cathedral has been at the forefront of the Black Lives Matter Movement. So often we call minorities in this country..."dogs." We might not say it out loud...but we say it by our actions...we say it by how we spend our money...we say it by the things that we leave unsaid and undone. You think you are any better than Jesus??? Jesus got called out. The Syrophoenician woman reminded Jesus that there is nothing queer about racism and Jesus responded. Jesus had to be reminded that there is nothing queer about racism in order to be healed. The Syrophoenician woman brought Jesus along...and there is another woman who is very glad that she did. Jesus was made queerer in that moment and a few months later he met a woman...

You see there was a woman who was caught in adultery. The Pharisees said they caught her in the very act. How long where they looking? After the Pharisees got over their watching...they got back to their accusing...and threw the woman at the feet of Jesus. In the prior revelation of queerness, Jesus learned what it looks like to stand with the marginalized and oppressed. Jesus was ready to be queer. Jesus was ready to stand with the hurting. So what does Jesus do when the woman is thrown at his feet? Jesus doesn't say a damn thing. You know what he does? Jesus throws his body to the dirt. Jesus places his body on the line. Jesus is ready to die so that this woman might live. That is the answer to the questions, "What does it mean to be queer? What does it mean to follow God? What does it mean to follow Jesus?" You cannot be queer until you are ready to place your body into the conversation.

Jesus gives his body to make a difference. Jesus shows us that one has to be different in order to make a difference.

In the story and beyond, Jesus shows us what love looks like in action. Ultimately, Jesus died so that others might live. The path of queerness is about doing the same. We are called to be different. Stop trying to be like everyone else! Be queer.

We are called to love our neighbors as ourselves. There is a famous theologian out there by the name of RuPaul who consistently asks, "How in the hell are you going to love somebody when you can't love yourself?" You have to live into your queerness. You have to be the queer that God created you to be. You have to love your neighbors queerly. You have to grow queerer and queerer.

...and then we will finally be able to fully love into each other as we queer the world.

Amen.

September 16, 2015

The Last Visit

I only met Juan Garcia once. I was asked to visit on September 15. For a couple of hours in a cold room, we talked. With an unforgiving deadline approaching fast, the last things were at the forefront of our minds. For most people, eschatology or the study of destiny is a theoretical conversation. When one is scheduled to be executed on October 6, you're not all that concerned with the theoretical.

"Do you think I'm going to die?" The question was the toughest I'd ever encountered. Despite the fact that I knew the answer, I had to name it. "I cannot imagine a circumstance in which you won't be executed." Though I felt like my response was cold, the words loosened Juan up. We began our journey back to the future.

The stories of persons on death row always begin far before the murders. Drugs and abuse are common elements. In a short period of time, Juan tried to tell me all that he could. On multiple occasions, I got lost in the intensity of it all. When Juan expressed his regret over the murder, I looked him straight in the eye and said, "You're forgiven."

"What is salvation?" I don't think about the definition of salvation too often...I'm too busy living it. Nevertheless, I blurted out what came to my mind first, "We are saved when we place our faith in love." Since God is love, I have always believed that love is our only way of knowing the divine. "I choose love." Even as time has put distance between us, Juan's answer festers in my soul.

The last topic was one we all think about...whether we admit it or not. "What will the judgment be like?" Growing up, I was always terrified of death. Our pastors constantly talked about fire and damnation. I was never able to shake the belief that the flames were for me. When I accepted the call to ministry, I promised God I would never talk like that. I haven't. After a quick silent prayer, I leaned in and declared, "Imagine encountering a love so powerful that it burns up all the evil within you and transforms all the love within you into something eternal." Juan's eyes started to water up. "I believe." In the power of that moment, I knew that I did too.

Knowing that our time was coming to a close, I didn't know how to say goodbye for the first and last time. In the agony of trying to think of the right words to say, I was paralyzed. Sensing my timidity, Juan smiled and said, "I think I know what will draw us together again."
Our shared faith in love remains.
Amen.

September 17, 2015

The Danger of Pride

"It's not for them." The words fester in my ears. When I asked about the consistent exclusion of people of color and transgender persons in the Dallas Pride parade and festival, a prominent gay citizen made it plain for me. While I was very aware that the entire event is marketed to wealthy white people and their allies, I couldn't believe that two of the most oppressed groups of people in our city were dismissed with four simple words. Perhaps, most others wouldn't forget their gentility and decide to be a little less blunt. Regardless, the exclusion of a variety of groups and identities in the parade and festival is consistently glaring. To that end, the danger of Dallas Pride is the solidification of normative excuses and prejudices. "It's not for them" sounds like the language of the oppressor not the oppressed. Liberation that is only available to some is not liberation.

Amen.

September 22, 2015

Joseph Hutcheson Federal Civil Rights Complaint

*This is a copy of the civil rights complaint I constructed and filed jointly with the Hutcheson Family against the Dallas County Sheriff's Department on September 22, 2015. Due to technical limitations, I had to leave out the still pictures contained in the incident section of the original complaint (that section should be read while following along with the video).

COMPLAINT

An encounter with the Dallas County Sheriff's Department on August 1, 2015 at the Lew Sterrett Justice Center in Dallas, Texas led to the demise of Joseph Hutcheson, we the undersigned believe his civil rights were violated in three different ways.

First, we believe the Dallas County Sheriff's Department failed to properly train their deputies to encounter someone having a psychological or manic episode and that such lack of training violated Hutcheson's right to life. Second, we believe the Dallas County Sheriff's Department exercised excessive force in their treatment of Joseph Hutcheson and that such force violated Hutcheson's right to life. Third, we believe that the Dallas County Sheriff's Department failed to administer proper medical aid to Hutcheson and by improper training directly contributed to his death and that such ignorance violated Hutcheson's right to life. We have provided supporting evidence and documents. We further ask that you use your power to secure all evidence already collected in the Dallas County Sheriff's Department's own investigation. With the aforementioned reasons in mind, we sign this formal complaint and ask the Department of Justice to investigate the actions of the Dallas County Sheriff's Department in the homicide of Joseph Hutcheson.

Rev. Dr. Jeff Hood,
Executive Director of Hope for Peace & Justice

Nicol Hutcheson,
Wife of Joseph Hutcheson

Ruth Boatner,
Mother of Joseph Hutcheson

James E. Hutcheson,
Brother of Joseph Hutcheson

TABLE OF CONTENTS

I. INICIDENT
II. WITNESS QUOTES
III. MEDICAL EXAMINER SUMMARY
IV. INDEPENDENT AUTOPSY SUMMARY
V. INDEPENDENT AUTOPSY REPORT

I. INCIDENT
*In the original complaint, there are still pictures that accompany the text below. This section is better understood when read while following along with the video.
video: *http://www.dallascounty.org/department/sheriff/video/lsjc_lobby.php*

On August 1, 2015 around 10am, Joseph Hutcheson parked his truck in the crosswalk on Commerce Street outside of the Lew Sterrett Justice Center in Dallas, Texas. Behaving erratically, Hutcheson stumbled up the hill into the main lobby. Entering the lobby, Hutcheson continues to act erratically and shouts out repeatedly, "My wife is trying to kill me!" On the video Hutcheson appears sick and disoriented. Having failed to receive the care that he needed at Parkland Hospital earlier in the day, the Hutcheson family believes that Hutcheson entered the jail desperate to get help after suffering from the effects of drug use and heart trouble. Regardless, there is no question that Hutcheson entered the lobby in desperate need of help.

People in the lobby were frightened of Hutcheson. To which, according to witness April Berryhill (http://www.dallasnews.com/news/crime/headlines/20150801-authorities-investigating-after-man-dies-in-dallas-county-jail-lobby.ece), Hutcheson responded, "Don't be scared of me. I just need some help." One deputy initially approaches Hutcheson and then multiple others join him. At this point, Hutcheson appears to be breathing heavily, walking oddly and acting strangely in obvious duress. Running up aggressively, a single deputy later approaches Hutcheson and violently forces him to the ground (2:16). By failing to properly identify Hutcheson as someone in need of medical attention and responding with excessive force, we believe the Dallas County Sheriff's Department began to violate Hutcheson's civil rights.

We were surprised to know that the only training that the Dallas County Sheriff's Department has for dealing with someone who is manic is blunt force. Hutcheson was in the lobby for a little over two minutes before the deputy decided to take this action. When the deputies got Hutcheson to the ground, other deputies piled on. At this point (2:25) it is obvious that the deputies have Hutcheson contained; yet they still continue to exert great force on him.

With knees to the back and neck, the officers begin to restrict Hutcheson's ability to breath. We believe that the amount of force shown in the video is excessive and a violation of Hutcheson's civil rights.

Around 3:20, officers appear to have Hutcheson contained.

Then, Hutcheson tries to turn over to breath (3:40).

While the deputy on the right acts nonchalantly, the two deputies to the left engage Hutcheson again. Both deputies come down on Hutcheson with unnecessary and excessive homicidal force.

We believe that Hutcheson was in critical condition around this point and the deputies kept going. The deputy places excessive force on the neck and chest of Hutcheson. If Hutcheson was such a threat, then why is this woman still acting so nonchalant?

Around 3:52, another deputy runs up and places his foot on Hutcheson's ankle.

A few seconds later (4:00), the deputy gives his legs a push to see if there is any life left in them. There is no push back. The deputy in the back then proceeds to lift up

Hutcheson's legs and push them to the front. We believe this further obstructed any chance that Hutcheson had to breath. At 4:25 there are six deputies around Hutcheson and one is still nonchalantly on her phone or radio, Hutcheson is not a threat and excessive force is still being used against him. Deputies are still on top of him and obstructing his ability to breath.

Around 4:51, we believe the deputies started to realize what they did. The deputy who placed his knees on the neck and throat of Hutcheson puts his arms out to absolve himself of responsibility.

The deputy is told to leave soon after.

For well over three minutes, the Dallas County Sheriff's Department used excessive force on Hutcheson. When they realized what they had done, they tried to save him. Unfortunately, the deputies didn't seem to have training on how to do that either.

Around 5:40, the deputies started to lift Hutcheson to his knees. When you first learn about first-aid, you are taught to lay someone in medical distress flat on the ground not to lift them up. It seems obvious that holding someone up makes it more difficult for someone to breath.

Over the next few minutes, deputies pull and tug at Hutcheson. There is no question that they know he is in medical distress. Regardless of their intentions, the deputies continue to block Hutcheson's airway by holding him up and failing to administer proper lifesaving techniques.

At 8:50, the deputies have still not secured Hutcheson proper medical care.

At 9:26, deputies begin to get more worried.

At 9:56, over FOUR MINUTES after Hutcheson is unresponsive, the first medical professional arrives (in a facility that has a fully functioning medical clinic).

On the advice of the medical professional, deputies remove the handcuffs at 11:02 (over FIVE MINUTES after Hutcheson was unresponsive).

Hutcheson is finally laid on his back at 11:28.

Hutcheson has already pissed himself.

The lobby is cleared at 11:50. For almost twelve minutes, the deputies allowed the lobby to stay open. If Hutcheson was as dangerous as all of the force he received indicates, then why did they keep the lobby open? CPR was started around 12:04. In a facility supposed to be filled with people who know CPR, Hutcheson got help SIX MINUTES after he became unresponsive.

Around 13:40, a full EIGHT MINUTES after he became unresponsive, a deputy places hands of aid and not harm on Hutcheson for the first time.

Nurses and Dallas County Fire and Rescue arrived to offer aid. After consistent interventions to try to save his life, Hutcheson was transported to Parkland Hospital (40:10).

Joseph Hutcheson was pronounced dead at Parkland Hospital not long after leaving the Lew Sterrett Justice Center.

To add insult to injury, authorities responded to public concern about the tragedy by releasing Hutcheson's criminal background and speculating that they could see narcotics in his truck. Later, the Dallas County Sheriff's Department had to go back and said there actually were no drugs in the truck.

II. WITNESS QUOTES

*While there are many other witnesses who have been interviewed by the Dallas County Sheriff's Department, Berryhill and White are significant because they were amongst the first ones to give statements after the incident.

April Berryhill

"He came in saying, 'Don't be scared of me. I just need some help.' They just tackled him as if he'd threatened their lives," Berryhill said. "He didn't have a weapon. He wasn't swinging at the officers. He just needed help."

– http://www.dallasnews.com/news/crime/headlines/20150801-authorities-investigating-after-man-dies-in-dallas-county-jail-lobby.ece

"They had him in handcuffs, he wasn't fighting back, he wasn't, not letting them restrain him, he was saying, 'I can't breathe, I can't breath,'" said April Berryhill, who was also waiting in the jail's lobby.
"One of the officers had him down on the ground with his knee on his neck."
The county says a nurse was called while Hutcheson was handcuffed and unresponsive. CPR was performed until Dallas Fire-Rescue paramedics arrived to take Hutcheson to Parkland Memorial Hospital, where he was later pronounced dead.

– http://www.wfaa.com/story/news/local/2015/08/01/man-unresponsive-after-dallas-jail-scuffle/30986151/

"They had him on the ground trying to get him handcuffed," said April Berryhill, a witness. "They got him handcuffed, and one of the jailers had his knee blocking [Joseph Hutcheson's] airway. In between the breaths, the man is going, 'I can't breathe. I'm sorry. Please don't kill me.' Then you didn't hear anything from him anymore."

Berryhill says Joseph Hutcheson turned blue and urinated on himself. At one point, she approached an officer, telling him that it didn't look like Joseph Hutcheson was breathing.

"He said, 'Oh, he's faking it,'" Berryhill said, adding that it took about 20 minutes before medical assistance was provided.

http://www.wfaa.com/story/news/local/dallas-county/2015/08/17/questions-mount-family-man-who-died-dallas-co-jail/31884433/

Tiffany Todd White

"When a person is asking for help, someone should reach out and help them...try and see what's going on with the person before you go in and start treating him like a dog," said Tiffany Todd White, a visitor at the jail who saw the incident.

http://www.wfaa.com/story/news/local/2015/08/01/man-unresponsive-after-dallas-jail-scuffle/30986151/

III. MEDICAL EXAMINER SUMMARY

On August 31, the Medical Examiner in Dallas County declared Hutcheson's death to be a homicide based on the "combined effects of cocaine and methamphetamine, compounded by hypertensive cardiovascular disease and physiologic stress associated with struggle and restraint."

http://thescoopblog.dallasnews.com/2015/08/death-of-man-in-dallas-county-jail-lobby-ruled-a-homicide-according-to-dallas-county-medical-examiner.html/

IV. INDEPENDENT AUTOPSY SUMMARY

In her report, Dr. Amy Gruszecki ruled the death of Hutcheson a homicide based on "combined effects of mechanical asphyxia; the physical stress associated with struggle and restraint and toxic effects of cocaine and methamphetamine."

September 24, 2015

A Cosmology of Darkness

The darkness was. The darkness is. The darkness will be. The darkness is God.

The voice of all voices calls to us. Staring past the stars. The heavens speak and we hear. The abyss reminds us.

The deeper we go. The closer we are drawn. In the darkness is infinity. Eternity is your home.

What was first? Darkness. What is now? Darkness. What is then? Darkness.

God is. Embrace the magic. Embrace the mystery. Become...darkness.

Amen.

September 26, 2015

The Immigration Question

*Interaction from the Hope for Peace and Justice "Imagination: Immigration 2" Panel I served on today (9/26).

Q: Where should our efforts to solve the immigration crises begin?

A: We must stop treating people like shit. We must learn to love our neighbors. The problem is that we don't even know who our neighbors are. I bet most folks wouldn't even be able to identify Mexico on a map. The level of ignorance and lack of concern exhibited on immigration in this nation is absolutely appalling. How can any person of conscience live comfortably behind the walled fortressed boundaries of the richest nation on the planet? So, I guess one can't begin until they repent of their nationalism and get saved from our borders.

Amen.

September 27, 2015

The Premeditated Murder of Kelly Gissendaner

In February of 1997, Greg Owen stabbed Doug Gissendaner until there was no life left in his body. Can you hear the screams? Can you smell the blood? Can you imagine the horror of it all? Make no mistake...this was an act of pure evil. Though not even present for the crime, the mastermind was Kelly Gissendaner.

Prosecutors often argue that the mastermind is more culpable than the person who actually carries out the murder. In order to secure a death sentence, prosecutors convinced a jury that Gissendaner was motivated by greed and used Owen as her weapon. Even at the last minute, Gissendaner could have even changed her mind and tried to save her husband's life. I find these arguments highly convincing. I believe that Gissendaner played the pivotal role in this tremendous act of evil. Even more than that, I agree with the prosecutor and think she deserves to die.

For the last few months, fellow Christians worked tirelessly to save Gissendaner's life. With the hashtag #kellyonmymind on constant display, we were reminded over and over that Gissendaner received a theological education, reconciled with her kids, mentored other inmates and repented. The problem is that all of these arguments and actions are probably going to fall short of saving her life. The reality is that this is not about Gissendaner. This is a woman who committed a crime so heinous that she deserves to die. The only question that remains is the only question that could've saved Gissendaner's life. Who deserves to kill her?

People have been planning the execution of Kelly Gissendaner for a long time. The premeditation has involved perfecting procedures, securing drugs, finding accomplices and even convincing people to watch. Through both inaction and their elected officials, the entire State of Georgia will be responsible. These actions are not all that different than the premeditated murder that Gissendaner masterminded. The fallacy of the death penalty is that it turns an entire state into the premeditated murderers that they are executing. I remember Jesus saying something about, "Whoever is without sin cast the first stone."

The campaign to make Gissendaner into a sympathetic figure has been very successful. The problem is that niceness doesn't save lives. We have to remind people of their complicity in the premeditated murder that is about to take place. While I am sure that Gissendaner has changed, the only way to save lives is to convince people to drop the knife.

Amen.

September 29, 2015

Christians Killed Kelly Gissendaner

1.75 million Southern Baptists forced her down the hallway. 619 thousand United Methodists strapped her to the gurney. 596 thousand Roman Catholics pushed the needle in. 566 thousand Evangelicals assured everyone that this was God's will. As the poison started going in, there were millions of Georgia Christians participating in the homicide. Within minutes, Kelly Gissendaner died and Christians were the ones who killed her.

Upwards of 85% of Georgians identify as Christians. When Gissendaner was prosecuted, Christians pushed for the death penalty. When Gissendaner was sentenced, a jury of Christians sentenced her to death. When Gissendaner sat in prison, it was Christians who imprisoned her. When Gissendaner's final appeals were denied, it was Christians who pushed her to the execution chamber. When

Gissendaner was executed, it was Christians who did the deed. Make no mistake...Christians killed Kelly Gissendaner.

There are some who might contest my categorizations with the fact that Christians are the ones who've been most involved in trying to save Gissendaner's life. I would argue that some of these persons are the ones most responsible for her death. What would've happened if this type of energy had been put into Gissendaner's case a decade ago? What would've happened if this type of energy would've been put into abolishing the death penalty altogether? I believe Kelly Gissendaner would still be alive. Christians love trying to save someone at the very end. What would happen if Christians started getting involved in the beginning? Over the next three months, there are 18 people facing death around the nation. Will they be on our minds? I hope so.

Amen.

September 30, 2015

Richard Glossip is Scheduled to Die for Our Sins

Over and over, Justin Sneed slammed a baseball bat into the flesh of Barry Van Treese. Blood splashed all over the Best Budget Inn until there was no life in Van Treese left. Oklahoma City was appalled at the horrific nature of the crime. Upon admitting to the crime, Sneed convinced prosecutors and two juries that motel manager Richard Glossip ordered him to kill Van Treese. Sneed got life and Glossip got death. After killing a man with a baseball bat, Sneed once again got to decide who lived and died.

The State of Oklahoma is about 85% Christian. You can't blame anyone else for this execution other than Christians. Richard Glossip is scheduled to die for our sins.

We allowed for death to remain a punishment option.

We must repent and abolish the death penalty.

We refused to reform our criminal justice system.

We must repent and seek real justice.

We promoted theologies of death.

We must repent and cling to theologies of life.

We are responsible for the scheduled execution of Richard Glossip.

We must repent.

May our repentance lead to life.

Amen.

September 30, 2015

Kim Davis Can Save Us

"Love your enemies and pray for those who persecute you..." -Matthew 5:44

Kim Davis can save us.

Amen.

October 2, 2015

F*** Your Guns

To put it bluntly, I'm over the ridiculous arguments against sweeping gun control. Charleston, Newtown, Columbine... People keep dying and cowards keep talking about the need for more guns. Earlier, Christians were forced to identify themselves and shot. Due to our loose gun laws, today Roseburg sounds more like ISIS than the US. Deranged people have unlimited access to guns. Congratulations gun lobby...you just caused another mass shooting. Unless we stand up to those who love guns more than people, we will continue to see these horrific tragedies. Followers of Jesus are called to, "Love your neighbor as yourself." I don't believe you can love anyone and keep providing unlimited access to guns that kill their family and friends. There will be those who still argue that they want unlimited and uninhibited access to buy their guns, I know I stand with Jesus when I say, "Fuck Your Guns."

Amen.

October 2, 2015

Walk to Stop Executions: A Preflection from Ohio

"...tell the Gissendaner family that I am so sorry. That amazing man lost his life because of me..." Just after midnight on September 30, 2015 after her final words of apology, the State of Georgia began to execute Kelly Gissendaner for the murder of her husband Doug. After the process started, Gissendaner began to sing. *Amazing grace! How sweet the sound that saved a wretch like me! I once was lost, but now am found; was blind, but now I see.* The confluences of Gissendaner's remorse scramble around my brain like ants running around their home.

Tomorrow morning, I will start walking 83 miles from the Ohio Execution Chamber in Lucasville to the Ohio State Capitol in Columbus. A few months back when abolitionists in Ohio asked me to help lead their **Walk to Stop Executions**, I couldn't say no. Placing one foot in front of the other is the only path to abolition. Jesus walks too.

When I walked 200 miles across Texas in 2014, the executed haunted me. This week will be no different. I will hear Kelly Gissendaner. I will feel Troy Davis. I will touch Kimberly McCarthy. I will experience Willie Trottie. I will speak Dennis McGuire. I will know Cameron Todd Willingham. I will experience them all. Like a fierce wind they will rage around me, speaking the words of God, "Prophesy to our breath!" I will...

While I am walking, my friend and fellow Texan Juan Garcia is to be executed on October 6. I clutch his picture right now. We only met once. I will never forget our powerful conversation. For two hours, we talked about the enormity of the love of God. I know that we deny the love with every execution. We got to get saved.

One day, we will stop our murderous rampage of vengeance...in Texas...in Ohio... and everywhere else. Until we do, I'm going to keep on walking.

Amen.

October 4, 2015

The Finger

Car after car sped by. I looked into the eyes of every face. The image of God looked back. I spent the day walking for the abolition of the death penalty in Southern Ohio. Every once in a while, someone would slow their car down, honk their horn and raise their middle finger as high as they could. Their mouths made sure their meaning was not lost, "Fuck You!" I got discouraged. Then, I got a word. The middle finger was pointing up to God as a reminder to pray for their ignorant asses.

Amen.

Mile 13 of 83

October 5, 2015

The Dangerous Views of My Professor Dr. Heath Lambert

Throughout my life, I've experienced attraction to both men and women. Growing up Southern Baptist, I didn't have much room to talk about sexuality. We were just told that if we didn't have sex or masturbate we would be following God. I remained quiet. Later, I felt called to ministry. In the midst of my conservatism, I decided to attend the Southern Baptist Theological Seminary.

In the midst of my studies, I was reminded over and over that a complex sexuality didn't mix with my professors' ideas of what it means to follow Jesus. I fell deeper and deeper into despair. I found no more legalistic of a professor than Dr. Heath Lambert. In his class, there wasn't a stitch of grace. We were told that any diversions from heterosexuality or conservative constructions of gender would lead to hell. I felt worthless. Night after night, I struggled with whether or not I should take my life. I don't know if I ever got any closer than I did when I was in Dr. Lambert's class.

Presently, I am tired and sunburnt as I walk 83 miles in opposition to the death penalty in Ohio. I didn't plan on writing anything about the current meeting of the Association of Certified Biblical Counselors (ACBC) at the Southern Baptist Theological Seminary in Louisville, Kentucky. Honestly, I just wanted to ignore it. But when I saw my professor Dr. Lambert speaking in the media and on stage about his views on sexuality and gender, I couldn't. I had to share that his views almost killed me. I know I'm not alone.

Amen.

October 5, 2015

Texas Will Kill My Friend

In less than 24 hours, Texas will kill my friend. Though we only met once, Juan Garcia and I share a spiritual connection. I will never forget talking to Juan about the light of love. The conversation went deeper and deeper. Jesus is strange like that...

I see absolutely no reason to kill Juan. Regardless, I know Texas will. Texans are proficient at sucking the life out of people. Of course, killing is always evil.

I am praying for Juan. I pray that all he will know is love. Regardless of the execution, I know love will win. Juan already assured me of that.

Amen.

October 7, 2015

The Abolition Prayer at St. Joseph Catholic Church in Circleville, Ohio

Spirit of Love. Spirit of Light. Spirit of Justice. Fill us from the tips of our toes to the tops of our heads with the passion and commitment necessary to end the death penalty. May the powerful words of abolition never be far from our lips. When we exit through the great wooden doors of this church and march out into the streets, let our cry ever be... "Not one more!" "Not one more!" "Not one more!" "Not one more!" "Not one more!" "Not one more!" "Not one more!" "Not one more!" "Not one more!" "Not one more!" Let it be so. Let it be so. Let it be so. Hallelujah!

Amen.

October 9, 2015

Queer Cosmology and the Penalty of Death

Queer theorists and theologians push against boundaries and borders until they are no more and the individual is liberated to exist in the perfect freedom that is being. Cosmologists study origins and the development of the universe. Tonight, I intend to push us into a queer cosmological experience. The spiritual experience of thinking about the last questions of those on death row teaches us about our origins and helps us to think about how we can move to a space beyond boundaries and borders.

Just a few short weeks back, I spent a few hours visiting Juan Garcia. Though we only knew each other for a short time, I've loosely based my talk tonight on some of the questions that Juan asked in our final meeting.

"Are you prepared to stand by as they kill me?"

The enormity of our cause should never be lost. We are participating in a struggle to save lives. Often, we are the last line of defense. The question of effort is a spiritual question. Do you believe in life enough to do all that you can to save it? To cede the question of life to the forces of death is a spiritual disease that has afflicted us for far too long. We must get rescued from our malaise. We must learn to push against the borders and boundaries of our laws that allow for executions to continually execute our consciences. Will we allow the machinery of death to continue with no resistance?

"Do you believe in forgiveness?"

We can't expect to change the way that people think about the death penalty until we change the way that we think about ourselves. Some of the most hateful and unforgiving people I know are abolitionists. How are we going to encourage our society to show mercy to persons on death row when we refuse to show mercy? Did you begin in hate? Abolition begins pushing against the borders and boundaries within.

"Is there redemption?"

The death penalty is a moral cancer on our society primarily because it refuses to acknowledge the possibility of redemption. Redemption is a critical component of a morally and ethically healthy society. Redemption allows people to change and blows up our categories of good and evil. I believe redemption is the only way to guide people to love. Do you remember love?

"What will the end be like?"

In order to get where we want to go...we have to know what direction we are going. The eschatological question of the end is critical. Do you remember when we didn't have a death penalty? Do we want to be a society where all life is valued? I believe the end is love and that our job is to work toward getting there. Do you believe that abolition is possible? You must first learn to believe before you can start heading that direction. The borders and boundaries of the mind are always the most difficult obstacle to abolition.

Imagine that you have engaged all of these questions with someone who is condemned to die and the guard knocks on the door to tell you, "It's time." The doors open and you take the final steps with the condemned. As tears roll down your face...you enter the execution chamber. Walking up to the condemned on the gurney, you look down to offer one last word and you are shocked by the face you see...it is your child.

This is how serious we must begin to think about our origins and abolition of the death penalty.

Amen.

October 10, 2015

The Prayer at the End of the Walk to Stop Executions

Almighty God...We know you by many names...but today we gather for a primary purpose of abolition...but first we must repent. We repent that we wake up most days and don't give a shit about the death penalty. We repent that we've often mounted little resistance to the machinery of death. We repent that we've consistently supplied all the funds necessary...by way of our taxes...to carry out these executions. Oh God...we repent.

We thank you for the sweet spirit in this place...but God you know that we don't need any more sweetness. We know that it will take anger to abolish the death penalty. We know that we have to get angrier about these executions. Oh God...we pray for anger. We pray for anger so mighty that it turns into a rage strong enough to help us topple the whole damn system. We need anger against injustice. We need anger against killing. We need anger against the devaluation of life. We need anger...for we know that only anger and rage can lead us to a place of love. We have to overturn the gurney and execution tables Lord before we can learn to love the executioners. Help us Oh God!

Raise our dead bodies up. Lift our weary feet. Grant us passion and commitment. Push us further than we ever thought we could go. May our Walk to Stop Executions turn into the Sprint to Abolition...and let it happen yesterday.

Amen.

October 12, 2015

The Closing Prayer at WE ARE NOT AFRAID

*Prayer given on 10/11/15 at a rally to respond to recent beatings and murders in the Dallas Gayborhood.

Almighty God...you are known by many names and found by many paths...we thank you for your presence with us tonight. Let us first apologize to you and our neighbors. We repent for all the times that we have sat on our asses and done nothing about the violence that has far too often afflicted our community. We repent for supporting and belonging to establishments and institutions that care more about our money than they do our lives. We repent for spending too much time in closets and failing to get out in the streets. Oh God...we repent.

On this day we join together in prayer for that great heavenly crowbar. Wedge that thing between our asses and our seats...push down with all your divine might and eject us from our places of comfort...and into the struggle for liberation. Then oh God we pray that you will take that crowbar over to all the bars and restaurants that line these streets and wedge it between the ass and the seats of all who are comfortable tonight in the midst of such grave injustices. Wake us up. Then I need you to take that crowbar to one more place oh God. The churches that fill up the Gayborhood too often talk about love but do nothing to save lives...oh God we need you to take that crowbar and get underneath the holy asses that line those pews...get them stepping for justice.

Lastly, oh God...I know that you have heard all of the prayers for love and peace tonight...so I won't spend all my time there...but I am going to ask you for something that you gave your son Jesus...rage. Help us to rage against injustice God. We know that you are the God that went into the temple and tore shit up. Help us to tear up injustice oh God. We are far too comfortable and complacent right now God...we need rage. We need to feel like these beatings and murders happened to us or those we love...oh God grant us a fiery rage.

We know that you are the God who is the eternal fire. Keep that eternal fire right up under our asses as we depart tonight. Let it not go out until that day that we see justice.

Hallelujah! and...

Amen.

October 12, 2015

God Give Us Rage

We open the doors to our sanctuaries. Ushers greet us with a program. Pleasantries always fill the air. Slowly, we walk to our favorite pew. By the time the preacher arises to welcome us, we know what's going to happen next and next after that. The service is always the same. Music fills the air. Hymnals are opened and closed. People rise up and down. The preacher preaches words that are just bland enough for us to ignore them. The offering plates are passed around to levy a tax for our experiences. By the time the invitation comes, we are just happy to stand up and leave the pews for a brief moment. Rushing to lunch, we laugh at all the cheesy jokes that we have heard over and over. Skipping the receiving line, we briefly watch the preacher shake every hand, forget names and try to act like they have real concern for all the souls who pass them by. Less than an hour after the service, we remember very little about what has just taken place. We practice the same irrelevancy over and over.

On a memorable occasion, Jesus interacted with a space of worship similar to ours. Before the organist got around to the invitation, Jesus destroyed their tables, slung their money out on the floor and pierced the air with a whip made of chords. Rage transformed the worship experience. Desperate for change, Jesus raged until the people were out of their seats and into the street.

Last night, I encountered the people of God in the streets of Dallas, Texas. These are not people you will ever meet at your church. Regardless of how great your programming is...these folks ain't coming...yet the spirit of God was mighty in their presence. The people were gathered to protest a series of beatings and murders against the LGBTQ community. When I was asked to deliver a closing prayer, I didn't really know what to say. I decided not to prepare anything. Usually, that is when I am most prepared for God to take over. I kept thinking about Jesus slinging that whip around. When my tongue loosened and my mouth opened, I knew that Spirit had taken over and that the words were hers:

> "Almighty God...you are known by many names and found by many paths...we thank you for your presence with us tonight. Let us first apologize to you and to our neighbors. We repent for all the times that we have done nothing about the violence that has far too often afflicted our community. We repent for supporting and belonging to establishments and institutions that care more about our money than they do our lives. We repent for spending too much time in closets and failing to get out in the streets. Oh God...we repent.
>
> On this day we join together in prayer for that great heavenly crowbar. Wedge that thing between our asses and our seats...push down with all your divine might and eject us from our places of comfort...and into the struggle for liberation. Then oh God we pray that you will take that crowbar over to all the bars and restaurants that line these streets and wedge it between the ass and the seats of all who are comfortable tonight in the midst of such grave injustices. Wake us up. Then I need you to take that crowbar to one more place oh God. The churches that fill up our city too often talk about love but do nothing to save lives...oh God we need you to take that crowbar and get underneath those holy asses that line the pews...and get them stepping for justice.
>
> Lastly, oh God...I know that you have heard all of the prayers for love and peace tonight...so I won't spend any time there...but I am going to ask you for something that you gave your son Jesus...rage. Help us to rage against injustice God. We know that you are the God that went into the temple and tore shit up. Help us to tear up injustice oh God. We are far too comfortable and complacent right now oh God...we need rage. We need to feel like these beatings and murders happened to us or those we love...oh God grant us a fiery rage.
>
> We know that you are the God who is the eternal fire. Keep that eternal fire right up under our asses as we depart tonight. Let it not go out until that day that we see justice face to face.
>
> Hallelujah! and...Amen."

When I finished, multiple people told me the prayer caused them to feel something in their bones. Although these folks would never go to church, I knew they were feeling the spirit of God far more than most of the folks who go to church do. When people said they wanted to go to church, I kept telling them, "Don't go to church! You already are the church. The church is right here." Jesus said, "What you have done to the least of these you have done to me." The least were out in full force and they didn't need buildings, pews, hymnals or offerings to experience God. The longer we sit in our pews and spend exorbitant amounts of money on irrelevance the longer we will miss Jesus. Oh God, I pray that you will help us destroy our churches so that we can meet you in the streets. God give us rage...

Amen.

October 18, 2015

The Times I Lose My Mind

I once spent over $14,000 on books in one month. I sold and spent anything I could get my hands on. I would've done anything to buy more books. In fourth grade, I was paranoid of tornadoes. Day after day, I fought anyone who attempted to force me outside. I once tried to cut down the largest tree in my backyard by ramming it with my car. For multiple early morning hours, I tried over and over. Multiple people threatened to call the police. Throughout my life...in numerous instances and in a variety of ways...I have lost my mind. Those who treat me call it Bipolar Disorder. I call it crazy. Regardless of the terminology, I'm prone to dangerous bouts of mania and paranoia without proper medication. Matthew Ajibade was too.

On New Year's Day of 2015 in Savannah, Georgia, Matthew Ajibade lost his mind. When officers arrived to the scene, Ajibade's bloodied girlfriend told them that Ajibade was having a mental breakdown and desperately needed the medication she was giving them. Instead of seeking treatment, the officers took Ajibade to the Chatham County Jail. During the booking process, Ajibade remained combative and broke the nose of a Chatham County Sheriff's Deputy. As payback, deputies beat the shit out of Ajibade and placed him in an isolation cell. Once Ajibade was compliant and strapped to a restraint chair, deputies took a Taser, pressed it to his genitals and shocked him with 50,000 volts. For multiple hours, no one monitored or checked on Ajibade. Around 1:38am, deputies discovered Matthew Ajibade dead. The Chatham County Coroner ruled the death a homicide by blunt force trauma. Though nine deputies were eventually fired and three deputies were found guilty of midlevel criminal offenses, justice wasn't served. The Chatham County Sheriff's Department tortured Matthew Ajibade to death. The Dallas County Sheriff's Department acted similarly with Joseph Hutcheson.

On August 1, 2015, Joseph Hutcheson was mentally ill suffering paranoia and on drugs. Hutcheson lost his mind. Desperate for help, Joseph Hutcheson parked his truck on the curb of the Lew Sterrett Justice Center in Dallas, Texas and ran inside. Upon entering, Hutcheson screamed, "Don't hurt me, I just need some help." Deputies tackled him. As Hutcheson screamed that he couldn't breathe, a witness described one deputy restraining Hutcheson with "a knee on his back" and another deputy restraining him "with a knee on his throat." Hutcheson's face turned from white to blue. Around 11:30am, Hutcheson was pronounced dead. The Dallas County Medical Examiner ruled the death a homicide. No one involved has faced any repercussions over the incident. The Dallas County Sheriff's Department tortured and choked the life out of Joseph Hutcheson.

Forget overseas, the terrorists are right here and they target the least of these. Law enforcement continues to torture and kill those who lose their minds and are in desperate need of help. I suffer from Bipolar Disorder just like Matthew Ajibade. When I am off my medicine, I experience paranoia just like Joseph Hutcheson. What happens if I lose my mind again? Will I be the next one in need of help murdered?

Amen.

October 20, 2015

The National Association of Evangelicals/Executioners

For years, I've heard rumors that the National Association of Evangelicals was planning to change their stance on the death penalty. When I heard that major evangelical figures were lobbying the organization to move to abolition, I grew more and more excited. Yesterday, I saw evangelical writer Jonathan Merritt's post, "This is HUGE news on #deathpenalty from America's largest evangelical Christian body." I knew this was the statement I'd been waiting on. Opening the link, I was thankful until I realized what the statement actually said. Having been for the death penalty since the early 1970s, the National Association of Evangelicals had now decided to take a moderate stance that allows for multiple legitimate views on the subject. In a day in which the evil nature of the death penalty is beyond obvious based on socioeconomics, systemic injustices, moral concerns, cost and a whole host of other factors, the National Association of Evangelicals continues to teach that one can legitimately follow Jesus and love your neighbor as yourself by executing them. In the name of Jesus... What the fuck? Let us remember that the greatest promulgators of evil are those who stand aside in times of murder. For this bullshit attempt at relevant moderation, the National Association of Evangelicals should be called the National Association of Executioners.

Amen.

Read the Full Statement at:
http://www.christianitytoday.com/gleanings/2015/october/evangelicals-divided-death-penalty-nae-capital-punishment.html

October 21, 2015

The Heresy of Quiet Times

"Jesus happens in quiet times." Growing up, I remember a minister consistently using this line to guilt us into regular quiet times. We were told that these daily times of personal prayer and Bible study were what made us Christians. We were not alone. Throughout the Christian faith, there exists this strange idea that quiet times are the base line of Christian practice. This is heresy. When Jesus declared that he would be incarnate in the least of these, we were shown what the base line of Christianity is...speaking up. While I am by no means opposed to personal prayer or Bible study, I am opposed placing a supremacy on quiet times. In a world where people are regularly being oppressed and marginalized to death, we need less quiet times and more loud times of prophetic resistance. "Jesus happens in loud times."

Amen.

October 21, 2015

The Greatest Narcissist of Them All: God

For the last few days, I've been involved in the gathering of a new progressive evangelical organization called OPEN. Throughout our time together, we've been asked by hipster music leaders to stand up and sing with all our might. In song after song, we sing about how awesome, wonderful, majestic, amazing and powerful God is. One of the thoughts I've long had hit me again like a ton of bricks. Why does God need us to sing all this shit? Is God the greatest narcissist of them all? This week, I've chosen to stop singing. I've simply realized I believe in the God beyond the God that everyone is singing about.

Amen.

October 22, 2015

Prayers from the Road

What happened? What was that? I felt something. It was more than something. It felt like a kick in the soul. I was overwhelmed. The blades turn. The few cabin lights interrupted the dark of this cold night. In the tiniest seat I have ever crushed my ass into, something happened. The intercom radios final instructions. I didn't give a shit. I just wanted more. Something grabbed me in the darkness... Did anyone see it? I am alone. What in the fuck was that? I can't even describe it. What grabbed me? I can't tell what is real right now. Why can't I get it back? We are airborne. I just want it back.

The air is cold. Don't freeze. The sudden bumps bring us closer to death. The baby cries out. Life is so fragile. We will live. The lights dim. The darkness comes back. I know you're there. I sense you coming closer. Is this a game of hide and seek? You're gone again. You're good at that. Stay with me for just one extended second. I can't take the constant in and out. Either stay or go. I'm sick of this. Why am I afraid? You taught me that.

Fasten your seatbelts. The plane is rocking violently back and forth. Is this what happens when you pitch a fit? Is this a mortality reminder? I don't need any reminders. I think about it all the time. I'm tired of the games. Let's see some proof of life. Fasten your seatbelts. The turbulence only grows stronger. Where in the fuck are you? No smoking. Forget it. I'm already on fire. Something smells like bullshit. I'm surrounded. Where? When? How? There has to be more than this.

Slow down. We begin to fall. The lights approach faster and faster. Our time is drawing to a close. The watches tick rapidly. Is this a crash? Everything is shaking. Why is the ground so close? The smoke rises. I grab for the elements. We skid to a stop. We're alive. I guess you're here. Maybe? Why is there always turbulence when I'm with you?

Amen.

October 27, 2015

The Complicity of Silence

Even in a society comfortable with violence, the video stands out. In the midst of a classroom dispute at Spring Valley High School, Richland County Sheriff's Deputy Ben Fields grabbed the desk of a young female student (14) and slammed her backward to the ground. If that wasn't brutal enough, the Deputy then drug her multiple feet across the floor before pouncing on top of her. Most in the room sat in stunned silence. In the midst of the chaos, one student named Niya Kenny spoke up. Upon demanding the assault stop, Kenny was arrested and charged with disturbing the school. Around our nation, there are many who sit in stunned silence after watching this video. While shock is an understandable reaction, we do not live in a time where anyone has the privilege of silence. To be silent now is to be complicit in the assault. May we all garner the courage of Niya Kenny and speak out.

Amen.

October 30, 2015

Standing in the Need of Prayer

What happened? What was that? I felt something. It was more than something. It felt like a kick in the soul. I am overwhelmed. The blades turn. The dim lights interrupt the dark of this cold night. In the tiniest space I have ever been forced into...something happened. The final instructions come in from the sky. I don't give a shit. I just wanted more. Something grabbed me in the darkness... Did anyone see it? I am alone. What in the fuck was that? I can't even describe it. What grabbed me? I can't tell what's real right now. Why can't I get it back? We gain altitude. I just want it back.

The air is cold. Don't freeze. The sudden bumps bring us closer to death. The baby cries out. Life is so fragile. We'll live. I know it. The lights dim even further. The darkness looks familiar. I know you're there. I sense you coming. Is this a game of hide and seek? You're gone again. You're good at that. Stay with me for just one second. I can't take the constant in and out. Either stay or go. I'm sick of this. Why am I afraid? You taught me to fear.

Fasten your seatbelts. We rock violently back and forth. Is this what happens when you pitch a fit? Is this a mortality reminder? I don't need any reminders. I think about it all the time. I'm tired of the games. Let's see some proof of life. Fasten your seatbelts. The turbulence only grows stronger. Where are you? Don't let rage creep up. Forget it. I'm already on fire. Something smells like bullshit. I'm surrounded.

Slower. We begin to fall. The lights grow brighter and brighter. Time is drawing to a close. Watches tick rapidly. Are we crashing? Everything is shaking. Why is the ground so close? Smoke rises. I grab the elements. We skid to a stop. We're alive. Are you?

Amen.

October 30, 2015

Three Months After the Death of Joseph Hutcheson: Words

We gather three months to the day after the Dallas County Sheriff's Department murdered Joseph Hutcheson. We are not far at all from the spot where Joseph pulled his truck up on the curb in desperate need of help. We can see where Joseph walked up that hill in desperate need of help. We know that on up that hill are the doors to the lobby where Joseph entered in desperate need of help. Instead of help...Joseph was slammed to the ground and murdered.

It seems fitting that we would gather on Halloween. While everyone dresses up in costumes and goes out tonight for the latest scare, we the gathered here know that the real house of horrors is right in there. In his hour of need, Joseph Hutcheson received death. I hold Sheriff Lupe Valdez responsible. There is nothing more frightening than the deputized bullies who killed Joseph and their powerful protector.

On this day...make no mistake...we are strong and want the world to know that we will not stop fighting for justice for Joseph Hutcheson. God is with us.

Amen.

October 31, 2015

God Damn these Hate Crimes and the Institutions that Fail to Act to Prevent Them

Just a few months ago, trans woman of color Shade Schuler was murdered in this community. Shade's body was in a field over in the Medical District so long that it was difficult for the police to identify her when someone cutting grass found her. We forgot about Shade. When I heard about the horror of it all, I didn't want to forget again. I decided to organize a vigil and communion at the exact spot where Shade was found. To my surprise, when we walked up to the spot...you could see the black outline of Shade's body. When I bent down to touch the place, you could feel the stickiness of rotted human flesh. As I lifted up the wine and bread to the heavens, I declared with all my might that this was the body and blood of Shade Schuler. When we drank and ate that night, I believe we were filled with the spirit of Shade. You see, I don't believe in death without resurrection. I am out here tonight in the exact same robe and stole I had on then to lift up the spirit of Shade. I believe she is here with us. When you march for light and against hate tonight, may you feel the resurrected spirit of Shade Schuler in a mighty and powerful way.

Even more than being the Executive Director of Hope for Peace & Justice, I am an old Baptist preacher. I still believe in fire and damnation...I just don't believe we have directed it in the proper direction. With so many hate crimes having taken place in this community over the last few months, I want to bring a little fire and damnation down to Oak Lawn... I pray that God will damn all the businesses in this community that continue to step over the bodies of marginalized and oppressed peoples to make a buck. I pray that God will damn those churches that step over the bodies of marginalized and oppressed peoples to conduct their services. I pray that God will damn any and all institutions that step over the bodies of marginalized and oppressed peoples to conduct their business. Oh God damn these hate crimes and all the institutions that do nothing to prevent them. No more will we sit back and allow this community to be brutalized. No more will we act like nothing is going on. No more will we stand aside as the least of these are brutalized. God we pray that you will send your fire down into our hearts in a powerful way...then send a little bit of fire down beneath our asses to keep us stepping for justice. Hallelujah! Hallelujah! and...

Amen.

November 5, 2015

The Failed Construct of Diversity

Diversity is a failed construct. The idea of diversity as sacrosanct is deeply problematic because it is falsely predicated on the notion that having a bunch of different identities in one place means that there is real difference represented. For decades, we've accepted and promoted diversity as a means of solving problems of exclusion. We've been taught to believe that as long as the space appears diverse then there is room for everyone. History shows us that this is certainly not true. Tokenisms have always run wild in our ideas of diversity. Even more than that, what was once called diverse we would now call oppressive. Truly, some of the most hateful spaces I have encountered have been the most diverse. People often learn to hate very quickly even in the midst of tremendous diversity. In fact, wide diversity often masks macro and micro aggressions against the oppressed and marginalized. True queerness forces us to think deeply about what it looks like to have the room to be different. We don't need wider diversity...we need wider authenticity.

Amen.

November 5, 2015

The Real Queers

Claiming an identity or category doesn't make you queer. Anyone can claim anything and be just as normative as anyone else. Oppression is always the chief marker of normativity. Queerness and oppression don't go together. The real queer shuns oppression for the sake of transformation. Over the last few weeks, I have watched many fake queers lead the campaign for the Houston Equal Rights Ordinance. Over and over again, persons of color were treated like their voices didn't matter. Trans persons were pushed aside in favor of more normative representations of the community. Poor people never got in the door to even have the conversation. Women were consistently asked to move aside in favor of the worn out arguments of men. I am tired of seeing representatives of the so-called queer community act just like those they claim to oppose. The Human Rights Campaign once again proved they're not a friend of anything queer. The white gay boys who ran this HERO campaign might as well have been shouting the words of

George Wallace, "Segregation now, segregation tomorrow, segregation forever." Because over and over the most marginalized and oppressed members of the Houston community were segregated out and informed that they didn't matter to the campaign. I am reminded how frail, normative and brutally oppressive identity politics intrinsically are. The old normativity always makes way for a new normativity. Will the real queers please stand up?

Amen.

November 7, 2015

The Right to Not Be Offended: Common Ground with Dr. Mohler

The inscription in my copy of Dr. Albert Mohler's 2008 book *Culture Shift* reads, "May God greatly bless you. I am thankful God called you to Southern Seminary." At the time, I was a fervent disciple of the President of the Southern Baptist Theological Seminary. Now, some might consider me to be an enemy. While there is no question that my views and theology have changed dramatically since I sat in the classrooms Dr. Mohler presided over, I have often wondered what common ground is left. While browsing my library a few weeks back, I stumbled on my copy of *Culture Shift*. For an hour or so, I read through the fundamentalist pages. I found little I agreed with until I came across this line, "There is simply no right to not be offended, and we should be offended by the very notion that such a right could exist."

We live in an age where the mythical right to not be offended is valued above all else. If someone is offended, you're expected to stop saying or doing whatever you're doing immediately. There is no room for discussion or dissent. Society becomes powerless to move. I find it all incredibly stifling. My faith teaches me that there must be room in our lives and interactions for robust and passionate disagreement and offense. Truth be told, you can't follow Jesus without offense. There is nothing more offensive than asking people to give their lives for the betterment of their enemies. There is nothing more offensive than demanding love in a society filled with hate. There is nothing more offensive than declaring God to forever be on the side of those we marginalize and oppressed. The Gospel of Jesus offends sensibilities and rationalities consistently. I can't stop following and proclaiming the truest and most offensive construction I have ever known. For those who believe they have a right to not be offended...I guess I should warn you to stay away from me.

Amen.

November 8, 2015

Opening Prayer at the Fellowship of Reconciliation Centennial Gala

Oh God, we thank you for 100 years of pursuing peace and justice in our world. This room is full of energy and ideals...but sometimes we can be a little slow. So...God we ask that you take the fire that is in all of our hearts tonight and manuever it underneath our backsides so that we will race into the next 100 years.

Amen.

November 8, 2015

The Institutionalized Jesus & the Lie that is Our Churches

Going to church was never part of the plan. In fact, church was less something you went to and more something you were supposed to become. Why do we spend so much time and money keeping up institutions? Jesus simply said, "Follow me." We are the church. We don't need anything else. We just need to follow Jesus.

How did being the church turn into our present institutionalized nightmare? The short answer is that we lost sight of Jesus. The long answer is about control. The institutionalized Jesus is much easier to control than the wilder real one. Our churches exist to keep Jesus contained. We don't want to sell everything we have. We don't want to house and feed the poor. We don't want to love our neighbors. We don't want to fight for the marginalized and oppressed. We love the contained Jesus because our safety is more important than anything else...which is why our churches have become lies. The truth is much more simple than our current functioning. Jesus will always be out there on the margins living dangerously beyond our budgets and bulletins.

Amen.

November 9, 2015

My Kids Tell Me Everything I Need to Know About Your Church

A few weeks back, our family opened the doors of an old church and sat down. I was invited to share with the congregation about my work and told that my family was more than welcome. From the moment we walked in, the sneering glances and pursed lips informed us that this congregation was most interested in robotic children who don't make a peep before they dutifully file out after the children's sermon. Our children are not like that.

For clarity sake, let me break it down for you. We have 5 very rowdy kids under the age of 3.5 years old. Our oldest children are a set of incredibly rambunctious twins. Our only single is a very demanding 2 year old. Our youngest set of twins are 7 months old and do what babies do. My kids tell me everything that I need to know about the churches we visit by the way they are treated.

The realm of God is made for the shrieks, howls and wild audacity of children. We must learn to join them. In Matthew 19:14, Jesus rebuked the child despising disciples with the following words, "Let the children come to me..." This don't sound like the believe and behave method of most of our churches. How you treat children in your church tells me everything that I need to know about what you believe about Jesus. If you think that Jesus is most concerned with the uninterrupted ordering of your service...I encourage you to reread the Gospels. Jesus was always interrupting and on the move. So why do we expect our children to function differently?

Amen.

November 10, 2015

Stop Going to Church

*appeared in Baptist News Global on 11/10

There was an expansive agricultural nursery across the street from the large Southern Baptist church I grew up in. Each Sunday, everyone who attended our fundamentalist church had to drive by the Jewish family who owned it on their way out. On multiple occasions, I remember different people from our church leaning out their windows and screaming at the top of their lungs, "Go to church!" Such actions were a natural outgrowth of our strategy to evangelize our community or to get more people into our church. While we were busy talking about how to grow our space, the hungry in our community knew they could always go to the Jewish family to get free food. During the quarterly budget meetings about the millions and millions of dollars needed to keep our facility going, I often thought about the juxtaposition of the Jewish family across the street feeding the hungry and our church members screaming at them to "Go to church!"

The more I have thought about this story from my youth, the more I realize that it is an adaptation of an old parable for the modern church. There once was a guy leading a minority religious community. One day, he led his disciples to some good food in the wheat fields. The day being the day that was normally reserved for worship, leaders of the majority religious community came by and demanded that they "Go to church!" or something like that. Jesus sought to make sure that those around him were fed and these idiots were trying to get more people into church or follow their lead.

"How do we grow our church?" Since my youth, I have heard this question asked over and over in a variety of spaces and contexts. The biggest fear of the modern church is decline. Why? I think we actually believe the church is going to die without our budgets, bulletins, buildings, baptisteries, branding and a whole host of things that have become so sacrosanct to us. I doubt we can get much more foolish. While we have spent our time pushing people into our churches, the world is still crumbling and demanding answers to the questions...

How can you tell someone to go to church when they are busy searching for something to eat...due to our concern about adjusting the temperature in our church and not to the changing climate that is destroying crops on the outside?

How can you tell someone to go to church when you know that they are far too strange...to fit into the normative ways that you consistently practice?

How can you tell someone to use their energy and resources to get to church when they don't have a home...due to the economic inequalities that have contributed to the growth of our edifices and the shrinking of our hearts?

How can you tell someone to go to church when they are locked up...because we have done nothing about mass incarceration?

How can you tell someone to go to church when they know that their clothes smell like shit...and all your people will do is complain about the stench?

How can you tell someone to go to church when they are sick and dying...due to churches refusing to engage in healthcare advocacy?

The question "How do we grow our church?" is offensive and disgusting in a world of injustice like ours. Those who keep asking the question do so at their own peril. For concentrating on growing the church means that you have ceased to concentrate on what it means to actually be the church in a world of crippling injustice. We don't need more budgets. We don't need more bulletins. We don't need more buildings. We don't need more baptisteries. We don't need more branding. We need Jesus and that is all.

The greatest heresy of all is that going to church was a part of the plan in the first place. The idea of church has always been more about becoming something than going somewhere. Why do we spend so much energy and resources keeping all these institutions up? How did being the church turn into our present institutionalized nightmare? The short answer is that we lost sight of Jesus. Jesus simply said, "Follow me." I invite you to stop going to church and learn to follow. Jesus will always be out there on the margins living dangerously beyond our budgets, bulletins, buildings, baptisteries, branding and...

Amen.

November 10, 2015

The Death Penalty & The Dallas County District Attorney: An Encounter

*A recreation of a public question and answer dialogue I had with Dallas County District Attorney Susan Hawk at her town hall last night.

JH: Good evening, my name is Rev. Dr. Jeff Hood and I serve on the Board of Directors of the Texas Coalition to Abolish the Death Penalty. We have talked about a number of issues involving race tonight and I wanted to ask you specifically about the death penalty. With persons of color much more likely to receive the death penalty than anyone else...isn't it time to abolish the death penalty?

SH: My office has completely changed the way that death penalty cases are handled. We take death penalty cases very seriously.

JH: There is no question that there has been improvement in the Dallas County District Attorney's Office since you took office but there is also no question that the death penalty is still on the table for you. These cases are unbelievably expensive to try. If someone murders five people in most counties in this state they are not going to get the death penalty because the counties can't afford to try the case. Why don't we take the option of the death penalty off the table and save the taxpayers an enormous amount of money? Will you commit to an impartial study that looks at the functioning of the death penalty in Dallas County?

SH: I cannot do that. The death penalty is the law. I will however add this...are you aware that we have not pursued a single death penalty case since I have been in office?

JH: I am and make no mistake...I'm going to pray that is stays that way. Thank you for your time District Attorney.

Amen.

November 10, 2015

I Don't Believe in Celebrating Veterans.

Ray Hood was a hero of mine. Late at night, he would gather us around and rip sideways on the harmonica. We danced as only children can. The older we got the more we loved his stories. None of us could believe that he was on a boat for months at a time. "Harry Truman saved my life!" If there'd been an invasion, he would've been on the first wave in. The older I got the more I thought about his love for the atomic bombs dropped on Japan. It is strange to grow into a place of conflict about someone you love. By the time I studied theology, I knew that Jesus wouldn't serve in the military. The old war stories started to sound strange. Though, I couldn't disregard all that he'd taught me about Jesus. Before he died, I told him that I no longer believed in war. Laying in bed, he couldn't respond. When I saw the flag draped over his casket, I grew angry at the thought that this blanket of nationalism was erasing my loving grandfather. I don't believe in celebrating veterans. I believe we shouldn't be warring in the first place. I believe in celebrating the love of God found in people. I believe in the ambiguity that was Ray Hood. I miss my grandfather terribly.

Amen.

November 12, 2015

The Reincarnation of Jesus Christ

In the beginning was Love, Love was with God and Love was God. There is nothing greater than Love... for God is Love. For God so Loved the world that Love gave Love's only begotten Love, that whosoever believes in Love will not perish but have everlasting Love. Love your enemies and pray for those who persecute you. Jesus Christ is the incarnation of Love. Love declared, "Love Love with all your heart mind, body and strength and Love your neighbor as yourself." When the time of death approached, Love climbed upon that cross and declared Love for all the world. After three days, Love rose again. Death could not kill Love. Love commanded, "Go therefore into all the world and make disciples of Love, baptizing them in the name of Love and of Love and of Love, teaching them to observe all the Love that I have shared. And behold, Love is with you always, even to the end of the age." Since those days, Love just keeps coming back. The reincarnation of Jesus Christ cannot be stopped for Love is all encompassing and eternal. Love wins.

Amen.

November 12, 2015

The Real Serial Killer: Our Categories

We sit at a profound moment in history. Daily, we are privy to images of social upheaval broadcast into our consciousness from all over the world. We regularly see the consequences of our fictitious categories. We've created more monsters than we can count. We thought that skin tones said something innate about who or what someone was. We continue to be so wrong. We thought that sexual orientation said something innate about who or what someone was. We continue to be so wrong. We thought that ability said something innate about who or what someone was. We continue to be so wrong. I could go on and on. Our categories have failed. We sit in the midst of hate of our own creation. We must find a way out of all of these lines that we have drawn between each other or we will suffocate under the weight of trying to live into the hateful categorical expectations that we have become enslaved to. Hate divides and kills.

"*Hate* provides a bitter fruit upon which to feed and slowly it poisons the whole being…Hate also wills the nonexistence of another human being. It is not the same as willing the destruction of another person; such is often the aim of bitterness and hostility. Hate is at another and more profound level; it undermines the very being of the other by affirming his nonexistence and accepting this affirmation as true and authentic. It is a withdrawal of sanction of the other as existing…This is refined evil."

-Howard Thurman, *This Luminous Darkness*, 45-46

Hate is what fuels the creation of categories and our desire to live into them. We believe that we can empower our category by excluding other categories. We are foolish. In our attempts to create exclusive safe spaces, we are perpetuating the hate that we claim to stand against. Make no mistake, all gatherings exclusive of other categories perpetuate the hate that were used to create the categories in the first place. I do not believe that peace or reconciliation or equality or justice can exist as long as we kill each other with our categories. On this day, I must declare that I will not participate in anything that excludes any categories. I do not believe that the segregation of categories will do anything but create more hate. Our categories are failing us and love is the only answer.

"Hate cannot drive out hate, only love can do that."

-Martin Luther King, Jr., *Strength to Love*, 37

Love is the only antidote to our addiction to our hateful categorization. Love is a process of radical inclusion not exclusion. We must love beyond the hate that is our foolish categories.

Amen.

November 14, 2015

I am a Terrorist

Early this morning, I shot up in bed. Even in my sleep, I couldn't get the images of Baghdad, Beirut and Paris out of my head. How is a follower of Jesus to respond to these terrorists? I thought about it for hours. Then I realized something. Jesus said, "Love your neighbor as yourself" & "Love your enemy." We are commanded to "love our enemies as ourselves." We cannot love our enemies as we love ourselves and not become our enemy. We are commanded to "love the terrorist as we love ourselves." We cannot love the terrorist as we love ourselves without becoming the terrorist. If we want to follow Jesus, we are commanded to become what we want to save. Is this not the lesson of the incarnation of Jesus into our evil world? Truly, those who are following the path of Jesus will embrace their enemies so fully that they will bind their person to them. In the coming days, our cry of love for our enemies must be, "I am a terrorist."

Amen.

November 16, 2015

The Pilgrimage for Raphael Holiday is The Pilgrimage for Abolition

This Wednesday, Raphael Holiday will be executed minutes after 6pm at the Walls Unit in Huntsville, Texas. Unlike many of those I've encountered on death row, I believe that Holiday deserves to die.

In early 2000, Raphael was partnered with Tami Wilkerson. Together, they lived in a secluded log cabin in Madison County with their infant daughter Justice and Tami's young daughters, five-year-old Jasmine and seven-year-old Tierra. In March, Tami discovered that Raphael had sexually assaulted Tierra and filed charges against him. Raphael was forced to move out. Despite the protective order, Tami let Raphael occasionally see his daughter. In August, Raphael started to assault and terrorize Tami incessantly. When she cut off all communication, things got worse.

Late in the night of September 5, 2000, Tami saw a figure coming through the woods. By the time family arrived to help, Raphael was in the house. Tami's aunt Beverly Mitchell rushed the oldest girls to the car. Though her uncle Terry Keller had a gun, Raphael choked Tami and made him hand it over. Raphael was unsuccessful in his attempts to burn the car with the girls in it. In the midst of it all, Tami rushed to a neighbor's home for help. By the time she returned to the log cabin, the structure was engulfed in flames and all three children were locked inside.

Though Raphael Holiday tried to argue that he didn't mean to kill the three little girls, I don't believe him. The jury didn't either. Now, the hour has come for the punishment to be carried out. I still believe that he deserves to die. There is only one question left to ask. Who deserves to kill him? I've sat with this question for many hours. I believe I know the answer.

There once was an execution scheduled. The authorities threw a woman that committed a capital offense at the feet of Jesus. As they raised their stones to kill her, Jesus got down in the dirt to join her in her fate. Looking up, Jesus declared, "Whoever is without sin can cast the first stone!"

Over the next two days, I will pilgrimage over 40 miles carrying the cross between Death Row/Polunsky Unit in Livingston and the Execution Chamber/Walls Unit in Huntsville not because I believe that Raphael Holiday is innocent...but rather because I know he's not. Jesus taught us to "love our neighbors as ourselves" and Holiday has already shown us that there is no love in killing. May we show Holiday the mercy that he didn't show his victims. Throughout my journey, I will pray that we will stop emulating the killers we claim we are punishing and stop this foolishness of executions once and for all.

Amen.

+ You can get hourly updates/prayers from the pilgrimage on Facebook at https://www.facebook.com/revjeffhood/ and on Twitter at @revjeffhood

November 20, 2015
The Church and Climate Change

When I think about climate change, the message of Jesus comes to mind. We are called to love our neighbor as we love our self. Our actions and lack of action continue to destroy the homes of billions. When it comes to climate change, it seems that we don't know the first thing about love. Jesus also talked about the least of these. We know that climate change is affecting the poorest of poor and the most marginalized amongst us at a much faster rate than anyone else. With the United Nations Climate Change Conference coming up, I urge followers of Jesus to stand up and speak for justice. Here in Dallas, one of the few things connecting First Baptist, First Methodist, Cathedral of Hope and a wide variety of churches large and small is that none are speaking out on climate change. I call on these churches to stand up and save our planet. Speak out! Act up! Follow the example of Pope Francis! Follow the example of Jesus! In this moment of crisis, silence is complicity in the continued destruction of our planet.
Amen

November 20, 2015

The Call of the Muslim Jesus

When Jesus bound his body and ultimately became the stranger in Matthew 25:35, he left no doubt that he was calling us to do the same. Since the Paris attacks, Muslims have been strangerized over and over. From calls for registration to violent language around refugees, the rhetoric has grown worse and worse with every day. Jesus is bound to the stranger. Jesus becomes the stranger. In our Islamophobic society, I have no question that Jesus is so intimately incarnated with and connected to our Muslim friends that he has become one. If we want to walk with Jesus in this moment of extreme oppression and marginalization, we will too.

Amen.

November 21, 2015

The Puppet in the Pulpit

For the third time in a week, I received a phone call from a prophetic and transformative friend who either resigned their pastorate or was bullied into silence by the governing board of the church. In an age of increasing injustice, our churches have become the great bastions and protectors of the status quo. The most praised ministers in this environment are those who talk a big game without ever actually doing anything transformative. Churches love the puppet in the pulpit. Everyone just gets to sit back, clap and enjoy the show. The puppets keep everyone from actually following Jesus and assure all who will listen that they're actually doing the opposite. Make no mistake, these puppets come in all kinds of identities and make up the majority of our ministers. If you want to know if your pastor is a puppet, just look for who is pulling the strings.

Amen.

November 22, 2015

Words from the Oak Lawn to DPD, Rally for Change

There is always a difference between talk and action. I doubt you will find many people from the community who would say that they are for what has been happening in Oak Lawn. On the other hand, we must also realize that very few people from this community have actually been engaged in the Battle for Oak Lawn. While I guess I could continue on with generalities...this being the Lord's day...I would be remiss if I didn't speak to the churches that dot the landscape of the community.

This morning thousands of people gathered for worship in and around Oak Lawn. These institutions went through the motions and went home. Though I seriously doubt it, some might have acknowledged the murder of Shade Schuler and the recent assaults of all of these precious children of God. Even if they did, there is a difference between talk and action. There are some very powerful churches in the community who could really change things if they decided to take to the streets. When blood is pouring down the sidewalk, I don't have much patience. I think the greatest evil imaginable is to be silent or slow in the midst of what we are seeing in this community. Since most of our local pastors and churches are chickenshit and refuse to stand up for your lives in the Battle for Oak Lawn, I say to hell with all of them...you yourselves are the church and pastors this community so desperately needs.

Since you have now been ordained by the Spirit of God to be the real pastors and churches of Oak Lawn, I need to talk to you about something. How did Shade Schuler lay in that field in this community for so long without anyone noticing that she was gone? We have got to talk about the racism and transphobia that exists in this community. You see the pastors have to make sure they don't lose any of the flock. You see the church is supposed to be the place where everyone has a seat at God's table. You keep talking about being a family...so be one...be the church and pastors of the transformative power of love. We forgot about Shade...let's make damn sure that we don't forget about anyone else ever again.

One last thing...if you will truly be the pastors and church of love and justice the community is so desperate for...we finally won't have to give a shit about waiting for the rest of them.

Amen.

November 24, 2015

The Courage to Be Queer: Trinity Presbyterian Church in Denton

I start all sermons that I give at the beginning. Progressive Christians struggle with the beginning. It's as if we've ceded that space to the Fundamentalists and their crusades for literal interpretations of the creation myth. We don't know how to believe that there is still tremendous power in these stories even when we don't take them literally. I have often wondered what it would look like if we stopped fighting the fundamentalists on all this creation stuff and just started to champion our own creative liberation centered interpretations.

There are some big questions that pop up in the beginning. Who is God? What is God? In the beginning was God...but what was there in the beginning. We have spent all of our time trying to anthropomorphize God. We have tried to make God into our image instead of remembering that we are made in the image of God. That is a big disconnect. When we go astray... When we don't fight for justice like we should... When we don't love our neighbors like we should... When we spend years talking about inclusion... it's because we have forgotten that all are created in the image of God. What does that image reflect?

I am a big fan of Paul Tillich. I consider his book *The Courage to Be* to be one of the most formative books of my theological journey. He talks about the importance of being to the spiritual life. Think about it...God is. God's being is enough. To ask the question... What is God? is to constrict God or at least constrict our ability to engage with God. What is God? God is. We think, hope and dream about a God that is beyond our wildest imaginations and yet we are always trying to bring God down to easy explanations. We believe in the God that is beyond God. We seek the God that is indescribable and uncontainable. That majesty. We get too used to singing all these songs. Many of our songs and hymns talk about God in this way...they talk about a God beyond category and restriction.

Think about the word...queer. The word describes that which is different and beyond description...that which is not normative...that which is other...that which is outside of our categories. You see...God has always been queer. God has always been beyond our categories. God has always been beyond our ability to describe. We've been arguing for many years about including queer people in the life of the church or not. What we are really arguing about is whether we are going to include God in the life of the church or not. The question of inclusion is actually one of exclusion. The way we engage the question matters. We have convinced ourselves that if we do enough we will become something...we forgot our being. We are created in the very image of God. We have all that we need. We were made to be something holy...something queer...from the very beginning. Why do we spend so much time on definitions, categories and exclusions that take away from our being? We are rejecting our creation. We are rejecting our birthright. We are rejecting our being. We are enough.

What happened that made everything fall apart? How did we loose our queerness? Do y'all remember that old snake in Eden? That old snake slithered up and changed everything. What does the snake say? The snake says, "If you eat of the tree, you will be made like God." The first sin is always forgetting that we were made like God in the first place.

Now you know I am a Baptist preacher...so I'm going to run on real quick to Jesus. I've also already been told that y'all don't like long sermons. Thank about the possibilities, John 1:1, "In the beginning was the Queer, the Queer was with God and the Queer was God." When we talk about difference...you have to remember that difference is the only thing that has ever made a difference. Queerness...pushing against lines and borders...Jesus shows us what it looks like to be queer. The further that Jesus pushes into queerness...pushes into this border and boundary busting...the more Jesus is reviled and shunned. Jesus was prepared to meet the woman caught in adultery by another woman.

Do y'all remember the Syrophoenician woman? That woman that Jesus called a dog...and if you have an imagination you can imagine a more colorful modern translation. Because she was of a different race, Jesus called that woman a dog. Jesus sinned. Jesus was a racist y'all. I'm glad that we can overcome our worst moments. I'm thankful for that Syrophoenician woman...for if it hadn't been for her...I don't know if Jesus' heart wouldn't have been formed to deal with the least of the least. She reminds me of many of the Black Lives Matter activists who have taken to the streets around our nation. These folks have the courage to be different in order to make a difference. They are queer in the most beautiful senses of the word. These activists are interrupting our lives to help us grow...to help us be queerer...to be more like Jesus. I thank God for them. By the time that Jesus got to the woman caught in adultery, he was prepared for the moment...he was ready to be queer.

Everyone loves to run to the end of the story of the adulterous woman. People love that old command, "You who are without sin cast the first stone!" We love it. That just makes us feel so good don't it. We can just imagine all those people looking at us with their stones and being able to look at them to proclaim, "You who are without sin cast the first stone!" We also love that moment where Jesus is writing in the dirt. We like to imagine that Jesus is writing the names of all the people that the Pharisees are fooling around with. Unfortunately, in our rush to get to the good ending of the story...we leave out the best part.

Before we get to that best part, I do have to add a couple of pieces that always get left out. First, how long where the Pharisees looking when they caught the woman in the act of adultery? Second, what happened to the man when they pulled her out of that bed? These questions always run around in my mind when I think about this story. Do you know what I'm saying? Nevertheless, this woman is slung in the dirt at the feet of Jesus. In that moment, Jesus has a decision to make. Jesus could have stayed standing and tried to convince the Pharisees not to throw those stones...but he didn't. This is the best part of the story. Jesus places his very body into the dirt with the woman. If the stones had started flying...Jesus would've been dead. Jesus was not dumb. Jesus was prepared to die with this woman. There is a difference between doing the work of justice and embodying the work of justice. I know this is a congregation that does much doing...you are well known for all of your doing...but I want to make sure you don't lose your being in the process. We think that being comes from doing. This is not necessarily true. Being comes from claiming who God created you to be in the first place. Being comes from being prepared to give your life so that others might have life. Being comes from being queer.

Jesus is there. There is nothing queerer than being prepared to give your life for those that society has said are worthless. There is nothing queerer than to give your life for those that society has called out of bounds. Jesus travels on from the dirt with the adulterous woman and commands us to love our neighbors as ourselves. Do y'all know that great theologian RuPaul? I love that great question she often asks, "How the hell you going to love somebody when you can't love yourself?" That Syrophoenician woman taught Jesus how to love his neighbor as himself. Jesus was able to get in the dirt with the woman caught in adultery because of that Syrophoenician woman. In this moment, Jesus teaches us what love in action looks like...Jesus teaches us what it looks like to give your body to the conversation....to grow queer enough that we can give our self away. Loving yourself is the key to following Jesus. We can't be queer without believing that God's queer creation in us is and will forever be enough. This is how you change the world...believing that you were created queer so that you can make the world queerer.

Do y'all remember when Jesus told Nicodemus that he had to be born again? Y'all probably don't talk about getting born again much here...but I wanted to give you another way of thinking about it. I invite you this morning to be born again. I invite you this morning to go back to the beginning...to the queer that you were made to be. I invite you to embrace that you were created in the image of a God that is queer beyond our wildest imaginations. Follow the God who consistently dies with those who we marginalize and oppress...for there is nothing queerer. Be born again...grow queerer my friends...and in that space your being will create the doing that can actually change the world.

Amen.

November 26, 2015

Frances Hood: The Last Thanksgiving

I recounted the following story after I found out my grandmother died last year:

Though I have had many beautiful conversations with my grandmother, I will always cherish the last one. My grandmother has never been able to understand my activism and progressive ministry. While I was at home for Thanksgiving, my grandmother brought up "the gays" (in her words). I asked her, "Have you ever been attracted to a woman before?" My question was simply too much for her. Though my grandmother was known her whole life for her ability to talk loudly and consistently, the question left her speechless and astonished. After a little back and forth, I backed off the question. The next day, we were about to leave to drive back to Texas. I had just loaded our kids into the car and was ready to go. Before I hit the gas, I thought to run inside her house next door and see my grandmother. When I knocked on the door, she opened it and said, "I was hoping you would stop and see me one last time before you left." I walked in and told her just how much I loved her. I prodded her to let me take a picture before I left. Leaning in, I gave her a soft kiss on the forehead and snapped a selfie. Though the picture was special, the interaction grew divine based on the last words she ever spoke to me, "I thought about our conversation, I want you to know that I am very proud of you and love is going to be what sees us all through." Though I will miss her with all my heart, I believe her last words to me. Even in the face of death, I know that our love remains and will sustain us both until we meet again.

These words cycle in my head often. One year later, I am thankful that at 89 my grandmother was still open to be moved and transformed. While there is no question that she was a racist, homophobe and many other things until the day she died, God was still moving in her life and I have no question that the God who began a good work in her was faithful until such work was complete. I pray that there will be many conversations around dinner tables today like the one I had with my grandmother. I pray that God will continue to transform hearts and our world. In the midst of all the hate that is going round, I'm not worried anymore...for I know that the author and perfecter of all that is will be faithful until the work is complete.

Amen.

November 26, 2015

The Praying Old Man

Throughout Thanksgiving dinner, I kept looking at an iconic photograph hanging on the wall at my wife's grandfather's home. Though I have seen the photograph all over the country and beyond, I couldn't help but stare this time. The photograph is of a old man praying over a simple meal. Rocking back and forth in my chair, I kept wondering what he was praying for. Then it hit me. The old man was praying to be saved from racism. I think we all should too.

Amen.

November 27, 2015

A Theology of Rain

The walls couldn't contain the energy of us all. Everyone wanted to go outside. Some of us did for a few minutes but never for much longer. I couldn't remember any holiday ever being this wet. Walking through the house, I blurted out, "It feels like God is pissing on us." "Maybe we deserve it," replied my wife. When I walked outside, looked to the heavens and let the rain hit my face, I wondered.

Amen.

December 1, 2015

God Has AIDS

Our God is born of flesh. Our God lives in flesh. Our God dies in flesh. Over and over, the incarnation of our God plays out in flesh. We are born of flesh. We live in flesh. We die in flesh. Over and over, the incarnation of our God plays out in us. We have AIDS. God has AIDS. Do you give a shit?

Amen.

December 7, 2015

The Turn: A Primer on Mixed Race Conversation in the South

Most genteel mixed race public conversations begin with a turn toward each other. Whether the turn occurs based on sports, cars or something else that can be easily agreed upon, the purpose of the initial turn is to find some means of communication. This phase of the conversation can be meaningful but does not lead to deep engagement. Unless there is a relationship between the conversationalists, the engagement can only last so long. The conversation breaks down based on either running out of words or the inclusion of a word about family, religion, politics, race or something that causes the conversationalists to turn away from each other. To not turn away, would be rude. Southerners are taught to reject impolite conversation. At this point, the conversation usually collapses or grows increasingly heated. This is the problem with mixed race conversations in the South...we still don't know how to turn back to each other. Our suggestion is to turn back to where we started the conversation and try again. In the midst of all the Bible reading, I think we all forget as Southerners that love has to be patient. With all of our baggage, how can we expect to learn to be different without a turn?

Amen.

December 8, 2015

The Great Deceiver

*appeared in Baptist News Global on 12/8

Fear was a consistent companion. Sleep was elusive. Terror regularly stopped by. The Tribulation Trail was a haunted walk through an interpretation of the Book of

Revelation hosted by a church across town. Our annual visit always ushered in months of study and speculation about the end times. During the Trail, there was always a movie projected on a huge sheet that illustrated how close we actually were to the end of the world.

Though I tried to convince myself that I didn't believe any of it, I was always shaken to my core. Every year, I regretted that my parents forced me to go. Though I couldn't shake the fear, I committed to erasing all of it from my mind and not believing any of it. In the last few months, I have changed my mind.

From his attacks on Mexicans to his support for roughing up a black protestor to his calls for a national database for Muslims to his passion for bullying, Donald Trump has provided us no shortage of evidence that he is both a bigot and a racist. Just today, Trump declared his support for barring Muslims from entering the United States. If he weren't so consistently evil, I would think this was some kind of sick joke. Unfortunately, the joke is up. Millions of other racists and bigots have flocked to join forces with him. These are scary days. Back when I was growing up, we were told that the Antichrist would be the opposite of Jesus and gain millions of followers quickly. While I think there are many antichrists who raise their ugly heads throughout history, I have no doubt in this contextual moment that Donald Trump is the chief opposite of Jesus.

The great deceiver has convinced millions of people that the best way to love your neighbor is to wall them out, shake them down and put them in their place. This is the opposite of the love of Jesus. The great deceiver has convinced millions that the best way to love your enemies is to bomb them into submission over and over again. This is the opposite of the love of Jesus. The great deceiver has convinced millions that the down and out deserve our contempt rather than our help. This is the opposite of the love Jesus. The great deceiver has convinced millions that bullying is the way to get ahead. This is the opposite of the love of Jesus. The great deceiver has convinced millions that those who are hungry deserve to be hungry. This is the opposite of the love of Jesus. The great deceiver has convinced millions that those who thirst should've thought ahead and prepared better. This is the opposite of the love of Jesus. The great deceiver has convinced millions that the stranger is our enemy. This is the opposite of the love of Jesus. The great deceiver has convinced millions to laugh at those who are without clothes. This is the opposite of the love of Jesus. The great deceiver has convinced millions to work to deny the sickest and poorest amongst us health care. This is the opposite of the love of Jesus. The great deceiver has promised to lock up more people. This is the opposite of the love of Jesus. The great deceiver has ridiculed the disabled. This is the opposite of the love of Jesus.

The great deceiver is named Donald Trump and he is working for the exact opposite of what followers of Jesus should be working for. What has and will be done to those standing in the line of fire of Trump has and will be done to Jesus. Those who stand against Trump at this perilous hour stand against the Antichrist.

Over the last few weeks, I've watched pastors and preachers run to meet and get their picture taken with Trump. These pastors and preachers love their ministries far more than they love the God they claim to serve. In much of the literature about the end of days, preachers cozy up to evil and forget about Jesus. Looking around at churches, I am seeing this phenomenon happen to more than just leaders. Many years ago, I promised to never look at any of the rapture, tribulation or end of days nonsense I grew up with ever again. I thought it was all so silly and irrelevant to modernity. Now, I look at the evil that is Donald Trump and think twice.

Amen.

December 13, 2015

The Southern Progressive Sunday School Class

These are words overheard this morning...

We got to do something about climate change y'all.
We need to stop buying all this bottled water.

The world is getting tough.
Years ago, we used to have throwaway money to help all the poor children in Mexico.
Now, we don't have no more throwaway money.

Police brutality is getting crazy.
We've got to step up for the blacks.

We've got to make the crooked straight.
The browns do that so much better than we do.

The flesh makes us oppress and marginalize people.
I guess we just need to get rid of it.

The way to solve our problems is limiting our population.
I'm not suggesting genocide.

Please pray for the Southern Progressives y'all.

Amen.

December 16, 2015

Donald Trump is the Antichrist

Fear was a consistent companion. Sleep was elusive. Terror regularly stopped by. The Tribulation Trail was a haunted walk through an interpretation of the Book of Revelation hosted by a church across town. Our annual visit always ushered in months of study and speculation about the end times. During the Trail, there was always a movie projected on a huge sheet that illustrated how close we actually were to the end of the world. Though I tried to convince myself that I didn't believe any of it, I was always shaken to my core. Every year, I regretted that my parents forced me to go. Though I couldn't shake the fear, I committed to erasing all of it from my mind and not believing any of it. In the last few months, I have changed my mind.

From his attacks on Mexicans to his support for roughing up a Black protestor to his calls for a national database for Muslims to his passion for bullying, Donald Trump has provided us no shortage of evidence that he is both a bigot and a racist. Just today, Trump declared his support for barring Muslims from entering the United States. If he weren't so consistently evil, I would think this was some kind of sick joke. Unfortunately, the joke is up. Millions of other racists and bigots have flocked to join forces with him. These are scary days. Back when I was growing up, we were told that the Antichrist would be the opposite of Jesus and gain millions of followers quickly. While I think there are many antichrists who raise their ugly heads throughout history, I have no doubt in this contextual moment that Donald Trump is the chief opposite of Jesus...Donald Trump is the Antichrist.

The great deceiver has convinced millions of people that the best way to love your neighbor is to wall them out, shake them down and put them in their place. This is the opposite of the love of Jesus. The great deceiver has convinced millions that the best way to love your enemies is to bomb them into submission over and over again. This is the opposite of the love of Jesus. The great deceiver has convinced millions that the down and out deserve our contempt rather than our help. This is the opposite of the love Jesus. The great deceiver has convinced millions that bullying is the way to get ahead. This is the opposite of the love of Jesus. The great deceiver has convinced millions that those who are hungry deserve to be hungry. This is the opposite of the love of Jesus. The great deceiver has convinced millions that those who thirst should've thought ahead and prepared better. This is the opposite of the love of Jesus. The great deceiver has convinced millions that the stranger is our enemy. This is the opposite of the love of Jesus. The great deceiver has convinced millions to laugh at those who are without clothes. This is the opposite of the love of Jesus. The great deceiver has convinced millions to work to deny the sickest and poorest amongst us healthcare. This is the opposite of the love of Jesus. The great deceiver has promised to lock up more people. This is the opposite of the love of Jesus. The great deceiver has ridiculed the disabled. This is the opposite of the love of Jesus. The great deceiver is named Donald Trump and is working for the exact opposite of what followers of Jesus should be working for. What has and will be done to those standing in the line of fire of Trump has and will be done to Jesus. Those who stand against Trump at this perilous hour stand against the Antichrist.

Over the last few weeks, I've watched pastors and preachers run to meet and get their picture taken with Trump. These pastors and preachers love their ministries far more than they love the God they claim to serve. In much of the literature about the end of days, preachers cozy up to evil and forget about Jesus. Looking around at churches, I am seeing this phenomenon happen to more than just leaders. Many years ago, I promised to never look at any of the rapture, tribulation or end of days bullshit I grew up with ever again. I thought it was all so silly and irrelevant to modernity. Now, I look at the evil that is Donald Trump and think twice.

Amen.

December 16, 2015

Dear Editor,

Why do we keep on killing people who kill people to show that killing people is wrong? Logic like this is more twisted than a runaway tornado. I'm so tired of killing people. Thankfully, the Texas Coalition to Abolish the Death Penalty's "Texas Death Penalty Developments in 2015: The Year in Review" shows us that use of the death penalty is declining dramatically. Over and over, North Texans rejected the death penalty. God knows it's time. Why don't we just go ahead and be done with the whole thing? I thought Texans took pride in getting rid of failed government programs? This whole execution thing costs too much, kills people of color disproportionately, runs the risk of killing the innocent, is not applied throughout the state, is against our core religious and moral beliefs and is just flat out nasty. In 2016, let's join together and fix our government. Let's abolish the death penalty!

Rev. Dr. Jeff Hood
Board of Directors, Texas Coalition to Abolish the Death Penalty

December 17, 2015

Cpl. Stephen Bean Chose to Kill: Beware of Denton

Throughout the last few years, I've worked with families seeking justice in the midst of police brutality. Over and over again, I've watched law enforcement make decisions to kill people when they didn't have to. The killing of Ryan McMillan is just another example. Only a few seconds after Cpl. Stephen Bean of the University of North Texas Police Department encountered a hatchet toting and obviously disturbed McMillan, lethal shots rang out. After repeatedly watching video of the incident, I don't understand why a less lethal response wasn't utilized. Cpl. Bean is representative of the lethal ways of law enforcement across our country. Contrary to other parts of the world where law enforcement handle these situations without lethal violence, our police shoot to kill. Until our local law enforcement gets better training, maybe we should put up signs around the University of North Texas and the City of Denton warning people that any sort of breakdown could result in their execution by our police. Though I doubt there will be any consequences for Cpl. Bean, the truth remains that he chose to kill Ryan McMillan and didn't have to. Don't get unstable Denton.

Amen.

December 17, 2015

The Protector of Brutality in Dallas County

Desperate for help back on August 1, 2015, Joseph Hutcheson parked his truck on the curb of the Lew Sterrett Justice Center in Dallas, Texas and ran inside. Not long after entering around 10:24am, Hutcheson screamed, "Don't hurt me, I just need some help." The deputies tackled him and wrestled him to the ground. As Hutcheson pleaded that he couldn't breathe, a witness in the Dallas Morning News described one deputy restraining Hutcheson with "a knee on his back" and another deputy restraining him "with a knee on his throat." Hutcheson's face turned from white to blue. Around 11:30am, Hutcheson was pronounced dead.

Not long after Joseph Hutcheson's death, Sheriff Lupe Valdez allowed information to be released to the media that drugs were found in his truck. This information turned out to be a lie. Not long after falsely speculating about the contents of his truck, Sheriff Valdez also released Hutcheson's criminal background. One of the first signs that law enforcement has committed brutality is that they start to trash the victim. Sheriff Valdez is guilty as charged.

I got involved in the case not long after Joseph Hutcheson died. Having known of Sheriff Valdez for many years, I couldn't figure out what was making her bungle this situation so badly. Regardless, a coalition of us began to push. Sheriff Valdez refused to publicly engage the case. When it took months of pushing to get video of the incident, I realized that Sheriff Valdez was the protector of the brutalizers.

The Dallas County Medical Examiner ruled the death of Joseph Hutcheson a homicide. Though Hutcheson was on cocaine and methamphetamine, the deputies were the primary causes of his death. Regardless, Sheriff Valdez still has not released their names. Though the deputies were on alternative duty for a while, no one was ever told what that even meant. For all we know, the deputies are now back working in the lobby where they killed a man. Based on Sheriff Valdez's actions throughout the investigation, I wouldn't be surprised one bit.

Not long ago, Sheriff Valdez finished her investigation of the Joseph Hutcheson incident. Now, the Dallas County District Attorney's Office is investigating her investigation. Maybe someone over there is compassionate enough to recognize brutality when they see it. Sheriff Valdez certainly was not. Sheriff Valdez remains Dallas County's great protector of brutality.

Amen.

December 20, 2015

Outside the Inn with the Shitty God

*sermon delivered on 12/20/15 at The Beloved Community in Asheville, North Carolina

The incarnation of God is a shitty story. This speaks not of the quality of the story...but rather where the story takes places. Jesus was born in a stable full of shit.

The Christmas story is a strange tale. Don't let the commercialization fool you. Jesus was not white. Jesus was not born in a department store. Jesus was not Santa's baby. Jesus was born to one of the strongest women to ever exist. Jesus was born in an occupied territory. Jesus was born to bust down walls and destroy lines. The Christmas story is a strange tale.

This time of the year is not about deals. You are not going to find Jesus while shopping. Jesus came into the shit and that is exactly where you will find him today.

Do you know about this trip that Mary and Joseph took to Bethlehem? This woman was full with child. This woman was experiencing deep pains. This woman was about to deliver this baby. Can you imagine riding on anything in that condition? This woman was and is the truth.

Do you realize that Bethlehem is currently in the occupied territory of Palestine? If Mary and Joseph tried to make the trip today...they would meet the walls that the Israelis have built. We think walls will keep us safe...but all they actually do is keep God out. We must become a wall breaking people.

Can you imagine the questions Mary and Joseph got along the way? How long have you been married? Do you feel like you are old enough to have a child? Did she cheat on you? What's your address? Questions like these are still ruining lives. How many of you feel like you are discriminated against or marginalized based on reoccurring questions? I guess we just need to start telling folks it's none of their damn business and work for a world where they don't have the right to ask these oppressive questions.

The Christmas story is about those who have been left out. This story is about a God that was born in the midst of some wild shit.

We have a woman claiming that she is having a child without having sex. We have a man who believes her. Who is crazier? Sometimes I feel like I am...because I think it's true.

Mary carries God. No one else can make such a claim. Despite the fact that the church has spent thousands of years oppressing women...this was always meant to be a story about liberation. Before Jesus is born...God comes to us as a woman.

Protestants don't want to touch Mary because they know it can lead to the empowerment of women. Catholics can't get enough of Mary because they know if they talk about her enough then they don't have to talk about the empowerment of women. Both are wrong. Mary kicks down the walls for all women.

Mary and Joseph arrive in Bethlehem. Can you imagine if they arrived in Asheville, North Carolina? Can you imagine if they sought shelter at the Biltmore Mansion? Can you imagine? Nevertheless, Mary and Joseph talk to this innkeeper. Have you ever thought about this innkeeper? I don't feel like I have to think about him. I feel like I see him on television...his name is Donald Trump. This man is running around telling the world that the wealthiest nation on earth has no room in the inn. God is always outside the inn.

The police are our current innkeepers. Most would rather gun you down in the street than have to help you find a place to stay for the night. We've seen unarmed body after body shot down in our streets. If you're poor in America then you get shot down in the streets. If you're undocumented in America then you get shot down in the streets. If you're mentally ill in America then you deserve to get shot down in the streets. On and on and on... We keep on hearing that the police feel that their lives are threatened. Aren't they the ones with the guns? Many people have taken to the streets to resist. Let me tell you one more time...God is always outside the inn...in the streets.

The United States is the inn. We are the richest nation on earth. People keep knocking at our door. We keep turning God away.

When the innkeeper turns Mary and Joseph away...he is saying that he doesn't give a shit whether their child lives or dies. I don't care what your needs are...you aren't getting in here. The beds are full and I can't loose any money. This is the nature of capitalism. We live in a similar society.

The innkeeper gives Mary and Joseph a little piece and lets them stay in the stable. We do the same thing. We give pieces away to appease the marginalized and oppressed. We think that we can give enough pieces away that we wont have to deal with the real problems. Like the innkeeper...we feel like we can just put our problems out back.

The situation got shittier. Upon arrival at the barn, there was shit everywhere. Animals letting their shit rip all over the place. Can you imagine your last steps before you give birth being over and through piles of shit? Then...Jesus drops down right into the shit. We serve a shitty God! In the midst of the shit...Jesus shows us how to be the shit...by hanging around in the shit with God.

There wasn't any room in the inn for Jesus...it didn't matter...God was always out in the shit and that's exactly where we are called to be.

May this Christmas be the shittiest Christmas you have ever had!

Amen.

December 21, 2015

A Call to Action

Why do we keep on killing people who kill people to show that killing people is wrong? Logic like this is more twisted than a runaway tornado. I'm so tired of killing people. Thankfully, the use of the death penalty is declining dramatically. Even here in Texas, people are rejecting the death penalty. God knows it's time. Why don't we just work together to abolish the whole thing? Like Texans, I know that Georgians like getting rid of failed government programs. This whole execution thing costs too much, kills people of color disproportionately, runs the risk of killing the innocent, is not applied fairly, is against our core religious and moral beliefs and is just flat-out nasty. In 2016, let's join forces and fix government. Let's abolish the death penalty.

-Rev. Dr. Jeff Hood, Board of Directors, Texas Coalition to Abolish the Death Penalty

December 23, 2015

The Buddhist Madonna: A Christmas Miracle

Many years ago, I worked as a chaplain at a large public hospital. Late one night, I received a message to get to the lobby immediately. Christmas was only a week away and I ran past a nativity scene stuck to the glass. Jumping down the steps, I felt like I just didn't believe in all that bullshit anymore. Armed with multiple degrees, I felt like I was so far beyond the idea of miracles. My job was to tell the truth. When I finally arrived in the lobby, I found a large Vietnamese family circled around what appeared to be their matriarch lying in the floor. Seeking more information, I was told that she had a brain aneurysm and probably wasn't going to make it. Someone also told me that she was Buddhist. While I was with the family, the doctors came to the room and told us the woman had no brain activity. Immediately, the children asked me to pray. Hesitant, I tried to offer a few good words. Though they were Buddhist, the kids pushed back and demanded a prayer "in the name of Jesus." Approaching the bed, I placed my hand on her head and loudly demanded, "In the name of Jesus...you are healed." The family thanked me. Although I knew she was going to die, I didn't have the heart to pray more honestly. After my shift ended, I tried to forget about it. On Christmas, I got a phone call from a colleague telling me that the Buddhist woman just walked out of the hospital after making a miraculous recovery. Through it all, the woman credited a prayer from a young chaplain with saving her life. Dropping the phone in disbelief, I told God I would never fail to believe in the miraculous again. The Buddhist woman saved my faith.

Liberal Christians love to deconstruct around Christmas. I guess they don't ever get the presents they wanted. From Jesus not being the reason for the season to the Bible being false on the birth narrative to Jesus not being God to Jesus not being real, I've heard it all at this time of the year. Most of the folks who put this shit out there think they're doing us a favor. Truthfully, there is nothing more contrary to following God than a lack of imagination. Faith is the assurance of things hoped for. Hope is the only antidote in a world of deconstruction. Hope is about imagining and embracing the miraculous brilliance of the possible.

The Virgin Birth is a fairy tale. I hear it all the time. I've stopped engaging in these mutterings. I know that Mary carried and birthed God. I feel it deep down in my bones. Mary taught us how to believe in miracles. Mary taught us how to believe in the incarnations of God in our world. Mary taught us to believe. The Buddhist woman is the modern Mary for me. The Buddhist woman taught me how to believe in miracles. The Buddhist woman taught me to believe in the incarnation of God. The Buddhist woman taught me to believe. In that Christmas miracle many years ago, the woman became my Buddhist Madonna.

Amen.

December 24, 2015

The Douglas County Sheriff's Department and the Slaughter of the Innocent

When the frantic calls started to flood his phone, Bobby Daniels knew his son Bias was in deep trouble. In the midst of an emotional breakdown, Bias had a gun and had just held a hostage for 45 minutes. Desperate to save his son, Bobby rushed to the scene. Talking his son down, Bobby got his son to put the gun on the hood of a car. Having served in the Navy and as a security guard at CNN in Atlanta, this was not Bobby's first encounter with a volatile situation. When a Douglas County Sheriff's Deputy arrived, Bobby sought to swat the gun away. Seeing a black man close to a gun, the Deputy got his chance. Seconds later, Bobby was dead. Without missing a beat, the racist Douglas County Sheriff Phil Miller blamed it on Bobby picking up the gun and pointing it at the deputy. Witnesses from the scene declared these words to be exactly what they are...lies. Here in my home state of Georgia, no matter who pulls the trigger...it's always the black man's fault.

Christmas is a time to celebrate love realized amongst us. King Herod couldn't handle it. After the birth of Jesus, Herod was terrified that love would cause him to lose his power. Responding much like our law enforcement today, Herod moved to kill anyone deemed a threat. Jesus and his family were forced to flee. In the midst of the incarnation of the love of a father, the Douglas County Sheriff's Department followed Herod's lead and slaughtered the innocent. During this Christmas moment, may we all search our hearts and find a way to transform such evil into love. May Bobby Daniels show us the way.

Amen.

more info: https://www.washingtonpost.com/news/post-nation/wp/2015/12/23/he-was-trying-to-help-georgia-deputies-fatally-shoot-cnn-security-guard-as-he-was-attempting-to-help-his-deranged-son/

December 25, 2015

Poems

The Dark Water of Salvation

The grass is wet. My toes feel all of nature. Each touch is mysterious.
The rocks grow harder. My feet remember the origin. Each step draws me out.
The dock is old. My being remembers the waves. Each plank grows the fear.
The edge pulls closer. My brain tells me to turn. Each moment ends the last.
The bend is the spring. My heart pulls the trigger. Each second I fly.
The spash rocks the soul. My nerves let go. Each darkness manifests divine.
The water flows through me. My breath is gone. The dark water of salvation is all.

Amen.

The Storm

We drove

We dreamed
You loved you
You were blind
We gave
We sought
You electrocuted
You burned us
We prayed
We stopped
You thundered
You refused
We yearned
We desired
You destroyed

Amen.

December 25, 2015

Christmas in Dixie

When the frantic calls started to flood his phone, Bobby Daniels knew his son Bias was in deep trouble. In the midst of an emotional breakdown, Bias had a gun and had just held a hostage for 45 minutes. Desperate to save his son, Bobby rushed to the scene. Talking his son down, Bobby got his son to put the gun on the hood of a car. Having served in the Navy and as a security guard at CNN in Atlanta, this was not Bobby's first encounter with a volatile situation. When a Douglas County Sheriff's Deputy arrived, Bobby sought to swat the gun away. Seeing a black man close to a gun, the Deputy opened fire. Seconds later, Bobby was dead.

Growing up, I enjoyed the song "Christmas in Dixie" by Alabama. Riding back from our visit to Atlanta tonight, the song came over the radio. This being the first time I'd heard the song in a very long time, I turned it up. As the syrupy imagery flowed, I realized the song has nothing to do with the region I've always called home. Honestly, the shooting of Bobby Daniels is much closer to reality. Christmas in Dixie is about killing black people and going home to assure your white children that they're safe. Make no mistake...Jesus lives in Dixie. Jesus lives with those being slaughtered by the white supremacy of the region. Jesus lives with the family of Bobby Daniels. On this night, Jesus is standing outside the Douglas County Sheriff's Department demanding an end to the genocide of black people. How is that for a Christmas in Dixie?

Amen.

December 26, 2015

Love your neighbor...BE QUEER. : A Sermon from the First Congregational Church of Fort Worth, Texas

When you stop to consider the absence of information that we've got about the childhood of Jesus, these passages about a young Jesus in the temple are incredibly profound. After a young Jesus leaves the temple, there is another huge gap (18 years to be exact) in the narrative. There is a reason that these passages stand out. They are the only information we have about the adolescence of Jesus. These are strange passages for strange people.

Over the last few days we have spent much time celebrating the birth of Jesus...but how much time have we spent celebrating the womb that carried God? The womb is a place where divinity meets divinity. God the creator works to create God's image. Let's not forget to celebrate the womb. One cannot understand the adolescent Jesus until you understand the womb from which he came.

The wise men came a few years into the tale. Why don't we ever talk about the wise women who came? Do you think there were wise women there? Surely? I know I am thankful for all the wise women in my life...including your pastor Rev. Lee Ann Bryce. I've got to believe that there were women in the life of Jesus who were incredibly instrumental in his upbringing. I think that the sexism of the writers of the narratives shines forth when we see such a glaring absence of influential women in the early narratives about his life. I guess that is just another gap in the text. When will we make room for the wise women amongst the wise men?

We treat wombs and women so terribly in our churches. When will we reverse the curse that proceeds out of the way we have talked about wombs and women since the beginning?

Under the gun, we know that a young Jesus eventually has to flee to Egypt. We have people fleeing violence all over the world right now. We should be able to relate. Unfortunately, most of us are too comfortable behind the safety of our borders to actually give it much thought. Truth be told, we've caused so much of the violence in the world. What wicked people we are. How can anyone claim to follow Jesus and live behind the borders of the richest nation on the planet? We don't care. We just keep on pillaging and screaming over and over, "There's not enough room for you!" The institutional church does the same thing. By institutionalizing our spaces we wall people out and declare, "There's not enough room for you!" We must repent.

These passages about a young Jesus in the temple are so strange. Can you imagine if a child came in here and wanted to deliver the message today? We don't believe that children have a message. We believe that children belong in their place. Do we value order more than we value the word of God?

I believe that this was Jesus' coming out moment. For many years, Jesus was developing. I believe that God whispered in Jesus' ear, "Step out of that closet! You can be everything that I have created you to be. You don't have to wait. Now is the time." Jesus was ready. In an instant, Jesus fully embraces the totality of his being and steps out as queer. The womb, the wise people and the experience of being a refugee prepare Jesus to be queer. The closet couldn't hold him back.

The queerness of Jesus causes great anxiety for Mary and Joseph. Jesus responds by telling them that he was about God's business. Without fail, the business of God is always queer. If one is not engaged in queer work, then they are not engaged in the business of God. You can't work for God in the Devil's closet. Too often, we respond like Mary and Joseph because we have denigrated the womb, we have denigrated women, we have denigrated refugees and we have denigrated all things that don't fit our idea of order. By simply being queer, Jesus repels any denigration. You can too.

While this is a nice story in the temple, I am particularly curious today about where Jesus was from this point until thirty. Like any good rabble rousing southern preacher...when there's a gap in the text...I just make it up. I got three things that I believed happened.

First, I think that Jesus had deep sustained interaction with scholars and practitioners of nonviolence. The Gospels are full of the most nonviolent passages the world has ever known. "Love your neighbor as yourself." If we lived like this, we wouldn't have violence. We don't. Jesus assures us that our destiny is tied to the other. Do you believe that?

We live in a society where everyone has a gun. We even pay people to walk around with guns to protect us. Everyone is ready to shoot. How can you love your neighbor and live in such a society? We say that we're nonviolent. I don't believe us. The church is one of the greatest promulgators of violence. Have you read the Bible lately?

Many decades ago, Thomas Merton boldly declared, "The modern man is walking around with a loaded gun in his hand. The only question that remains is 'Will they shoot their self or someone else first?'" That's the world we live in. We see it play out in shooting after shooting after shooting. How can anyone love Jesus and own a gun? To be queer in a world full of guns is to refuse to ever pick one up. Stand down Christians!

Second, I believe that revolutionary teachers helped form Jesus. We are living in revolutionary times. Throughout our nation, activists are dismantling our infrastructures of oppression. Why are we not joining in? Why are we not examining our own souls? Do you believe that black lives matter? To answer this question, one has to look no further than this stained glass window towering over us at this very moment. While you are not alone in having a white Jesus in your sanctuary, surely we know that such a depiction is a product of racism and a desire to whitewash Christianity. Friends...Jesus is not white. Far too often, we create God in our image instead of believing that all of humanity was created in God's image. We must repent of the white Jesus and get it out of our lives.

Lastly, I believe Jesus engaged deeply with the mystics. Jesus walked with the God beyond God. Jesus sought the unexplainable. Jesus sought something magical. Jesus sought the indescribable. Jesus sought something alien. Jesus never stopped seeking...for in the seeking is the knowing. Knowing that he was created in the image of the God beyond God, Jesus sought the self beyond the self. Do you? I encourage you to trade your explaining in for some being. Stop doing a bunch of stuff and learn to be what you were created to be in the first place...the very image of God.

Love your neighbor...put down your gun.
Love your neighbor...open your borders.
Love your neighbor...embrace the revolutionary spirit of our age.
Love your neighbor...be queer.

Amen.

December 29, 2015

Tamir Rice and Our Sin

Our laws allow for our police to shoot first and ask questions later. The murder of Tamir Rice is the consequence of our actions and inactions. We are an evil people. Our hands are covered in blood. I don't see how anyone can follow Jesus and see this situation differently. Who's going to be our next victim?

Amen.

December 31, 2015

Happy New Year! : White Folks Are Here to Save Us

"All the white folks on my team!" The game was kickball. Before we could begin, we had to pick the teams. Will demanded that we divide by race. Even at the age of six, I knew this was wrong. Though Will was much bigger and stronger than me, I knew I had to tell the teacher. Immediately, Will was sent to the principal's office. Being the first black teacher at our school, Ms. Ellington was well positioned to teach us a few words, "Division is the child of hate." Though it took me a few years to figure out what these words meant, I continue to cling to them.

Over the last year, I've seen a surge in language concerning the need for white folks to organize. From the Ku Klux Klan, I've heard that white people must organize to save the white race. From white only activist organizations, I've heard that white people must organize to atone for our sins and save black people. From a wild assortment of people and groups, I've heard what white people need to. With all this talk about white people, one would think that white people are the solution to the all the problems in the universe. It's as if we should all be shouting, "Happy New Year! : The White Folks Are Here to Save Us!" I don't believe such bullshit for a second. So, why should white people organize as if such words are true? Our systems of oppression have a diversity of actors. If we are going to overthrow and deconstruct such systems, there will be a need for a diversity of actors.

Over the years, I've learned to run away from white only groups. In my soul, I've always known they're evil. Why would I start joining such groups now? In the coming year, I commit to not joining any group that is white only...whether it is the Ku Klux Klan or one of these white only activist organizations. I don't see any of it as beneficial or helpful. Instead of sticking with their own race, I hope that white folks out there will join with a diversity of actors to fight a diversity of evils. We don't need any more all white groups. We have enough. Truthfully, I think our present white groups have already fuck everything up enough.

Hate is diverse and so too must we be if we are going to see Justice.

Amen.

www.ingramcontent.com/pod-product-compliance
Lightning Source LLC
Chambersburg PA
CBHW071143300426
44113CB00009B/1067